The Heart of Desire

Keys to the Pleasures of Love

STELLA RESNICK, PHD

WILEY

John Wiley & Sons, Inc.

To Alan
My favorite human

Design by Forty-five Degree Design LLC

Published by John Wiley & Sons, Inc., Hoboken, New Jersey ·
Published simultaneously in Canada

The information contained in this book is not intended to serve as a replacement for professional medical advice. Any use of the information in this book is at the reader's discretion. The author and the publisher specifically disclaim any and all liability arising directly or indirectly from the use or application of any information contained in this book. A health care professional should be consulted regarding your specific situation.

For general information about our other products and services, please contact our Customer Care Department within the United States at (800) 762-2974, outside the United States at (317) 572-3993 or fax (317) 572-4002.

Wiley also publishes its books in a variety of electronic formats and by print-on-demand. Some content that appears in standard print versions of this book may not be available in other formats. For more information about Wiley products, visit us at www.wiley.com.

Library of Congress Cataloging-in-Publication Data:
Resnick, Stella, date.
    The heart of desire : keys to the pleasures of love / by Stella Resnick.
      p. cm.
    Includes bibliographical references and index.
    ISBN 978-0-470-58235-0 (paper); ISBN 978-1-118-20491-7 (ebk);
    ISBN 978-1-118-20492-4 (ebk); ISBN 978-1-118-20493-1 (ebk)
      1. Love. 2. Desire. 3. Sex (Psychology) I. Title.
  BF575.L8R47 2012
  306.7—dc23

                                2011046738

Printed in the United States of America

10 9 8 7 6 5 4 3 2 1

Contents

Acknowledgments

To start with how this book came into being, I have to first thank the agents and editors who looked upon the early stages of the manuscript as a proposal and rejected it. One critique said that I had good ideas but that I would have to remove all references to childhood sexuality, because it was too controversial. I was stunned to discover that the thought of a child having sexual feelings was still a taboo topic among educated people. That in itself was very informative.

I'm also grateful to those who rejected the proposal for good reason. They didn't see what was particularly unique about my perspective that low sexual desire in a committed relationship starts in childhood. Their criticism showed me that I needed to better articulate what was unique (and even controversial) about the ideas in this book.

Rejection always hurts, but because I was an experienced writer at that point, it also had the salubrious effect of increasing my resolve. I was determined to write this book and to solidly support my view of the underlying influences on intimate relations by cross-referencing information and research from a variety of scientific fields that are not typically integrated or seen as linked.

I am particularly grateful to my agent, Judith Riven, for recognizing the significance of this book, for her valuable suggestions in shaping the proposal, and for her efforts in finding the right publisher. I found her by chance thanks to my cousin-in-law Liz Tagami. I got lucky.

I'm also grateful to Tom Miller, my editor at John Wiley & Sons, for his valuable comments and for his standards of excellence that put me through several rewrites, each of which resulted in substantial improvements. My thanks also go to editor Christel Winkler for spotting the worthiness of this project, Jorge Amaral at Wiley for his help in the logistics of the editorial process, production editor Lisa Burstiner, and the excellent copy editor, Judith Antonelli.

For all that I have learned from my clients, I especially appreciate all of the women and men who have graced my couch and explored their innermost feelings in my presence. I have learned so much from their questions, desires, and revelations and from witnessing how our work together has helped them to blossom. I'm grateful to be able to use details of their stories as examples—carefully disguised, of course—in my anecdotes.

I'm indebted to the Society for the Scientific Study of Sexuality and to the American Association for Sexuality Educators, Counselors, and Therapists for bringing together outstanding colleagues at quality conferences and providing opportunities for me to present and test this material with informed and lively professional audiences.

As an embodied Gestalt therapist—practicing a form of psychotherapy that is present-centered and focused on observing bodily experience—I'm grateful to the Gestalt community, and to the international conferences presented by the Association for the Advancement of Gestalt Therapy, for supporting the continued evolution of Gestalt work—an elegant psychotherapeutic method for self-discovery and personal growth. I particularly thank Anne Teachworth, a dear friend and colleague, who brought me to New Orleans to share my work with stimulating groups of clients, friends, family, and colleagues. Thanks, too, to Dan Bode for his gracious southern hospitality.

I am grateful to Esalen Institute and to the staff for all of the opportunities I have been given in four decades to offer Gestalt seminars and, more recently, couples workshops with my husband. The beauty of the Big Sur environment, between the mountains and the Pacific Ocean and graced by gardens and hot springs, is matched by the spirit of the people who are drawn from all over the world to be inspired and to learn. I am honored to share a history with this exceptional educational institution.

I am especially grateful to Marion F. Solomon, Matthew Solomon, Bonnie Goldstein, and the Lifespan Learning program at UCLA for a decade of annual conferences on attachment theory and cutting-edge research presented by luminaries in the field. From the first conference in 2001 to the present, these exciting scholarly meetings have had a major impact on my understanding of the childhood influences on the adult brain and the nervous system and on the resulting capacity to love and enjoy intimacy.

Some of my dearest friends are also esteemed colleagues, and I offer heartfelt thanks for their continual encouragement as this book progressed. Carol Cassell, as always, has been the go-to friend for her honesty, clarity, professionalism, and wisdom. Patti Britton has graced me with her generosity and deep appreciation for my work. Robert Dunlap has been a generous resource for technological information. Diane Rapaport has been a source of encouragement and feedback since my earliest attempts to put ideas on paper. Betty Dodson, a friend, mentor, and outrageous human being, manages to both support and challenge me at the same time.

My heartfelt thanks go to Ron Kurtz, a dear friend and colleague, who passed away in 2011, for his consistent generosity and appreciation since we were graduate students at Indiana University. He was right. We should have taped our conversations. I will miss him.

Some of my most cherished friends are always there for me, and I for them. We have seemingly known one another forever, have witnessed one another at life's landmarks, understand one another deeply, and cherish one another's company. I continually learn from them about deep love in long-term relationships. Besides the aforementioned friends, I am grateful for the love and unequivocal support of Adrienne and Mark Tobin, Gloria and Barry Blum, Carol and Bob Cassell, Diane and Walter Rapaport, Morgan Alexander and Kate Mack, Lolita Sapriel and Joe Metscher, Margot Winchester and Arthur Schimmel, Lenore and Mel Lefer, and Jorjana and Roger Kellaway.

I'm grateful to my loving family: my brother, Lou Siegel; my sister-in-"love," Deborah Bornstein; my nephew, Isaac Siegel; and my niece, Emma Bornstein, for making me proud of our DNA. A special note of gratitude goes to my loving in-laws, Jean and Jerry Haserot, for making me feel so welcome into their extended family.

Finally, I most especially thank my husband, Alan Kishbaugh, for his constant encouragement and expert editorial suggestions throughout the whole journey of birthing a book. I am grateful beyond words for his unwavering love and friendship and for taking such good care of me for all these years.

Introduction

This book has been written for all the men and women seeking to enjoy more emotionally fulfilling sexual pleasure with the ones they love. I have you in mind whether or not you have ever seen a therapist or have ever considered it. This book will surprise you with new information to think about.

I have you in mind whether you have ever been in individual therapy or couples therapy. This book, with its emphasis on the body and becoming more attuned to moment-to-moment experience, will complement your personal discovery and your growth as part of a couple.

I also have you in mind whether you are a psychotherapist, sex therapist, psychologist, psychiatrist, physician, bodyworker, health professional, teacher, or social worker—or any of the number of people who provide assistance to those seeking guidance or healing. This book will help you to do that.

Pleasure Informs

In my last book, *The Pleasure Zone: Why We Resist Good Feelings and How to Let Go and Be Happy*, I showed how pleasurable experiences nurture us as individuals and help us to thrive in life. Here, once again, I take a body-mind approach to how pleasure can be a great teacher. This time we focus on enjoying a highly fulfilling, affectionate, sexy, and intimate love relationship.

This is a detailed study of the many body-based factors that can affect a couple's ability to enjoy loving sexual pleasure. The book demonstrates clearly that what's important is not just how well we communicate verbally but also what two bodies are saying to each other when they're together, whether the message is mentally registered or not.

When we look deeper at the body's response to love and sexual feelings, we find that things get a bit complicated. Your response has to do with whether or not you learned to separate emotional attachment from sex, how secure or insecure you feel, how you deal with stress in a relationship, how comfortable you are in your own body, how playful you are about anything, how well informed you are about sex, and how skillful you are as a lover.

Part I: Love and Romance

Part I begins with an exploration of what I call the love-lust dilemma, the disappointing fact that due to our sexual programming, the commitment of love itself can undermine sexual desire. I show how early childhood history with sexual feelings typically programs the brain and the nervous system to inhibit any arousal in the presence of family and to direct sexual interest toward strangers. That's a good thing. But when you make a commitment, the "beloved" becomes "family." The more the partners start to act like family with each other, the more likely there will be an automatic physiological tendency to cut off desire for him or her.

This reaction is body-based, and you can't be talked out of it. Inhibitory responses are minute muscle tensions that may be set off by a fleeting thought of self-doubt or a partner's microsecond gesture that is reminiscent of parental disapproval. But you can become aware of the body-mind process that opens or closes you to sexual love.

This part continues with a scientifically based view of romance and the critical role it plays in generating feelings of desire. It shows how a certain kind of romantic play can turn on the erotic body and transform a partner from a family projection into a sexually appealing playmate.

Part II: Sexual Pleasure

Part II begins with a definition of sexual health and the importance of sexual gratification to general health and the health of an intimate relationship. It examines the factors that can get in the way of letting go to sexual pleasure and how body-based intimate attunement with oneself and with a partner can break through barriers and spark sexual enthusiasm.

This part continues with an exploration of the kind of erotic play that can keep sexual feelings alive. It offers a detailed description of sexual activities that can be experienced with greater presence, expertise, and gratifying pleasures.

The Ten-Step Loving Sex Program

This book doesn't just talk about the factors that make up loving sex; it also offers a ten-step program for putting the information to use.

Each chapter concludes with a step in the program that can provide you with a personal experience of the material presented in that chapter. The step offers further comments, one-person exercises, couples games, and experiments to do on your own or with a partner. These explorations are to be taken in the spirit of play and adventure and are designed to bring pleasure while providing insights about yourself and your partner. Although it would be best to do some of these exercises with your partner, you can also gain insight and skill by doing the partnered exercises alone, using mental imagery, fantasy, and felt-sense awareness (this will be explained in chapter 1).

If you are between partners, you may be able to do some of these exercises with a good friend, setting boundaries as you go along and being clear when an exercise feels beyond the parameters of your physical relationship.

An Evolutionary Process

This book represents an evolutionary process that can deepen the capacity for emotional and sexual intimacy. Wherever we start, and with whatever history, we can be in charge of our own emotional and sexual evolution.

This has been my own story, and I offer myself and not just my clients as an example of how it can be done on an ongoing basis.

In August 1964 I had completed my course work toward my doctorate in clinical psychology at Indiana University, and I arrived at the University of California, San Francisco, as an intern at the UCSF Medical Center's highly regarded Langley Porter Neuropsychiatric Institute. I should have been thrilled to be there, but instead I was severely depressed.

I had been married for about two years, and my young husband and I had just separated. We decided to separate because we seemed incapable of making love in any way that was fulfilling for either of us. I loved him deeply, as I'd never loved anyone before, and I cried every day because I was so lonely and missed him so much.

We were both twenty-two when we married, and although we seemed perfect for each other in many ways, the sex was inept and such a terrible disappointment. We decided that he would remain in Bloomington for the year of my internship and that we would each have other lovers. We thought that with more sexual experience we would come back to each other better able to work out our sexual problems so we could stay together forever. This was, after all, the sixties.

As luck would have it, Langley Porter was located on the top of a hill overlooking Haight-Ashbury, a modest neighborhood with no hint yet of notoriety, and I found an apartment with a working fireplace and a view of the bay and the Golden Gate Bridge. So here I was: a heartbroken and sexually yearning young woman in my early twenties, plunked down in what was about to become a vortex of the Sexual Revolution.

I met my first real lover at a folk dance and was immediately attracted to his exuberant spirit, his graceful dancer's body, and his physicality. I will never forget the first time we made love on the bed in my flat: candles aglow all around us, a fire shimmering and crackling in the fireplace, shakuhachi flute and koto music playing softly on the stereo, and foghorns moaning in the distance. It was magical and everything I had ever hoped to experience sexually. It lasted for hours and became the gold standard by which all other sex was measured.

In fact, this beautiful young man and I made wonderful love together for more than a year, even though he knew I was married and planning to return to my husband. We loved each other but expected nothing of each other.

We lived together only once for about three weeks. That happened right after my husband wrote to me that he was in love with another woman and wanted a divorce. I was overcome with grief. My lover took me to the flat he shared with a friend, put me to bed, and held me silently for hours on end as I cried in his arms over another man.

So in truth, while I was surrounded by the sexual peregrinations of all my friends in Haight-Ashbury and learned a lot from them, I had a single great lover while I was there, and I was quite content.

When I got back to Bloomington, with my newly acquired liberation and spite for my ex, who was now living with his girlfriend, I felt driven to chalk up sexual victories. I wanted to be free and try everything everyone else was trying. But in my heart I still longed for love, and I believed with all my being that sex in a loving relationship was the best sex of all.

I did finally meet the man who was to become my life partner. It was at the end of 1978. We were at a Christmas party. He clearly liked me, but I was unimpressed. He was not my type— he was too thin, too blond, and too nice. Two weeks later, when he called, I agreed to a date only because I had nothing else to do on the Friday night he asked me out. I've been with him ever since. I never did find a reason to say no to him.

This relationship has taught me more about myself, life, love, sexual desire, passion, orgasms, commitment, joy, and peace than anyone or anything else I've ever experienced. It hasn't always been easy. He's been his own man, and I'm my own woman. As it's turned out, that has been our greatest asset. I've come to appreciate that the difficulties we've had have pushed us to grow. Here we are now, more than three decades later, reaping the benefits of what we've learned, weathered, and supported in each other.

When the Professional Is Personal

Clearly, the subject matter of this book has been more than a professional and intellectual study; it's been a lifetime commitment. My personal insights have informed my therapeutic approach. The insights I've gained at the office and in studying the research have helped my partner and me at home. This book is the culmination of all of the work I have done so far to integrate everything I know about love, sex, and the body.

Enjoy the journey!

PART I

Love
and
Romance

1

The Love-Lust Dilemma

Feelings of love can kill libido. Today's big relationship challenges—sexless marriages, low desire, infidelity, compulsive use of pornography, chronic conflict, and marital boredom—are all linked to this unfortunate reality. It's a basic dilemma for the contemporary man or woman. It manifests in different forms, but what's common in each instance is this: as the emotional attachment in an intimate relationship grows, the sexual desire often dwindles, yet without desire, the relationship is at risk of failing.

I call it the love-lust dilemma. There's a wealth of scientific data from research in brain biochemistry, sexual science, anthropology, and sociology to support this assertion. As a therapist with more than thirty-five years of practice in couples therapy and sex therapy, I also have plenty of anecdotal evidence to offer.

In my view, the love-lust dilemma is not an inherent aspect of human sexuality but rather an artifact of a society that unwittingly primes us from childhood through adulthood to separate love from sexual desire.

Sexless Love as a Social Phenomenon

Consider the plight of so many couples: the well-publicized trend of sexless marriages or lack of interest in sex. Low sexual desire reached national prominence several years ago when *Newsweek* ran a cover story titled "No Sex Please, We're Married." The article proclaimed the number of sexless marriages to be a problem "of epidemic proportions," and it suggested that the level of sexual activity in a marriage serves as a reliable measure of whether the relationship will last.

We might expect this problem from couples who have a lot of stress in their lives or from older people who have been in the same relationship for decades. But as a therapist with a specialty in sexual concerns, I can tell you that this development is just as true for couples without much stress and for twenty- and thirty-year-olds in relatively new relationships. Some men and women lose their desire for their partners even within days of moving in together.

One frustrated young woman in her twenties wondered what she could do to jump-start her sex life with her live-in boyfriend. Ever since they had moved in together only eight months earlier, their love had grown stronger but their sex life had died. She loved cuddling with him and considered him cute, but the passion was gone.

A despondent man in his thirties was crushed when the only woman he ever really loved left him because he lost interest in her sexually. She said it wasn't good for her self-esteem that he couldn't see her as a desirable woman. Whenever they went out, she could see him lusting after other women. He said it had been that way with every woman he'd ever cared about.

Loss of Desire at the Earliest Stage

Then there are individuals who lose sexual interest in someone practically within *minutes* of merely liking him or her.

One good-looking young man in his early thirties came to see me about his late-night habit of computer sex. His high-paced business kept him on the run and stressed-out with ten-hour days. He lived alone, and his way of relaxing was to come home, eat something, and get into the world of Internet porn. He called for an appointment right after a sobering experience with a woman.

It was the only time he had ever been fixed up with a woman in which the two of them had really hit it off on the first meeting. They saw each other a few times that week for coffee or a drink and made out one time briefly in his car. A week later she invited him over to her place, and he went. They kissed for a while on the couch and moved onto the bed. As he turned to put his arms around her he had a sudden realization that he felt nothing. What he really wanted was to get home, relax, and cozy up with the screen and keyboard.

In this instance and others like it, people in new relationships are complaining about a sexual issue—a loss of libido in one or both partners—that we usually associate with long-term relationships.

In Lust but Not in Love

Whereas one side of the love-lust dilemma is the inability to desire the one you love, the other side—the inability to love the one you desire—is equally limited. Some people throw away the possibility to have what they say they want most—sexual excitement *and* true love—because they find it hard to love the person they're in lust with.

I've heard some men and women say that the people they are most turned on to are not the type of people they care to love. I heard it from a young woman who was holding back sex from someone who could be a potential mate while gleefully giving in to the seductions of a man she never wanted to see again.

One man began therapy because he was seeing a woman he had a great sexual relationship with but didn't feel capable of loving. They had been together for more than a year, and she gave him an ultimatum: make a commitment to her or she was going to move on. He didn't want to give her up, but he couldn't commit, either. When he talked about her, he said she was a good woman and he didn't want to hurt her. But then he seemed reluctant to acknowledge her good qualities, like her intelligence and kindheartedness, and he even faulted her for her high sex drive.

When these men and women come for therapy, they are often well aware of their disconnect between love and desire, and they recognize it as a pattern that keeps them from committing to a relationship.

Low Libido in Loving Couples

Finally, there are the poster children for sexless marriage: people who love each other but have lost interest in sex. They may feel emotionally close and even be affectionate with each other, but for one reason or another the sexual part of their relationship reached a low point and never quite picked up again.

It can happen at various stages in a relationship, such as in the early years, with the stresses of young children, or after a decade or two together. Mature couples may take a loss of interest for granted as something to be expected even though they still miss the sexual side of their relationship.

Same-sex couples are not immune. Two gay men in their forties, celebrating nearly five years together, mourned the loss of their passionate sex life that had turned into a deep bond—cozy but sexless. They came for therapy, they said, because they loved each other and wanted to avoid the "easy" solution of having sex with others.

There are also people in long-term relationships who love their mates but have never really had any sexual interest in them. One woman said she loved her husband of nine years, that he was a good man and a good father to their six-year old daughter, but she had never had an orgasm with him. She was considering having an affair with a man she desired who, she was convinced, had the mojo she needed to climax. When I suggested that with some focus she might be able to achieve the elusive orgasm first alone and then with her husband, she cried out in horror, "Oh, no. I don't want it with *him*!"

I have also seen long-term relationships break up after one person confessed to the other, "I love you, but I'm not *in* love with you." It's as though being *in* love is tantamount to being in lust, but just loving is platonic: warm and friendly and, by definition, nonsexual.

Obviously, none of these seemingly uninterested men or women really had a low libido. Rather, their libido was just not directed toward their committed partner.

All of this is so opposite to what we have been led to expect or would want. How can it be that so many find it easier to turn on sexually to a complete stranger or a figure on a computer screen than to the man or woman they love or could love?

The Love-Lust Dilemma

The answer lies in the fact that although our beliefs, attitudes, and values about sex have changed a great deal in the last fifty years, how our bodies are programmed to respond to sexual feelings hasn't changed much at all.

In our formative years, most of us learned more about stifling our sex drive than about celebrating our desires, particularly in the presence of family. The paradoxical result, contrary to what society or our family intends, is that once a romance turns into an emotional attachment, our brains and bodies are wired to inhibit sexual excitement in ourselves.

There is now a great deal of neurological, biochemical, and psychological evidence to show that feelings of love and sexual desire often operate antagonistically and drive us in opposite directions. It all starts with our earliest programming.

Love and Attachment

The first stage in our ability to love is what neuroscientists who specialize in infant development call *attachment*. We begin life with an undeveloped brain and nervous system and a need to bond with one person only. Usually that's the mother, who feeds, holds, and rocks us in her soft, safe arms.

At this point, only the right hemisphere is active—the emotional, intuitive, nonverbal side of the brain. The left hemisphere, associated with language and logic, doesn't begin to function until about the eighteenth month of life. It's in the interaction between mother and child that the right brain and the nervous system begin to forge neural linkages in the brain that activate or calm the nervous system.

This early bonding experience is our first intimacy. It's a nonverbal interaction, with mother and infant mutually attuned to each other's bodily rhythms.

At one end of the spectrum, the closeness is based on need: the mother's warm, intuitive responsiveness alleviates the infant's discomfort. When the infant grows hungry, fearful, or stressed, the mother's breast, soft cooing voice, and attentiveness calms and soothes the baby.

At the other end, it's a closeness born of playfulness: the mother and the baby gazing lovingly into each other's eyes, kootchy-cooing, smiling, and laughing together. Their play energizes them both, and the mother's presence helps the infant to tolerate and enjoy high levels of playful stimulation.

When Attachment and Desire Disconnect

As the attachment system comes into play, another inborn motivational system is making an appearance.

We know that babies are born sexual. Male babies have erections in the womb, and soon after birth they can have erections—which they take obvious delight in—while being bathed or diapered. Female babies exhibit vaginal lubrication within the first three days of life. Anyone who spends time around babies and young children can't help but notice the enjoyment they take in discovering their bodies and stimulating and playing with their genitals.

With all of that holding and touching, it's natural for an infant or a toddler to direct sexual feelings toward family members. But parents can become uneasy when a child shows any sign of sexual interest. We live in a society that believes that babies and children are not *supposed* to be sexual and that parents should not encourage children's sex play.

It's a legitimate dilemma, and even the most well-meaning parents are likely to give off tense messages in their facial expressions and body language whenever a child shows any interest in sex. The parents may reflexively hold their breath, purse their lips and look away, or suddenly cut off physical contact.

Parents who believe the cultural myth that children are sexually "innocent" until puberty may be even more overtly disapproving. A client recently told me about a time her mother was visiting and watching as she changed the diaper on her six-month-old son. The little boy was obviously enjoying the process and grabbed his penis, cooing and giggling. My client was horrified to see that her mother had instinctively raised her hand to slap the baby's hand away. She grabbed her mother's hand just in time and believed that she had just protected her son from a sanctioned form of sex abuse.

We do want children to channel sexual energy outside the family. Yet the effect of disapproving or harsh gestures can be not only to cut off sexual feelings in the presence of family but also to associate *any* sexual feelings with fear or shame.

When we are adults, any sign of disapproval or discomfort in a partner can trigger old sense memories that can shut down sexual responsiveness. Commitment itself can initiate a process of projecting unresolved emotions from our original family onto our new attachments. Once that starts, the same sexual inhibitions we felt for family are reactivated in our adult bodies toward our partners. All of this takes place to a large extent on a nonverbal, unconscious, and physically numbing level.

Parenting: A Big Risk Factor for the Sex Drive

When two people get married and have children together, they really are parents. She's not his mom and he's not her dad, but seeing each one act as a parent can easily shut down the partner's sexual responsiveness. Witnessing him or her scolding the children or setting rules for them can be a big turnoff, especially if it brings up old feelings toward one's own parents. When the partners disagree, they are unlikely to be aware of how they may be acting out their own parents' relationship—treating each other as their parents treated each other when they were under stress.

Many parents, especially decades ago, were often careful not to show any signs of sexual interest in front of their children, modeling a proper, nonsexual interaction. However the partners' parents behaved when they were children becomes triggered in front of their own children. The less time they spend alone, or show any signs of affection or playfulness toward each other, the lower the libido drops.

By the time a couple gets to the point where the kids are grown and parenting is less of an issue, the partners may have neglected the sexual side of their relationship and find it hard to get it back. That's especially true if they've gotten into the habit of treating sex like an occasional nighttime ritual, a sleep aid to help them doze off.

Seeing all this intellectually is one thing. Recognizing the projections and how they affect the body is the real challenge.

Better Communication Is Not the Answer

For all of the people I've described, talking about their concerns with me or with their partners was very helpful. Certainly there is a clarity that comes with being able to articulate your feelings and to understand yourself and get your partner to understand the difficulties you're having. But while talking about it is necessary, it's not sufficient for breaking the body-based inhibitions to feel love and desire for the same person.

When two emotionally attached people start to treat each other like family, one or both of them may notice a loss of sexual interest. But what's causing it is happening on such a deep level—relating to how the brain and the nervous system are programmed—that it's typically not something anyone can put into words.

Research shows that automatic body-based inhibitions are triggered at the neural level in nanoseconds and are often experienced as faint visceral sensations. At the same time, they are communicated to the partner at an implicit or unspoken level, revealed primarily through micro-expressions on the face and in subtle body language: a dry versus wet kiss, a pat on the back instead of a suggestive caress, or a sudden discomfort with nudity.

We may not consciously know what our brains are responding to; we just know we're getting turned off. Some of these factors may even limit how good the sex can be for partners who do have good sex. Understanding the issues that limit sexual arousal is a good start, but that alone is not enough to increase desire. Telling your partner what you like sexually is always good, but that's not enough, either.

The problem with words is that they keep you focused in your head. What inhibits desire is not just a mind-set but also a body-set, habitual tensions that can numb the sexual body even as your affection for someone grows. No amount of talk can unlock a closed-off pelvis, particularly when the minute reactions to a sexual possibility are too subtle to be consciously registered, let alone verbalized.

What's a person to do? If talking about it doesn't go deep enough, what will? Once we get comfortable with each other, is it possible to bridge the gap between the nurturing calm of love and the thrills of a lusty appetite?

Changing Our Programming

I say it *is* possible to love the one you desire or to reignite sexual desire for someone you care for, but not by resorting to superficial gimmicks and quick fixes. Years of rote practice have gone into keeping love and lust separate, not just in our own lifetimes but also culturally for centuries. Changing our programming is nothing short of a personal sexual revolution, an intentional sexual *evolution*.

Personal Evolution

The process of personal evolution is very different from "curing a sexual disorder." You don't call something that occurs naturally a *disorder*. As we're finding, it's rather common to lose your libido for your partner as your emotional attachment grows. It's natural to find your heart race and your juices flow for sexy strangers. It doesn't serve us to deny it.

The love-lust dilemma may be natural, but it's (literally) not desirable. Twinges of excitement for sexy strangers can be fun and exciting, particularly if those people remain strangers. But we want to be able to unite affection and passion in the same person—ideally, for the life of the relationship. When the sex is good, people rate the nonsexual aspects of their relationships as more satisfying than people who say that their sex lives are lacking.

Partners who love each other but don't express it sexually know that having a passionate sex life together would do them a lot of good. It would enhance their love, put more spring in their step, give them energy for each other, and even engender a more positive personal outlook.

Women who are turned on by sleazy guys they would never marry yearn to have sexual passion with someone they respect and admire. They just don't think they can. Men who spend at least an hour or two a day with Internet porn have intense sexual experiences and explosive orgasms with themselves. But it bothers them that they can't have that with someone they care for.

Partners who have been together forever, or what feels like forever, in their heart of hearts would love to have scintillating sex with each other—especially if it was better than ever before.

The Evolutionary Process

The truth is that we *can* have it all, but to do so we have to be willing to break through centuries of old programming that's wired into our brains and nervous systems. Recognizing this takes us beyond the narrow perspectives of treating loss of libido as a sexual dysfunction or simply requiring greater imagination in bed. This is about breaking free from a socially induced affliction and evolving as individuals and as a couple. It's especially about how we love and how we experience sexual feelings, in our bodies and not just in our heads.

As we explore the research, you'll get a clear sense of how love and sexual feelings are linked in the brain and the nervous system. You'll also see how being responsive to a subtle level of intimate experience between partners can essentially rewire the brain and the nervous system. There is now a great deal of scientific evidence to show that we can do this.

Columbia University psychiatrist and researcher Norman Doidge has amassed an astounding array of studies that represent a revolution in brain science known as *neuroplasticity*. Medical science has always taken as a given that once neuronal connections in the brain have been programmed to respond in a particular way, especially during critical periods in childhood, they are essentially hardwired and fixed.

Neuroscientists are now discovering that the brain actually changes all the time, perfecting itself. It can do this to the degree that if certain parts of the brain are damaged, other parts can take over and become rewired. Deaf people can sometimes learn to hear and blind people can sometimes learn to see through exercises that stimulate new neural pathways to build between sensory organs and the brain. The healing process, it turns out, capitalizes on the natural capacity to feel rewarded by playful activity by turning the ordinary life experiences that need to be relearned into games. As we shall see, the neuroplastic revolution, with its emphasis on our natural aptitude to evolve our brains, lends great support to our ability to evolve and to enjoy a sexy kind of love.

The Ten-Step Loving Sex Program: Your Own Personal Evolution

At the conclusion of each chapter in this book you will find one step of the Ten-Step Loving Sex Program. Each step offers experiments and games corresponding to that chapter that can stimulate new pathways to intimate pleasures for you. The program is designed so that each step is progressively more intimate than the one preceding it. Even if you don't actually do any of the exercises, you can still benefit from reading the exercises and picturing yourself doing them.

Loving Sex Starts with Love

As you will see, this loving sex program doesn't begin with a new way of understanding and enjoying sex. That comes later. Rather, this program begins with a new way of understanding and enjoying love and its essential pleasures.

Sex can be driven by emotions and motivations other than love. Sexual activity can be fueled by anxiety and a need for reassurance, by guilt and a sense of obligation, by shame and an urge to be punished, or even by anger and a desire for revenge. But for sex that is impassioned by love, we need to begin our exploration of loving sex as we do, by taking a new look at love and its erotic counterpart, romance.

For this reason, the first five steps of the program are dedicated to honing the pleasures of love and romance. The final five steps focus on developing the pleasures of skillful sexual activity and eroticism.

I'm a big proponent of psychotherapy and sex therapy. In fact, because of our collective repressive history, I think everyone would benefit from an enlightening course of sex education for adults and some individual and/or couples therapy. Most people have much to gain and to learn about themselves by expressing their feelings in the safe presence of a warm, intuitive, skilled therapist. This book and the loving sex program offered here are meant not to replace therapy but to complement it through body-based methods that support personal growth.

The Body-Mind Route to Loving Sex

As a society we have come to accept the mind-body connection. We recognize that how we think about things—whether we are essentially optimistic or pessimistic—affects our emotions, which in turn affect the physical body, health, immunity, and longevity. Systems of psychotherapy that are based on the primacy of thought—how changing the way you think can change how you feel and act—are called *cognitive-behavioral* approaches.

The body-mind perspective starts not with the state of the mind but with an awareness of the state of the body; it is often referred to as a *somatic-experiential* approach. Body-based psychotherapy, like Gestalt therapy, the method I was trained in by the founders, Fritz Perls and Laura Perls, emphasizes becoming more attuned to a person's inner felt-sense awareness, focusing on sensations, emotions, and muscular tensions to make discoveries about one's emotional truths.

Gestalt therapy is essentially based on a philosophical model of psychotherapy and emphasizes personal growth though self-exploration and body-mind awareness. It stands in contradistinction to traditional psychotherapy that is based on the medical model and typically treats emotional distress as a mental disorder.

Gestalt methods involve recognizing and releasing chronic tensions in the body, which can then reveal memories, mental imagery, and limiting thought patterns and emotional habits. Body-mind awareness confers physical-fitness skills that can be an even more direct route to health and longevity. Since some Gestalt therapists have become increasingly cognitive in their approach, those of us who emphasize body awareness are considered embodied Gestalt therapists.

Psychologist Wilhelm Reich is considered the originator of somatic, or body-based, approaches to psychotherapy and of any bodywork that aims to release blocked emotion through breath work, touch, movement, or sensory awareness. Writing in the 1930s and 1940s, Reich, originally a student of Sigmund Freud, predicted a future that held dramatic changes in sexuality, marriage, and the family. He named it the Sexual Revolution and clearly articulated the crucial role of women's liberation and ending what he saw as forced sexual abstinence in youth. Reich also was the first to make the connections among the inability to fully let go during sexual experience, the resistance to pleasure, and the inability to be happy in general and to fully enjoy life. He believed that this had repercussions beyond the individual level, affecting our entire social and political reality.

A Full-Spectrum Approach

The approach we are about to embark on for integrating love and libido combines all of the above into a cognitive-behavioral-somatic-experiential system. Anything less is only part of the picture.

We want to understand where our thoughts come from and how our thought (cognitive) processes affect our excitement and desire. Yet if we want new attitudes and behavioral patterns to take hold, we have to become aware of what's going on inside the body in the moment: the sensations, images, and emotions that are aroused by those thoughts.

That's the experiential part of the somatic-experiential approach. It has to do with reading what's going on inside your body in the moment and checking for sensations in the emotional center that runs from the head through the heart and the belly to the pelvis. Once you become aware of your true feelings—what's in your heart and your gut—and any tendency you have to react automatically and reflexively based on your programming, you will be better able to assess the situation and choose how you want to respond.

The Value of Pleasure and Play

A full-spectrum approach that uses all accessible resources involves learning through playful and pleasurable experience as well as through processing painful feelings.

Research in the neuroplasticity of the brain clearly demonstrates that new pathways in the brain and the nervous system grow primarily through accessing positive feelings, pleasure, and playfulness. One of the leading figures in the new field of neuroplasticity described by Norman Doidge is neuroscientist Michael Merzenich. Based in Santa Rosa, California, Merzenich has created a variety of programs to exercise the brain to help with (among other concerns), autism, language problems, rehabilitation after brain injury, and the prevention of the decline in brain function that accompanies aging. His studies show that it is possible to improve the capacities of the brain for all of these difficulties and for all of us throughout life. What is essential for enhancing the brain is to keep it engaged and attentive. Playfulness is one of the great ways to stay engaged and attentive.

As you will see, so much of what can be learned about love and sex is about promoting good feelings and enhancing the capacity for play. Our ability to feel good, to play, and to enjoy loving sex is intertwined with every aspect of life: physical health, emotional and mental well-being, loving relationships, and spiritual connection.

Know Thyself

These words were inscribed at the entrance to the Temple of Apollo in Delphi during the first millennium BC in ancient Greece, where the priestess known as the Oracle of Delphi gave counsel to the kings and other leaders of her time. The philosopher Socrates lived in Athens then. He was revered as a great teacher among the intellectuals of his time and was considered the wisest man in Athens, not only by his colleagues but by the oracle herself.

Socrates developed a method of teaching that involved simply asking his students questions. The purpose of the questioning was to lead them to achieve genuine self-knowledge by logically examining the popular beliefs of the time and thinking for themselves. For this he was charged with undermining the state religion and corrupting the youth. When he was brought to trial and condemned to death, the jury offered to spare his life if he would make a commitment to abandon his methods. To this he replied, "The unexamined life is not worth living."

Socrates at first rejected the oracle's pronouncement of his being the wisest man, but through utilizing his own method of asking himself questions and going deeper he ended up coming to the same conclusion as the oracle had. He reasoned that everyone he came in contact with thought they were so smart, but he could see they were fools. He, in contrast, *knew* he was a fool. Ergo, he must be the wisest man in Athens.

In esoteric systems, the fool is actually an archetype seen to be a source of wisdom. He is childlike, full of curiosity, and playful; unencumbered by conventional explanations, he spurs those who come in contact with him to think for themselves and to change.

Body-Mind Self-Attunement

If you ask yourself why something is happening, how you tend to explain it often stops the process of looking any further. In this process of self-knowing, we want to be able to steer clear of old explanations that bias what we focus on as solutions and to look for new ways of understanding. In a sense, we need to become the fool to trick ourselves to make deeper discoveries.

Step one of the Loving Sex Program offers some opportunities to know yourself more deeply. It starts with some simple useful questions about yourself and your partner. If you are not currently in a relationship, you can do this exercise with a significant past intimacy in mind.

You'll then move into your body to see what truths you can learn directly from self-observation. You'll learn the basic embodiment exercise and other body-based tools that help you to become more attuned to your inner state of emotional activation, stress, or relaxation.

Step One: Body-Mind Basics

Objective: To know and experience yourself in new ways

The life that's worth living is worth examining, not just in what you think but especially in what you feel. We begin our exploration with your thoughts about, and goals for, your intimate relationship. Then we look at what you can learn from your body.

You can write your answers down in a notebook you keep especially for these exercises, you can do these exercises in conversation with your partner or a friend, or you can just think about them and maybe take some notes afterward. In all of these exercises, if you are not currently in a relationship, answer with your last or a future partner in mind.

Personal Goals

1. Name three qualities you would like more of in your emotional life with your partner. Give some examples of how that might look.

2. Name three qualities you would like more of in your sexual life with your partner. Give some examples of how that might look.

3. How do you imagine your partner would have to grow to make those changes? Describe the skills he or she would need to learn.

4. How do you imagine you would have to grow to make those changes? Describe the skills you would need to learn.

As you continue reading, see whether your answers to these questions change.

Embodiment Exercises

Observations that start with the body and not with what we think or think we know are called a "bottom-up" system of inquiry rather

than "top-down." Sensations, feelings, images, or memories popping up in fantasy are the experiences of the present moment, to
observe now and to scrutinize later.

These exercises can help you tune in to any tightness or numb-
ness in your body, especially in the emotional center of your
body—the area from the top of your head to your pelvis. The exercises can help you to find your true feelings and reactions, heal old
wounds, and make choices based on the present and not on habits
formed in the past. Practice them for a few seconds or minutes a
couple of times a day.

BELLY ROLLS

The purpose of this exercise is to see if you unconsciously hold your
belly tense and to learn to relax and let it breathe. When you're sexually active, you want your belly relaxed or engaged rather than tense.
Tension in the abdominal muscles prevents blood flow to the pelvis.

1. Sit with your back comfortably straight in a chair and place your
   hands on your belly. Notice if you're holding your belly in or if
   the muscles of your belly feel relaxed. Now breathe and pull
   your belly in quickly three times. Notice that you automatically
   exhale every time you tug on your abdominal muscles.

2. Take a deep breath in, and blow out. As you exhale, pull your
   belly in and tense it up as much as you can. Hold your breath as
   you hold your belly. Tighter, tighter, tighter. Now inhale deeply,
   letting your belly go as loose and limp as possible. Take a breath
   in and out, and do it again. Tighten. Tighter. Tightest. Hold
   it. Now let go as you breathe in. Feel your belly relax as you
   breathe deeply. Do this exercise for about a minute.

BELLY BREATHING

If you have a tendency to suck in your belly and lift your chest
on the inhalation, learning to relax the belly on the inhalation is
a healthier way to breathe. This enables the diaphragm to flatten
as you inhale, which pushes out the belly and the rib cage and
makes room for the lower lobes of the lungs to fill. The more you
exercise your lungs fully, the healthier they remain. The object of
this exercise is to breathe primarily with only your belly and rib
cage moving. This way of breathing is also known as diaphragmatic
breathing. Practice this exercise for a few minutes.

1. Sit with your back straight in a comfortable chair, relax your shoulders, place your hands on your belly, and inhale deeply through your nose until your lungs are full, without moving your shoulders. Exhale slowly through your mouth, and focus your attention on your belly.

2. As you start your next inhalation, feel how the belly pushes out to make room for the lungs to fill. See if you can feel the movement of your breath in your lower back and spine. Make sure you don't lift your shoulders, because that indicates that your belly and diaphragm are tight. See if you can relax your shoulders as you inhale, and let the expansion of the torso come from the belly opening. Feel your belly contract as you exhale.

THE COMPLETE BREATH

The object of this exercise is to feel your breath fill your belly and move through your entire torso, through your rib cage and filling your chest; do this as much as you can without lifting your shoulders. Practice this exercise about a minute.

1. Sit with your back straight in a comfortable chair, relax your shoulders, place your hands on your belly, and inhale deeply through your nose, but this time, as the rib cage widens, bring the breath into your chest and feel it lift as you keep your shoulders down.

2. When your lungs are full, get to the top of your breath and blow out slowly through slightly puckered lips all the way down to the bottom of the exhale until you run out of air. If you notice that you have lifted your shoulders, drop them before you blow out. Pull your abdominal muscles in to push the last bit of air out of your lungs. When you have emptied your lungs as much as you can, the next inhalation will happen naturally. In this way your whole torso works efficiently as the bellows it's designed to be, taking in fresh air and getting rid of the old stale air.

3. Do this breath three times, and with each new breath see if you can increase movement in your abdominal muscles to get more motility in your torso. This breath is also known as a cleansing breath.

THE SIGHING BREATH

The object of this breath is to release tension and relax the body. This exercise will typically take about ten seconds.

1. After you have taken three complete breaths, take a quick inhalation with an open mouth and exhale through your mouth in a deep sigh.

2. Do two more quick sighs in this way and notice how this breath moves mostly in the upper chest and upper back. Don't lift your shoulders as you breathe, and don't hold your breath at the end of your inhalation. As you inhale and exhale, your chest quickly fills and releases, and your upper back widens and releases. The sigh is like an unvocalized *ha*. Hold your palm in front of your mouth and sigh as though you're going to clean your glasses. If the air coming out is warm, you're doing it right.

TAKING A FELT-SENSE INVENTORY

1. After you have taken several complete breaths and a few deep sighing breaths, tune in to the sensations in your emotional center, the area of your body between your head and your pelvis. Slowly focus on each of the five sections of the body identified below.

2. For each section you examine, close your eyes, tune in to that area, notice any sensations you may feel there, and make a mental note of it. This is called *felt-sense awareness*. Then open your eyes, read the next step, take a deep sigh, close your eyes, and feel the next section of your emotional center. This exercise will probably take you thirty seconds to a minute, once you get the hang of it.

   • Start with your head, forehead, eyes, cheeks, mouth, and jaw. Breathe deeply and see if any of these areas are tight. Make a mental note of what you observe.

   • Take a deep sigh and tune in to your throat. Sense if you have a grip or a lump in your throat. Make a mental note.

   • Take another deep sigh and check your chest. Sense if there is a weight on your chest, a band around your chest, or a grip in the center of your chest. Make a mental note.

- Sigh and feel for any knot in your solar plexus, diaphragm, gut, or belly. Make a mental note.
- Take a deep sigh and see if there is any tension in your genitals, thighs, anus, or butt. Make a mental note.

What does it all mean? Although people can store feelings anywhere in the body, there are some typical areas for feeling particular emotions. See if this outline helps you to understand the emotion behind your tensions:

- Tension in the head, forehead, and eyes is usually a sign of mental stress, thinking a lot, and a tendency to analyze situations to try to figure things out. Tension in the cheeks, mouth, and jaw is usually about holding feelings in and not speaking up. It can also be a sign of anger or disgust.
- A grip in the throat is often a sign of anxiety; a lump usually has to do with feeling sad or hurt.
- A weight on the chest usually suggests feelings of sadness, hurt, or disappointment. A grip in the center of the chest or a band around the chest may indicate anxiety or fear.
- A knot in the solar plexus, diaphragm, or gut can be a sign of guilt or self-punishment, feelings of responsibility, or heavy obligation. A knot in the belly can be anger or fear. A feeling of "butterflies" is usually a sign of dread about the future.
- Tension in the genitals, thighs, anus, or butt can indicate feelings of shame.

THE BASIC EMBODIMENT EXERCISE

This exercise may take about a minute to do, yet it's your basic tool for relaxing tension and knowing yourself more deeply.

1. Take three complete breaths and a few deep sighs.
2. Then take a felt-sense inventory starting at your head, face, and jaw, moving your attention into your throat, chest, diaphragm, belly, and pelvic area. Scan your emotional center for any tension, tightness, heaviness, or sensation.

The basic embodiment excercise is helpful to do when you're feeling stressed and overwhelmed. It's also good to do when you're feeling content and want to savor your enjoyment.

2

What Dampens Desire

Quick—picture a scene of hot sex between a man and a woman in a movie. I'll bet you flashed on something resembling a dam breaking: two people restraining themselves no more, swept away in a flood of overwhelming passion. They go at each other in a flurry of intimacies that likely includes ripping off their clothing, clearing a table with the sweep of a forearm or having sex against a wall, and the woman's face in rapture. A minute later it's over. That's what I call "frenzied sex."

Think of the first sex scene in the 1981 movie *Body Heat*. Kathleen Turner locks William Hurt out of her house. He pounds on the door as she backs against the wall, sweating and breathing heavily. Her eyes follow him through the window as an increasingly frantic Hurt in heat races around the porch, searching for a way in.

Finally he throws a deck chair at a window, shatters it, and climbs through. Hungrily they kiss big gaping kisses and claw at each other's clothes. They do it right there against the wall. The dam breaks.

The sex gets a lot less frantic and a whole lot hotter as the movie progresses. Yet subsequent filmmakers seem to have fixated on that first scene, repeating it, ad nauseam, for more than thirty years.

Another film from the same year, the remake of *The Postman Always Rings Twice*, starring Jack Nicholson and Jessica Lange, may be the first table-sweeping sex. Starting with a one-minute violent struggle, it continues against a wall with the ripping of clothing and ends with two whole minutes of urgent passion, hers as much as his, on top of a butcher-block table covered with flour.

Many tabletops have followed. As one Internet movie blogger wrote in an essay titled "9 Things I Learned about Sex from the Movies," number three was "The best sex takes place on kitchen counters." Besides mentioning *Postman*, the blogger also listed *Secretary*, *The Boss of It All*, and *Jackie Brown*.

The lesbian scenes in mainstream movies that I'm familiar with tend to portray slower and more deliberate sex, like the scenes between the characters in the 1996 movie *Bound* starring Gina Gershon and Jennifer Tilly. Still, though more sensual, I have seen a number of female-on-female make-out scenes against a wall.

For gay male characters think *Brokeback Mountain*—the requisite frenzy is still there. Recall the first sex scene between Heath Ledger's Ennis and Jake Gyllenhaal's Jack. It starts out violent and ends in rough hard sex that lasts less than a minute. And how about that de rigueur fifteen-second frantic reunion kiss in the alley against the wall as Ennis's wife, Alma (Michelle Williams), catches it through a window?

Could it be that one of the difficulties with married sex is the lack of imaginative use of wall space or tabletops?

Sexual Misinformation

Popular movies are not only a reflection of cultural beliefs and values, they also play a major role in shaping them—including our expectations about sex.

In the 1994 University of Chicago study "Sex in America," the researchers were stunned to discover the level of misinformation and myth among the nearly thirty-five hundred randomly selected participants. Almost everyone, the authors wrote, had questions about their sexuality. Most believed that everyone else was having a better time than they were.

The researchers suggested that it was understandable that people would feel "a sense of lingering dissatisfaction when the erotic sexual world of novels and movies turned out to be so different from the world of conventional sex in marriage." The consequences of these misconceptions, the authors observed, make it difficult for people to understand how their sex lives develop so they can realistically change the aspects they don't like.

I certainly don't think that the world of conventional sex in marriage is anything to aspire to. Besides, when movies are the main source of sex education for a badly misinformed public, we're in trouble. Two things we don't want to rely on the movies for are an accurate account of history and an informed depiction of sexual desire.

Twenty-first-century sexual attitudes haven't changed much from the past few decades. Many of the individuals or couples I see with concerns about their sex lives were born in the 1970s, 1980s, or 1990s. Yet when they start to talk about their beliefs, expectations, sexual histories, family histories, and sexual habits in their relationships, I can see a generational continuity that goes back to the 1950s.

A Multitude of Risk Factors

There are lots of risk factors associated with losing desire for the person you love. Some are obvious, but others are genuine dilemmas and harder to deal with.

Obvious Risk Factors

Some of the conditions that increase the likelihood that an individual will lose interest in sex are well known and often addressed in individual or couples therapy.

Stress

Today's financial climate and the pressures of work, money, and raising young children can strain a relationship and keep people on edge. One couple dealt with money tensions by getting angry, each partner blaming the other for the stress. The combination of pessimism, fear, arguing, power struggles, and resentment made the couple stop touching completely.

Depression and Anxiety

Despair and apprehension naturally wipe out enthusiasm for anything pleasurable, because depressed and anxious people have difficulty staying in the present moment—a big limitation when it comes to sex. Typically, depressed people are locked in the past while anxious people are busy worrying about the future. Sex has to be very here-and-now to be good.

Trauma

The unresolved emotional effects of sexual abuse can trigger a person to dissociate—to mentally split off from the body—when anything sexual seems imminent. One man I worked with who was molested as a young boy could keep his erection during intercourse with his wife, but he wasn't present emotionally with her. She could feel him drift away, and she interpreted his inattention as boredom and felt rejected. For sex to be truly satisfying and enriching, both partners have to be tuned in to their bodies and in contact emotionally, looking at and relating to each other.

Desire-Dampening Physical Conditions

Hormone deficiencies, the side effects of antidepressant medications, drug abuse, or illness can all limit spontaneous sexual interest. If there's limited physical energy—and especially when there's limited motivation for physical contact, hugs, or kisses with a partner—sex is not likely to be a high priority and thus not likely to happen.

Genuine Dilemmas

These are factors that can contribute to losing sexual interest for a committed partner that are more difficult to resolve.

Monogamy

Could it be that monogamy itself—and the expectation that sexual desire will last for a lifetime—has limitations? Rutgers University anthropologist Helen Fisher reports on cross-cultural research that shows that divorce everywhere tends to peak around the fourth year of marriage, a time that also corresponds to when the excitement of infatuation typically fades.

Although most of society would define monogamy as one partner for life, Fisher tells us that anthropologists don't necessarily equate monogamy with fidelity. Based on a multitude of studies around the world, from Western societies to island tribes, Fisher concluded that "adultery goes hand in hand with monogamy." Secret affairs and occasional cheating seem to be an indelible part of what we think of as monogamous relationships.

Infidelity

It's difficult to get a completely accurate picture of the prevalence of infidelity, because many of the same factors that cause straying men and women to lie to their partners also cause them to lie to survey takers. Studies vary, but most suggest that 50 to 60 percent of married men and 45 to 55 percent of married women have engaged in extramarital sex at some time, whereas only 25 to 35 percent of men and women whose spouses had cheated ever suspected any extramarital activity.

We've certainly witnessed a rash of high-profile figures caught up in scandals from being discovered in extramarital affairs. In many instances the shame was compounded by the fact that the errant spouse had been such a hypocrite by condemning other men caught cheating.

How compelling is the urge for sex and romance outside marriage that powerful men would risk everything for sexual trysts with sexy young women? Part of it has to do with the well-known fact that men with power have high levels of available testosterone. Another part of it has to do with a seemingly unlimited access to pretty young women who are hot powerful men.

Women cheat, too. I have heard many women with supposedly low libido confide that they haven't lost sexual desire, just the desire for "bad sex" with their partners. Increasingly, women confess to having outside sexual encounters that are passionate and playful beyond anything they ever had with their mates. One woman summed it up for me by describing her lover as more attentive, more romantic, more appreciative of what she does for him, and more focused on giving her pleasure than her husband is.

Men who cheat say the same. They say that their lovers are more interested in them physically, easier to be with, easier to please, and sexually more available than their wives are.

The Biochemistry of Romance versus Commitment

Romance is all about falling in love, head over heels, as we say. It's a time of great excitement, joy, and obsession. Studies show that the biochemistry of these experiences involves brain chemicals associated with reward: dopamine and norepinephrine.

Dopamine and norepinephrine are stimulants, generating feelings of euphoria. Both chemicals are also triggers for testosterone, the hormone of sexual desire for both men and women.

In contrast, once a commitment is made, the predominant biochemistry of the feelings of comfort and security is oxytocin and vasopressin. Oxytocin is a brain chemical associated with bonding, and vasopressin is a hormone linked to monogamy in males. Both can be sedating, and inhibit testosterone.

Bad news for young parents: babies are also testosterone inhibitors. Some studies have shown that just putting an infant on a man's chest for a minute will immediately lower the available testosterone in the man's blood. In one set of studies at Northwestern University that was reported in 2010, it was found that the fathers who spent the most time actively caring for their kids, feeding, bathing, and putting them to sleep, had the lowest levels of testosterone. It's good news for keeping the man around to protect the family, but not so great for mommy and daddy's sex life—especially since mommies are getting an overabundance of oxytocin from bringing up baby.

The Lure of Otherness

The late psychiatrist and sex therapist Dr. Helen Singer Kaplan first drew attention in 1979 to low sex drive as a growing issue for couples, and she bestowed upon it the clinical label *hypoactive sexual desire*, or HSD. She described the most common variant of it, situational HSD, as "an inhibited desire for one's spouse while, at the same time, a strong sexual interest in uncommitted partners, unconventional sex, or strangers." No surprise there.

Daily Proximity

Research in the last eighty years has consistently shown that daily proximity itself can dampen sexual interest. One set of studies was run on people raised collectively on Israeli kibbutzim during the late 1940s and the 1950s. It showed that among the thousands of marriages between these individuals as adults, it was rare to find any marriages between those who had been raised in the same group. No marriages had occurred between people who were raised together before the age of six. The researchers suggest that the greater the sense of familiarity, the less the sexual interest between people who are like family to each other.

What Chance Do We Have to Change Things?

Here we are, with a lack of good information about sex and with cultural associations that tell us that the best sex is the first time, if you hold yourself back until you can't stand it anymore, and then it's all downhill from there.

There may also be some built-in tendencies that limit long-term monogamous relationships. Anthropologists inform us that we may be biologically programmed to last for four years, suggesting that if we do nothing to counter that, there is a statistical likelihood of stale sex with a mate and passion for strangers.

Then, of course, there are the very real dampening effects of stress, feeling depressed or anxious, and maybe having bad associations with sexual activity. What's the possibility of getting past those feelings? What chance is there, really, for sustaining desire and passion with just one person for the rest of your life?

Resolving this dilemma sounds like a formidable task. However, if we take all of these factors into account and work with them rather than deny them, the chance of resolution is very good. That's because there is an underlying dynamic that, with greater awareness, can help to ameliorate these influences. It starts by recognizing the early programming of the love-lust dilemma during childhood and how that can result in "family transference" in an adult intimate relationship.

The Thorny Subject of Childhood Sexuality

We are born sexual. That doesn't mean that we want to have sex with our mothers or our fathers. Sex in infancy and childhood is nothing like reproductive sex, which doesn't manifest until puberty.

Infant and childhood sexuality is all about being playful and sensual and doing what feels good. Juvenile sex play, whether alone or with playmates, is a natural developmental phase for humans, just as it is for all primates and other animals. That place between the legs feels especially good. That's the true meaning of childhood sexual innocence.

Sigmund Freud called it "polymorphous perversity," but he did not intend the word *perversity* in the sense that we understand it, as deviance. Quite the contrary: he saw children's sexual explorations as natural, and he never retracted his view on the importance of infantile and childhood sexuality. Early in the twentieth century, he wrote the following:

> Sexual manifestations from the period before puberty have only attracted attention in connection with phenomena of degeneracy. In none of the accounts . . . of the psychology of this period of life is a chapter to be found on the erotic life of children.
>
> As long ago as in the year 1896 I insisted on the significance of the years of childhood in the origin of certain important phenomena connected with sexual life, and since then I have never ceased to emphasize the part played in sexuality by the infantile factor.

Yet for most of us, that delightfully exploratory phase of our sexual selves met with parental anxiety. Maybe we were punished and shamed. At worst, we may have been sexually mistreated. Maybe our parents were very involved or even intrusive in other respects, but when it came to sex they were completely AWOL.

Love for Family and Lust for Strangers

At some level, we've all been sexually injured by what is fundamentally a sexually stunted society. Some of us have been abused and truly wounded at a very early stage in our sexual development. Most of us are doing remarkably well, given the lack of information and guidance we've had at critical periods in our sexual development.

Abandoned to our own devices, we were left to negotiate the sexual mysteries by ourselves. We conspired with other ten-year-olds, whenever possible, to sleuth it out together.

We've been programmed to associate love with family and close friends and to reserve our lusty feelings for strangers, "bad" boys and girls. We've downloaded the history of our sexually skittish society through our parents in the covert negative messages they unconsciously transmitted to us about sex. We shouldn't blame them, though. They downloaded their uneasiness with childhood sexual interest in the same way, from their parents.

Covert messages are nature's original wireless transmissions: face-to-face, a widening or a narrowing of the eyes, a smile or a sneer, a hug or a cringe. Then, as adults, the pleasure or the pain associated with the aggregate of our sexual experiences to date goes into the mix.

How we feel about our bodies, any feelings of guilt or shame, what we learn to expect of anyone we love, what we want or think we want when it comes to sex, whom we desire or feel we *should* desire, when we desire, how we should express that, and what should happen next are all largely programmed during critical periods in the development of our personal sexuality, especially during the first five years and during adolescence.

Neurologists say that "neurons that fire together wire together." All of these early experiences wire our emotional and sexual neurons together in the subliminal and emotional right brain and in the language and logic-dependent, often faulty-premise-prone left brain.

It's in our nervous systems: how we respond to getting excited, whether we open or close to sexual feelings in the context of emotional attachment, and whether we feel excited or worried. It's in our habitual muscular tensions and how we hold ourselves in or let the energy flow.

The blocks that get in the way of complete sexual fulfillment are a sign not of disease but largely of arrested development during critical periods in our sexual histories. We're not sick, so we can't be cured. We may be wounded, some of us more than others, but with nurturing we can heal our wounded sexual selves. With good information and commitment to the process, we can set back in motion the natural maturation of loving sexuality throughout our entire life span.

Any barriers we may have to one of the most exquisite capacities of the human experience—sharing the heights of sexual pleasure in the context of love—are nothing more than opportunities to evolve our sexual selves, whether we're in our twenties, our fifties, or our eighties.

The Love-Lust Dilemma and Family Transference

Once a sexual interest becomes a potential or real mate, there is a strong tendency to begin to automatically transfer unresolved issues from your original family to the "new family figure." When you do, your body begins a programmed response of inhibiting sexual energy toward that person.

This is the underlying factor that turns people off sexually to someone they love or care for. It is an involuntary reflexive shutting down of sexual feelings as the emotional attachment to that person grows.

Here's an example of how it manifests even in the absence of many of the obvious risk factors mentioned earlier. This description is based on a few initial sessions in my office with an attractive woman in her early thirties.

When Love Trumps Lust

Teri sat on my cozy sea-green chenille sofa. I sat opposite her in my black leather chair, listening closely as she began her story. Teri had finally met the man of her dreams and was totally in love with him. Andy and she had been living together for more than a year and were making plans to marry. The only problem was that they had become "good buddies" and she had totally lost interest in making love with him. This had happened to her before, and it was the kiss of death for every relationship. She had come for therapy now to nip this "terrible thing" in the bud.

As Teri described Andy to me, I could tell that she thought the world of him. "He's a good, decent human being," she told me proudly, "and he's very cute. He's a fitness nut like me and has a nice body." She threw up her hands in a gesture of helplessness. "Why am I so blasé about him?"

When Teri and Andy first met, they had had really hot sex. But once they moved in together, they started having sex less and less often, and eventually whole weeks would go by without any sexual contact at all. "Poor Andy," she said to me. "He keeps trying anyway, but he's beginning to feel rejected." She shook her head sadly. "But what can I do," she said, more as a statement than a question. "I can't fake it."

When I asked her what she thought was going on, she told me that she didn't have a clue. She just knew that something must be terribly wrong with her, and she wanted to figure it out. Rather than digging further for answers about what she *thought* might be going on, I told her that she was more likely to find some clues by focusing on her body.

Teri agreed to the experiment, so I asked her to close her eyes, take a few deep breaths, and pay attention to her emotional body—the area between her head and her pelvis. Teri said she felt relaxed. When I asked her to get an image of Andy in her mind's eye, she smiled and said she could feel her heart swell with love for him. But when I asked her to imagine the two of them making love, Teri crinkled her nose and said it just didn't feel right. She could feel her diaphragm and belly tense at the thought.

In the next session, when I took Teri's family history, I learned that she came from a very close, loving family and had a brother just two years older. She and her brother were "good buddies" growing up, and she said that to this day she would do anything for him, and he for her. I remembered that Teri had used that same phrase for Andy in her previous session, so I told Teri that it seemed to me that she had turned Andy into her big brother.

Teri laughed when I said this, but she admitted that she did feel the same kinds of feelings for him as she felt for her brother. She admired them both. When we began to look at the kinds of men who had turned her on in the past, she picked up a toss pillow from the couch and playfully hid her face behind it.

Teri was clearly embarrassed. "I like bad boys," she confessed with some quick nods. Her last boyfriend was the kind of man she could never bring home: he was into motorcycles, his hair was wild, and he was covered with tattoos. "I had to break it off with him after only six months, but *wow*." She smiled and rolled her eyes, and her cheeks were getting redder by the second. "Was he ever hot!"

Teri had made a choice not to pick her life partner based primarily on sexual excitement. She had never considered sharing a life with her "bad boy" lover. Andy was different, and she loved him dearly. They had fun together and were there for each other completely. They stimulated each other intellectually, had similar values, and wanted the same lifestyle. She had made a good choice.

Teri and Andy once had a good sexual connection—naturally, without having to learn anything. Now they both had some powerful incentives to learn more.

The Pain and Pleasure of Love

A classic French song, "Plaisir d'Amour," warns that the pleasures of love last but a moment while the pain of love lasts a lifetime: *plaisir d'amour ne dure qu'un moment; chagrin d'amour dure toute la vie.*

In fact, we carry both the joys and the heartaches of love in the body, especially in the heart and the rest of the chest. Is it possible to be enriched by grief and come to terms with loss? How do the pains and pleasures of the past affect our ability to fully love and be loved in the present?

Step two of the program can help you to make some discoveries about how the pains and pleasures of love in your past have influenced how you give and receive love today.

Step Two: Making the Family Connection

Objectives: To recognize how your past is present in how you love and to explore some of the pleasures of love

Start and end each of these exercises with the basic embodiment exercises in chapter 1, taking a few complete breaths and two or three deep sighs. Take a felt-sense inventory and notice any sensations, emotions, memories, and images that come up, especially when you breathe into—and fully feel—your chest and your heart.

1. *Complete a family history chart.* This exercise could take anywhere from fifteen minutes to half an hour. Don't think about it too much. Take a few deep breaths, get centered in your body, and just let it happen intuitively.

   - Draw a diagram of your family as you were growing up, from birth until the age of twelve. Do it this way: assign a circle to every female in your family and a triangle to every male, and indicate their relationships to one another by showing how close or distant their symbols are in relation to one another. For example, if your mother and your father were very close, her circle and his triangle might be touching. If they were distant, their symbols would be wide apart on the page. If you were closer to one parent than to the other, put your circle (if you're female) or your triangle (if you're male) closer to that parent, and fit in any sisters or brothers accordingly. Label all of the figures with their names. This diagram will give you a clear picture of what your childhood was like. If something like divorce changed your life between ages one and twelve, do two diagrams, one before the divorce and one after, and give a set of descriptions for each.

   - At the bottom of the page, write three adjectives that best describe each of the following in terms of what you observed and felt as a child, not what you know now:

         What it was like for you to grow up in this family
         The relationship between your mother and your father
         The relationship between you and your mother
         The relationship between you and your father
         The relationship between you and any brothers or sisters

2. *Explore the possibility of family transference.* See if your partner is triggering any old feelings you may have had as a child (or even now as an adult) with anyone in your family.

- Does your partner remind you of anyone in your family as you were growing up? Name some positive qualities the two have in common.

- Does your relationship with him or her resemble your parents' relationship, and if so, how?

- Does your relationship with him or her resemble your relationship with a brother or sister, and if so, how?

- What are some of the typical or habitual family-type interactions between you and your partner?

- Of the list of risk factors for loss of sexual interest in a relationship, what do you think are the three biggest factors in your relationship?

3. *Write a letter to each parent.* It doesn't matter whether they are still alive. This is simply an exercise for *you*, and neither letter is to be mailed. Write these letters fast, in anywhere from ten to twenty minutes each.

- Start each letter with what you most love and appreciate about him or her.

- Talk about any resentment you may still harbor for how he or she failed you and what you would need to forgive him or her.

- End with an expression of gratitude for whatever good each parent gave you.

- Take a few deep breaths and check in with yourself. Do a felt-sense inventory and see if any feelings have been aroused, particularly in your throat, chest, gut, and diaphragm.

- Set the letters aside in a nearby file.

- You may find it helpful to also write a letter to each of your siblings, following this format. If you don't want to write to all of them, write letters only to those you have some unresolved issues with.

4. *Write a letter to your current partner or your most recent partner*. This also is not to be mailed but is simply an exercise for you.

   - Start with what you most love and appreciate about him or her.

   - Detail any resentment you harbor for how he or she may have failed or wronged you and what you would need to forgive him or her.

   - End with an expression of gratitude for whatever good he or she has given and continues to give you.

   - Take a few deep breaths and check in with yourself. See if any feelings have been aroused, particularly in your throat, chest, gut, and diaphragm.

5. *Compare the letters*. See what you can learn from taking some time to think about how your feelings have remained the same or changed over the years.

   - What are the similarities and differences between the letters to your parents and the letter to your partner? If you see any patterns, which parent or sibling do you notice your partner typically becomes a stand-in for?

   - Keep all of the letters in a file to review what you wrote and to monitor any change in feelings.

6. *List a few of their favorite things*. This is a little exercise that may get you in touch with warm feelings of familiarity. You may find it helpful to write down any feelings, sensations, thoughts, and images you discover.

   - Make a list of what you think were your parents' favorites, as you were growing up, in the following categories:

     Food or meal

     Way to relax

     Television or radio show

     Other entertainment

     Way to celebrate a special occasion

     Memory

     Time with you

- Make a list of what you think are your partner's all-time favorites (or answer for a former partner) in the following categories:

    Food or meal

    Way to relax

    Television or radio show

    Other entertainment

    Way to celebrate a special occasion

    Memory

    Time with you

Take a few deep cleansing breaths and a couple of sighs, and check in with your emotional center. How do you feel? What have you learned doing these exercises?

3

Love, Sex, and Stress

To tackle the love-lust dilemma, we have to first understand a little more about the biological roots of love. Research shows that the kind of attachment bonds we form with our parents from the very beginning of life can affect how we love as adults, whom we choose as partners, and even the quality of our sex lives. The key factor is how we learn to deal with stress.

UCLA neuroscientist Alan Schore has been a leading figure in highlighting how regulating stress and the emotions, also referred to as *affect*, is most critical in the early bonding between mother and child. A warm, intuitive mother who is attuned to her baby's rhythms of activity is responsive to his or her needs. When the baby becomes distressed, the attuned mother also becomes distressed, and when she attends to the baby's needs and the baby relaxes, the mother relaxes, too. In this way, mother and baby are a *mutual regulatory system*. An intuitive mother can fine-tune her baby's stress level, and when the baby is responsive to her effort, the mother calms down as well.

By about two months of age, an infant begins to take an intense interest in the mother's face, especially the eyes. Thus begins the first real communication: the gaze-avert game. Baby looks into mother's eyes (gaze); mother is there with a smile, and they both get excited; baby looks away (avert), and they both relax. Baby looks back (gaze) and, ideally, mother is there with a smile and a friendly voice; baby smiles and looks away (avert). And so it continues.

In the laboratory, when mother and infant wore electrode caps to show a printout of brain activity and electrodes to monitor heart rate and other physiological measures, the neuroscientists made a startling discovery. The measures for both mother and infant showed an identical activation in the same area of the right brain and stress levels that were completely synchronized. Both nervous systems were activated when the two looked into each other's eyes, and a relaxation response was triggered in both during the avert phase.

This is nature's original wireless connection. Mother and baby are essentially instant-messaging, left eye to left eye, right brain to right brain. The look in the mother's eyes, her tone of voice, and her smile or frown become the implicit nonverbal messages that signal safety or threat to the baby. In this way, mother and baby become a mutual stress-regulatory system.

But it doesn't stop there. Our parents' ability to regulate our stress in childhood can affect whether we are secure or insecure in a sexually intimate relationship twenty or more years later.

Attachment Styles in Childhood

This *affect synchrony*, in which mother and infant are energetically tuned in to each other, becomes the basis for a secure attachment in which the mother allows the baby to disengage and is present and available with an expressive face when the baby comes back to reengage.

A *secure* attachment style in a child tends to be associated with an attentive, warm, and intuitive mother who can allay her child's distress. Soft eye contact, smiles, and a warm and soothing tone of voice help an infant to achieve a sense of calm after being upset. These facial expressions and gestures become the unspoken, implicit messages that balance his or her nervous system and foster a sense of safety, self-worth, and trust.

An *insecure-anxious* attachment style tends to be associated with an anxiously intrusive mother who doesn't allow the child to disengage. Such a child lacks confidence and has a tendency to cry and be clingy and dependent. The implicit messages of threat here may be darting eyes, a tense and high-pitched tone of voice, and a tight mouth.

An *insecure-avoidant* attachment style may be the result of depressed, rejecting, or unavailable mother. These children may actively avoid their parents; they have learned to rely on themselves and take care of their own needs. Here the implicit messages may be an expressionless or detached face, avoidance of eye contact, and a tight downturned mouth.

An *ambivalent* attachment style is likely to develop in a child whose mother or primary caretaker is inconsistent or undependable. These children never know when they will be loved or wounded by the same person. They are likely to learn to be cautious about the temporary nature of love and suspicious of the likelihood that a good feeling can turn bad in an instant. Their parents' faces and demeanors can turn in an instant from being affectionate and nurturing to punishing and threatening.

Naturally, a warm and attentive father can have a major impact on an infant, especially if he shares in infant and child care or is more emotionally available than the mother. Sometimes the "primary caretaker" of an infant is in fact a male, so although I use the term *mother* in describing the earliest parent-child dynamic, a mother can be a "he." When parents follow more typical sex roles, a father still contributes to the attachment styles of his offspring but may have his greatest impact after infancy, at the toddler stage and later, especially in how he may affect mother's emotional state when she is caring for the baby.

Adult Attachment and Love Styles

Phillip Shaver, a research psychologist at the University of California at Davis, and his colleagues have provided solid evidence of the continuing influence of attachment style into the adolescent and adult years, affecting the mates we choose and how we interact with them emotionally and sexually.

Hundreds of studies provide ample evidence that the four basic attachment styles—what I'll simply call secure, anxious, avoidant, and ambivalent—persist into our adult years and affect how we interact in intimate love relationships. Essentially these patterns are neurologically wired "working models of relationship," or adult love styles. These love styles are our mental and physical habits in intimacy. They strongly influence our beliefs and expectations about intimacy. Our love style especially shapes how we are likely to deal with stress in a relationship and how that stress will affect our sexual responses.

Secure love style. According to the data, people with a secure love style tend to be at ease with emotional intimacy. They value closeness and have long, stable relationships. Under stress, they reach out for support and appear to be well equipped to handle painful emotions. They are likely to be supportive when their partners are distressed. Secure people tend to be comfortable with their sexuality and are likely to have sex both for pleasure and as an expression of love and caring.

Anxious love style. People with an anxious love style were typically raised by anxious and intrusive parents, which engendered in them self-doubt, a tendency to depend on other people's approval for a sense of self-worth, and a heightened fear of rejection and of being unloved. Under stress, these men and women tend to be needy and are apt to interpret relationship issues in a negative way. They are more likely than others to have emotional conflict in their day-to-day interactions. Anxious people are also more likely than others to engage in sexual activity for reasons other than for pleasure—perhaps to be reassured of their desirability or to safeguard a relationship. However, they also tend to be passionate lovers.

Avoidant love style. Avoidant men and women were typically raised by unresponsive, depressed, or distant parents. This could be a result of growing up in a large or troubled family or for any other reason that would make them learn to rely on their own resources at an early age. These people put a high value on self-reliance and are less comfortable with emotional closeness or expression. Under stress, avoidant individuals may shut down, shun intimate contact, and opt to be alone. Research shows that these men and women often report having a lower sex drive than their partners do. Under stress, they are also more likely than others to have sex out of a sense of obligation rather than for love or pleasure.

Ambivalent love style. These people were raised by inconsistent parents, perhaps loving one moment but harsh the next, and tend to have mixed feelings in relationships. They may desire warmth and intimacy but then get uncomfortable and feel engulfed when their partners try to get physically or emotionally closer. If their partners are anxious, these people may become avoidant; if their partners are avoidant, they may become anxious. Two ambivalents together can make for some really confusing nonverbal, implicit messages. A more seriously ambivalent love style, known as disorganized attachment, is the result of a traumatic childhood, where the caregiver was unstable or disturbed and both a source of comfort and fearful alarm. An adult with a disorganized attachment style, who is fearfully avoidant in a relationship, is unlikely to be able to sustain a loving relationship without the benefit of therapy that specifically works to unlock the trauma.

The Insecure Couple

When two insecure people get together, a common scenario is for an anxious person to pair up with an avoidant person. This is the familiar "pursuer and distancer" type of relationship. The anxious person pursues the avoidant one, pressing for more closeness and more sex to fulfill a need for reassurance. The avoidant partner then begins to feel smothered and needs more space but may consent to sex primarily to placate the other.

Under stress, the insecure coping strategies are triggered. The anxious partner needs contact; the avoidant partner needs to get away. Naturally, making love not for love or pleasure but for reassurance or out of obligation is not going to be very thrilling or sexually fulfilling for either partner.

Even if they're careful about what they say to each other, their bodies are in constant nonverbal communication: tense and critical eyes, a downturned mouth of disapproval, a lack of eye contact, sighs of impatience, and a kiss that is more of a kiss-off than a sign of affection. These rapid-fire facial expressions or gestures may occur in a microsecond and register on a subconscious level yet cut deeper than words.

Family Transference and Sex

I see people project their family issues onto their partners all the time. One woman who lost all desire for sex began to see that she had transferred her anger toward her father onto her husband. Her husband was very much like her father, she said. In one session, she came to realize that the constant criticism and resentment she leveled at her husband was the behavior she wished her mother had exhibited with her own husband (my client's father) in response to his emotional abusiveness many years ago. This client had seen her mother as a weakling and now saw her own willingness to complain to her husband as a sign of strength.

Family transference can be activated in the earliest stages of an intimate relationship. The fellow who was eager to leave a lovely woman he admired in order to curl up with his computer at home felt freer to be himself when he was alone. As soon as he got together with a woman he cared for, he felt a need to please her and to forget about himself. That's something he also always felt toward his needy and depressed mother. No surprise there.

Even under the best of circumstances, transferring family feelings to a committed partner is hard to avoid. Teri came from a loving, supportive family and developed a secure love style. Yet sex was never discussed, and she learned at a very early age to cut off her sexual feelings at home. Andy, her fiancé, had a less than ideal family situation and a more anxious love style. Teri said that after his parents divorced, Andy developed a special bond with his mother that Teri thought was a little too close.

Soon after he and Teri moved in together, Andy started to go through a hard time related to his work, and he reached out to Teri for support. That's when Teri came to see that in her mind, Andy had become her brother.

Implicit Memories

How exactly are these unresolved issues transferred? One way is through the subtle nonverbal cues sent back and forth between partners in daily proximity that signal "we are family."

Research has shown that infants establish memories even at the earliest stages of life. Although these cellular and tissue memories typically remain as neural foundations for the entire life span, they are not something we are aware of. They are *implicit* memories, imprinted in the neural network of the right brain as sense memories that influence eye contact and facial expression, smiles and frowns, body gestures, vocal tone, and heartbeat—our own and our partners'.

These implicit memories may involve sense memories like smell and touch; visceral sensations in the chest, stomach, or gut; nervous activation; muscular tension; sensations of pleasure or pain; and feelings of anger, fear, sadness, or excitement. It is very likely that Teri's comforting of Andy triggered sisterly memories in her that started a process of shutting off any sexual interest.

Since we don't have the ability to conceptualize these experiences or describe them, what is retained is implicit—experienced on an unconscious and emotional level. Yet they are significant aspects of a very primal, sensory process that underlies our bodily expectations and emotional triggers.

UCLA psychiatrist Dan Siegel has focused on the role that implicit memory plays in our everyday experiences. Implicit memories give us our subjective sense of ourselves and form mental models programmed in the brain that automatically interpret present events. Most important, minute sensory elements and similarities of a present situation with a past one can trigger implicit emotional memories from the earlier situation without our ever being aware that something is being recalled.

A couple communicates on this subtle level of nonverbal right brain–to–right brain messaging all the time, especially during sexual intimacy. A solicitous pat on the back can make you feel as though you're with a doting relative, and an instantaneous flash of disapproval can create a childhood sense memory of anxiety without ever registering what spurred that emotional reaction. These are the same kinds of micro-expressions, communicated in a nanosecond and picked up in a glance, that Malcolm Gladwell described in his bestseller *Blink*. In the coming chapters we'll look at how to recognize and learn from this subtle level of implicit communication.

Sex, Stress, and the Nervous System

When we talk about security versus insecurity and how people respond to the inevitable challenges in a relationship, what we're really talking about is how they respond under stress. To understand how stress can be so detrimental to loving sex, you have to take a closer look at the nervous system and at what it means, physiologically, to be stressed.

The autonomic nervous system (ANS) is a set of nerves that runs from the brain to the spine and to every organ, gland, and muscle of the body. It affects such functions as heart rate, respiration, digestion, perspiration, dilation of the pupils, and sexual arousal. The ANS has two subdivisions—the sympathetic nervous system and the parasympathetic nervous system—that act antag-onistically to either energize and activate us or to relax and calm us down.

Under threat, the sympathetic nervous system (SNS) shoots adrenaline and other stress hormones into the bloodstream and triggers the emergency fight-or-flight reaction. Every part of the body contracts, and the breath is held or shortened. Blood drains from the thinking part of the brain, the prefrontal cortex, and into the reflexive part of the brain, the amygdala, a cluster of neurons in the limbic system associated with anger and fear, and into sur-vival mode, automatically engendering either aggressive behavior or retreat and escape. For example, suppose you're walking down a quiet street and you see someone coming toward you who, for whatever reason, looks dangerous to you. You hold your breath. Your heart starts to beat hard in your chest, and you're thinking fast about what you could do in a pinch. You get more and more tense as he gets closer. The muscles in your chest and gut contract. You're hypervigilant.

Now let's say that as you approach your suspected foe, he smiles and nods at you, and his eyes look friendly. He passes you by and the danger is over. The first thing that happens is you exhale a big breath of relief. Whew! Next you may find yourself panting with excitement and feeling great about what just happened. You may even laugh about it. That breath—that *whew*—triggers the parasympathetic nervous system (PNS), which floods the body with endorphins, the body's natural opiates, and other biochemi-cals that induce relaxation and possibly jubilation. Whereas the SNS triggers fight-or-flight, a survival response, the PNS triggers a restoration response. The muscles and organs begin to let go, the blood vessels widen, breathing slows and becomes more rhyth-mic, and the eyes moisten and sparkle. The PNS is also known to be associated with a conservation of energy, because it regulates the combination of excitement and relaxation and balances your power output. When you are in autonomic balance, you are not squandering your energy by revving up more than necessary.

Stress is a natural, unavoidable part of life, but we need to be able to balance our stress with restoration, to relax and replenish our resources. People under chronic stress are in a persistent state of SNS hyperarousal, as though they are in constant danger. Their bodies are tense, they're hyperalert to any possibility of threat, and they're prone to knee-jerk reactions based more on past events than on being responsive to the present situation, which is the province of the PNS. All of these tendencies can make for very disappointing sex, because SNS stress prevents PNS restoration and replenishment.

Sexual desire, enthusiasm, and orgasm depend on both sympathetic activation and parasympathetic expansiveness. The rapid heartbeat and panting breath are sympathetic functions. Erection in a male and lubrication in a female, on the other hand, are parasympathetic. Orgasm depends on a high state of both sympathetic *and* parasympathetic arousal.

A Secure Relationship: An Antidote for the Deficits of Childhood

The evidence shows that the couples who are the most sexually satisfied in their relationships are most likely to involve individuals with a secure love style. Morris Eagle, a professor emeritus at Adelphi University, posited that an insecure individual is more likely to see the partner as a stand-in for one of the parents (or for a sibling) and to stop regarding the partner as a sexual person. The more unresolved the original attachment, especially when there are painful feelings of guilt, anxiety, or resentment, the more likely an insecure person will respond to an intimate as a parent or a sibling. In that case, the insecure person will either become sexually turned off or, as Andy did with Teri, turn off the partner.

There's an abundance of evidence that insecure people can become secure through a secure relationship. People who become secure as adults as a result of enjoying a nourishing relationship are often referred to as *earned secures*.

The major challenge for insecure couples is to create the kind of intimate relationship that promotes feelings of security and trust in each other's love. This is the kind of interaction that offers the greatest possibilities for emotionally gratifying sexual pleasure.

Those of us who grew up to be insecure adults were very likely not effectively nurtured through our stress when we were infants and children. Without parents who modeled comforting skills for us, we may not know how to do it for anyone else. And even if we do have partners who can be nurturing when we're under stress, we may still be uneasy with the closeness or suspicious of another person's motives for being so nice.

The neurological research shows that the brain and the nervous system are programmed to generate specific intimacy habits. These are often intergenerational patterns, handed down from grandparent to parent to child. Two people together can, however, overcome the deficits of their original attachment and free themselves to fully love and be sexual with each other.

The evidence shows that exposing ourselves to emotionally positive experiences and developing skills that foster intimate connection can break through the programming and rewire the brain and the nervous system. The result is a livelier, sexier, more loving relationship, along with an increase in each partner's sense of security in the world and his or her ability to take greater pleasure in everyday life.

Primal Intimacy

One of the best ways a couple can reduce each other's stress and generate a feeling of emotional safety is by holding each other for several minutes at a time and breathing deeply in each other's arms. The lying-in-arms that takes place between mother and infant—face-to-face, eye to eye, and heart to heart, with smiling, cooing, baby talk, and rocking together—is the basic unit of intimacy. It's also what lovers do when they fall in love. They lie face-to-face and heart to heart, sucking at each other's mouths and bodies, talking baby talk, and rocking together. Primal intimacy is all about a shared felt-sense of *mutual attunement*.

As adults, we have the same ability to become synchronized with each other and the same needs for playfulness and de-stressing as we did as infants. We also have the same potential to become mutual stress regulatory systems for each other. The same mechanisms of attunement that reduce an infant's stress and create a sense of safety and security in his or her body are still present and responsive in the adult nervous system. We crave an attuned other to reassure us and to play with us. A tender look, smiling eye contact, being held close to a warm body, and hearing a friendly reassuring tone of voice all have the power to trigger the PNS, stimulating pleasurable feelings and relieving debilitating tensions.

Partners in trouble are not in attunement, especially when they get into their areas of stress. Talking often raises each other's stress level rather than lowering it. Neither one listens, often both become dismissive, and they blame, shame, and criticize each other. Many times these people are replicating the kinds of conflict they witnessed between their own parents when they were growing up. Their bodies become defensive and closed off. If they would just shut up and hold each other, they might be able to calm down and become more open to listening to each other and working things out in fairness to both.

Heart-to-heart physical contact is a basic physiological mechanism by which we mutually regulate each other's stress. A warm hug is like a shot of good feelings. Holding someone in distress is the surest way to calm that person down, to soothe him or her and instill a sense of safety. The same interactive regulatory mechanisms that create security in an infant create security and peace in adults.

Many of us grew up without the benefit of this basic stress-reducing interaction. The skills addressed in the subsequent chapters are precisely the kinds of behaviors that can help to reduce stress in oneself and in one's partner and generate a greater sense of security and capacity to play and enjoy oneself.

Optimal Stress and Self-Regulation

From the moment we get up in the morning to the moment we get back into bed at night, our waking hours bring many opportunities to be stressed. A disagreement with a partner, hassles with the kids, rushing to work, disappointments or frustrations during the day, or even a positive experience like moving to a better office can all raise our stress level. Stress is natural and unavoidable, but there's an ineffective way to respond to the situation and an effective way.

There's a growing recognition that stress can be good for us. Even after we have gone through terribly difficult times in life, post-traumatic stress can turn into post-traumatic growth. A person who has suffered greatly can learn from and gain something valuable from a painful experience.

What's positive about stress is that it is adaptive: the body's physiological response to threat or change generates a surge of energy that helps us to survive. The ill effects of stress are caused by chronic hyperactivity of the emergency system and the survival mode and little PNS restoration.

Generating a level of continual alarm and readiness for danger produces a hypervigilance that sees threat everywhere and causes burnout. On the other hand, when stress is moderate and levels rise appropriately in response to a situation and then return to a resting state, stress can stimulate learning, memory, and problem solving.

Massachusetts psychiatrist Martha Stark has distinguished between traumatic stress and optimal stress. She has suggested that although traumatic stress disrupts growth, there is a level of optimal stress that provides the impetus for growth and transformation. If there's too little stress, there will be less of a tendency to explore opportunities or seek solutions to problems that can promote wisdom and maturity. Stark has even suggested that it's the mild everyday aggravations that stimulate the body's self-healing process. Ultimately, adaptive responses to stress enhance an individual's resilience, the ability to recover from setbacks.

The key to keeping your stress down to an optimal level of functioning is *self-regulation*. This consists of learning body-based methods that will help you to be responsive to the present situation rather than react with emotional habits based on the past. Some people learn self-regulation when they are children from comforting parents, particularly if the parents are able to manage their own stress. Many of us, however, have to learn this skill as adults.

The Principle of Relaxed Excitement

Of everything that I have learned throughout the years, the fundamental insight that has changed my life and deepened my work the most has been to recognize the critical energetic link between excitation and relaxation. It is essential to cultivate the ability to be energized and relaxed at the same time. This may well be the master key to all of our aspirations. I think of it as the key to success in everything!

For most people, especially those of us who have grown up feeling insecure and unsure, excitement and relaxation are often seen as opposites, but in fact they are intricately connected. Think about it. Certainly during difficult or troubling times, when we have to function at our very best, the key to success rests on our ability to be energized (even when we are scared and our hearts are pumping) and relaxed (thinking clearly, staying focused, quieting the racing heart) at the same time.

Maybe we're at work, dealing with a crisis or some offputting office politics, yet we also need to be effective and creative. Perhaps we have to deal with a disappointing or discouraging turn of events or a frustrating disagreement with someone we love. Maybe we feel anxious and insecure. Perhaps we have to do something exhilarating, like give a talk in front of a group of strangers. We want to be able to calm down and not be overwhelmed by our excitement.

This is especially crucial when it comes to achieving loving sexual pleasure. When people want to improve their sex lives, the very sense of urgency to reach a sexual goal can sometimes cause tension, which then militates against achieving the goal. By relaxing into the excitement, a person can function at an optimal stress level without the debilitating feelings of pressure and strain. This is what Canadian physiologist Hans Selye, the original stress researcher, called "stress without distress." It consists of being highly energized, focusing on the task at hand, and staying positive and hopeful. There are several methods that can help us to develop these skills.

Conscious Breathing

Just as the basic embodiment exercise you learned in the program can help you to discover your feelings, it can also help to calm you down and balance your nervous system. Conscious breathing is your fundamental embodied support and the key to relaxing into your excitement.

Stress is SNS activation, which is an impetus to act, yet what we often do under stress is try to hold everything in. We get tense and the pressure builds.

Conscious breathing is the primary somatic tool for tuning into as well as calming the internal body. Slow, deliberate, complete breaths and a few quick sighs are the most reliable ways to trigger the PNS and a relaxation response. Deep breaths expand the belly and the rest of the torso with each inhalation and relax those areas with each exhalation.

When we're tense, we automatically grip the chest and belly muscles by holding the breath and allowing only shallow inhalations and exhalations. When we inhale deeply, we can deliberately aim to fill the belly, stretch and widen the rib cage and upper back, and lift the chest. The increased movement in the torso and respiratory musculature awakens and amplifies visceral and muscular sensory perceptiveness.

When we're in a state of relaxed excitement, both sides of the nervous system are operating, and we experience what's called *autonomic balance*. As you will see, fulfilling sexual activity completely depends on high sympathetic and parasympathetic activation at the same time.

Deep breathing is also a highly effective method for pausing a knee-jerk reaction based on past experience and allowing you to assess the current situation before you act. The brain is programmed on the premise that the past is the best predictor of the present. Under threat, the brain in survival mode wants a quick reflexive reaction to escape danger. I think of it as the "feet-don't-fail-me-now" response. As a result, you may automatically read threat into a situation where there is none and react defensively or even with hostility and aggression. I see partners overreact to each other all the time. They "nuke" each other with emotional blasts that set off a proliferation of highly damaging counterblasts that they never fully get over.

If you take a few deep breaths, you might see that there is a better way to handle the situation. Breathing deeply allows you to stay energized yet relaxed and to slow down your response. That way you can take in more of what is actually happening in the present and choose a more appropriate and effective way to handle it.

Mindfulness

The term *mindfulness* is used to describe the kind of relaxed attentiveness that comes with the ability to be still and completely present in the moment-by-moment flow of the experience. Sitting in meditation, observing the mind in stillness and without judgment, is an essential Buddhist practice on the path to insight and personal transformation. Modern-day neuroscientists and medical researchers have shown that the ability to cultivate the quality of presence that comes with quieting the mind and calming the body is a critical factor in healing emotional and physical trauma and enhancing health.

Mindfulness is particularly important for being aware of what turns us on sexually, what happens when we get sexually turned off, and how to get turned back on again. Even just a few mindful

seconds, noticing the stressful feelings without immediately react-
ing, may be enough to handle things better, with wisdom rather
than by reflex.

Focused Attention

Giving someone your complete attention, listening as someone
talks without your mind wandering, or focusing on something
happening in real time and staying with it can be problematic for
people under stress. Focused attention is a valuable skill to cultivate in order to reduce stress and be fully present, especially when
there is some tension between people.

Sexual difficulties are often related to a person's inability to
stay present and be attentive to the pleasurable opportunities of
the moment. Instead, he or she is likely to be focused on imagining worst-case scenarios. I think of this as the curious habit of
mentally rehearsing exactly what you don't want to happen.

The ability to focus attention is especially critical as we get
older. Many of the problems of aging, like memory loss and even
hearing loss, have been attributed to a chronic habit of not paying attention. The brain's attention centers, which are primarily
in the regions of the temporal and parietal lobes, as a result, can
suffer from disuse and atrophy. The temporal lobe is involved in
auditory perception and memory, while the parietal lobe integrates all sensory information, especially with visual input. You
can see how hearing and memory would be affected by continual
inattention. Paying attention is made easier by being alert to your
senses—staying focused on what you can see, hear, smell, taste,
touch, and feel right now.

Evolution Is a Stretch

One of the things we often can't help but notice when we turn
our attention inward is how much tension, discomfort, and even
pain we hold in the body. You may feel yours in the neck and
shoulders, in the small of your back, in your thighs, in your hands,

or in your feet. Most of the time people try to shut out any awareness of the tension, but that will only keep you stiff.

Stretching provides an opportunity to take a quick break and
release some low-grade discomfort and pain. Unfortunately, that
may not be so easy. Our bodies learned in grade school to stop
fidgeting because we were reprimanded for doing so. The dictionary defines *fidget* as "to move around in a restless, absent-minded
manner." These days it can even get you a diagnosis of ADHD,
attention-deficit/hyperactivity disorder. It might also be contrary
to protocol in your workplace if, in the middle of a meeting, you
were to get up to stretch or touch your toes.

In 2005, medical researchers at the Mayo Clinic published a
study in *Science* magazine that concluded that fidgeting in meetings, getting up to stretch throughout the day, or being restless
may actually help one to be lean rather than overweight and to
stay energetic rather than become listless. Apparently, having "ants
in your pants" can be good for you—adding as much as two and a
half hours of movement a day, using up lots of calories, and very
likely releasing tension. The authors of the study suggest that
"despite admonitions to the contrary, people should be encouraged
to fidget." Fidgeting is now considered to be protective against
heart disease, diabetes, cancer, and other weight-related illnesses.

Self-Regulate with New Ways of Doing Things

Other ways to self-regulate may involve removing yourself physically from a difficult situation—talking a walk, sitting quietly in
a private spot, taking a few mindful moments to be with yourself
to stretch and relax. The goal is to calm the hyperactive mind,
replenish your energy, and get centered in the body.

Step three in the program offers exercises to identify your
love style and that of your partner and how each of you tends
to deal with stress. There are several exercises for self-regulating
stress and a few simple stretches that take only a few minutes to
practice.

Step Three: Self-Regulation

Objectives: To recognize your relationship patterns and
to practice methods for releasing tension in the body and
quieting the mind

You are likely to see yourself in one of these love styles. This is
not a definitive, scientific, diagnostic test. These descriptions are
merely suggestive, aimed at helping you find a gut feeling of the
style you relate to most. As always, start with the basic embodiment exercise: a few complete breaths, a couple of sighs, and a
felt-sense inventory.

Identify Your Love Style

Once you've identified your love style, you don't have to do anything about it. The most important thing is just recognizing your
patterns as they come up in your relationship. Pay particular attention to the sensations in your throat, chest, and diaphragm. (Note:
The descriptions of the parents may apply to only one parent or to
both of them.)

THE SECURE LOVE STYLE

My parents were attentive, loving, and helpful. Growing up, I felt
safe and had fun. I trusted my parents and could go to them to
share my concerns. Now I feel comfortable with myself and with
sharing my true feelings.

   In a relationship, I know that if my partner and I listen to each
other, we'll be able to work things out. I trust my partner. When
I'm under stress, I have faith in myself that I'll be okay, but it's
always nice to get a hug and reassuring words from my partner.

   I feel comfortable with my sexuality. I enjoy sex. When I'm in a
relationship, I enjoy sex for the pleasure it gives my partner and me
and as an expression of our love.

THE ANXIOUS LOVE STYLE

My parents were often uneasy and not always responsive to me
when I needed them. They could also be critical and hard to please.
I felt lonely as a child, and I doubted myself and my self-worth.
Now I have a tendency to share too much about myself with
people who probably don't really care.

In a relationship, I know I tend to be needy when I'm under stress. If my partner is not available when I'm looking for reassurance, I have a tendency to feel sorry for myself or get angry with my partner.

When my partner and I are having sex, I feel good about our relationship. When we're not having sex, I feel unsure about us.

THE AVOIDANT LOVE STYLE

I grew up in a large or a troubled family. My parents were not very available because they were either too busy or depressed. Still, I may have felt they cared about me. An older sibling or another family member took care of me, although I was left on my own a lot. Now I continue to value my independence, and I need my space.

I am most comfortable in a relationship that is not very demanding. I'm not into a lot of self-disclosure and intimate talks. When I'm under stress, I prefer to be alone.

My sex drive is usually lower than my partner's. I sometimes have sex just to please my partner and because it's good for our relationship.

THE AMBIVALENT LOVE STYLE

My parents were inconsistent. Sometimes they were there for me, and at other times they were abusive. I couldn't always tell which way they would be. Now I have mixed feelings in relationships.

Sometimes I need to be close to feel reassured, but then I may feel overwhelmed and need to get away. I don't always know what will make me feel better.

My sex drive varies a lot with my emotions.

Identify Your Partner's Love Style

If you are in a relationship now, and knowing what you know about your partner, how would you identify his or her love style? If you are not in a relationship now, look back at your most recent relationship, and knowing what you know about that person, how would you identify his or her love style? It might be helpful to look back to the last one or two relationships you had before the most recent one and see if you keep picking people with the same love style. If you do, what does that tell you?

Identifying your partner's love style may help to make you more forgiving of how he or she deals with stress. It may also inspire you to help him or her deal with stress. If you are in a relationship now and you share this information and he or she disagrees, drop it. No one ever appreciates being psychologically diagnosed by a mate. Take it from me.

As we go along in this program, you will find a number of exercises that are aimed to help you and your partner become more loving and more secure in your love.

Self-Regulate

Stress is a fact of life. There are all kinds of situations that are capable of triggering a fight-or-flight response in your daily life: family, work, money, and health are the leading contenders. Dealing with it under stress just makes it more difficult to resolve whatever real threat is present and gain a sense of safety, comfort, and satisfaction.

The most critical fact to remember about self-regulating your stress is this: stress is a nervous system out of balance; only half of the system, your SNS, is active. It has your heart beating fast, your blood pressure rising, your thoughts of danger escalating, and your gut in knots. Your PNS is underactivated.

Your muscles are tense because your body wants to run away, but your mind won't let it. The better you regulate and reduce your stress, the more effectively you can deal with your challenges and enjoy your pleasures.

The following exercises offer ways to consciously trigger your PNS and balance your nervous system. Once again, begin with the embodied basics: take some deep breaths and do a felt-sense inventory.

MINDFUL MINUTES

So much of our lives is compartmentalized: now we go to work, now we play, now we meditate, now we make love. This exercise is a way to weave meditative moments throughout the day as a way to find inner balance. We deepen our sense of ourselves when we simply sit still, turn our attention inward, and watch what's going on in there—even for just a minute. One quiet minute can be enough time to clear the head and find balance.

The object of this exercise is to spend one minute paying undivided attention to ongoing moment-by-moment experience. Read through the instructions first, then do the exercise.

- Wherever you are, sit in an alert posture, feet on the floor or cross-legged, and keep your chin parallel to the ground. Close your eyes and check in with your body. Notice any areas of tension or tightness.

- Focus your attention on your inhalation and your exhalation—as your breath comes in and goes out through your nose, or as your chest lifts and lowers. Just notice what's going on inside your body and how your mind can distract you from your body. Practice quieting your mind and staying focused on how the breath moves your body.

- You may want to set a timer to do a longer meditation for five or ten minutes or more once or twice a day.

S-T-R-E-T-C-H

Take a break for a few seconds and release some tension. These stretches are also meant to be woven into the fabric of the day—a minute or two or three, here and there.

People who stretch are often more likely to do it in the morning or at the gym and not stretch again for the rest of the day. But if you can find a little niche of time to sneak in a little stretch (discreetly, of course), it would probably go a long way toward relaxing your daily tensions.

Stretching while Sitting   There are many stretches you can do to ease tension without ever getting out of your chair. Here are just a few examples. They are described in sequence; that is, each one starts from the position of the previous one.

- *Look up.* Wherever you are sitting, make yourself symmetrical: both feet flat on the ground, both arms hanging at your side, and looking up at the ceiling or the sky. Close your eyes, take a deep breath in, and blow out through slightly puckered lips upward as you press your shoulders and fingers down. This stretch should feel pleasurable in the throat and neck. It will feel even better if you smile while you're doing it.

- *Interlaced fingers, palms up.* Inhale. Raise both hands up as you keep your chin parallel to the ground, interlace your fingers, invert your hands so your palms and fingers are being stretched—and blow out.

- *Waist pull.* Inhale. Hold your left wrist with your right hand and pull your left arm gently but firmly as high as you can and toward the right side of your head until you feel the stretch in your waist on your left side. Exhale. Then inhale and do it on the opposite side so you're pulling your right side out at the waist and blow out. This should feel good all along the sides of your arms to your waist.

- *Neck stretch.* Interlace your fingers and let them rest on the back of your head as you breathe in. Let your chin fall toward your chest, let your elbows fall toward each other, and let the weight of your arms stretch the back of your neck as you blow out.

- *Right and left neck stretch.* Inhale. Lift your head, lower your hands, keep your chin parallel to the ground, and slowly and gently look over your right shoulder and blow out. Inhale and look over your left shoulder and blow out.

- *Toe touch.* If you are sitting at a desk or a table, push yourself away so you have nothing in front of you. Keeping your back straight and your butt on the chair, stretch forward and drop your head as your reach for your toes and blow out.

Stand and Stretch   Any stretch you can do sitting, you can do standing. This will get your bottom half stretched, too.

- *Standing up.* A quick series of stretches as you come to your feet may include a couple of deep breaths to get a sense of relaxed balance. Make sure both feet are flat and parallel, knees slightly bent, shoulders relaxed, and chin parallel to the ground. From there you might enjoy just standing still and finding your balance or swaying slightly.

- *The slow toe touch.* Bend forward with your hands on your thighs, then let your arms drop and let the weight of your arms draw you down toward your toes. Straighten your legs as you touch your toes (or as close as you can get without straining) and blow out. Then slowly straighten up, one vertebra at a time, keeping your head down until the very end, when you are standing straight, relaxed and in balance.
- *Combination.* Interlace your fingers and do a palms up, a neck stretch, a waist pull, and a few squats or lunges—anything that feels good that takes three to five minutes.

SELF-REGULATION THROUGHOUT THE DAY

The hardest part of self- regulation is remembering to take a few moments every so often to focus your attention inward and to monitor your stress level. Here are a few quick exercises that can help you establish self-regulation as a daily practice.

- Periodically throughout the day, do some embodied basics and check in with yourself. Especially if you are tense or rushed, it always helps to take a few deep breaths, do a couple of sighs, and scan your body from the inside.

- Do a felt-sense inventory and see if there's any tension or holding anywhere in your emotional center, between your head and your pelvis. See whether you're in touch with any emotions or feeling tense or stressed. Then, if you can, take a few moments to walk around and stretch.

- If you feel some emotions coming up—such as anxiety, hurt, disappointment, resentment, frustration, or guilt—ask yourself whether there is anything positive and productive that you can do to resolve those feelings right now. Breathing into the chest is always a good way to find the courage and inner resourcefulness to deal with a challenging situation.

- Compartmentalization is another way to let go of stress. You allow yourself to shelve something that cannot be productively dealt with in the present moment. We can sometimes solve our problems just by letting them go temporarily. When we come back to the problem later, we may find that the brain has been subconsciously working on it and has come up with a creative solution.

THE MINI STRESS REGULATOR

As you can see, these exercises are not very labor-intensive or time-consuming. If you were to do them every day, they might take up fifteen minutes of your day at the most. Here's an even shorter version.

- It will take you about fifteen seconds to do one long complete breath and a quick sigh: the belly fills, the rib cage widens, the chest lifts on the inhalation, and everything relaxes as you slowly. Inhale again and sigh by exhaling slowly through the mouth.
- A quick felt-sense body scan can take another fifteen seconds.
- Add a mindful minute and a few stretches, and you've taken up less than five minutes of your day. Yet it can have a profound effect on your ability to relax, to tune in to and be present in your body.

4

Romance and Desire

It's assumed that the madness of falling intensely in love begins in adolescence, when the sex drive and the need to establish some autonomy from one's parents converge like gunpowder. In fact, romantic feelings are a natural part of the sex drive from its first appearance in childhood.

Budding Romance

Think back to when you had your first crush. One man I spoke with remembered his first crush as a girl he gave a box of candy to. She told him that she liked somebody else, but she took the candy anyway, thanked him, and walked away. He was nine years old and devastated.

A woman recalled her first crush as a boy who got her so angry in the schoolyard that she shoved his face into a snowbank. She was seven, and she was livid because she saw him pushing another girl on the swing. She could still see his thick eyeglasses fogged and flaked with ice and his look of utter shock as he came up gasping for air.

From playground attractions to first loves and infatuations to the declaration of undying affection and commitment, romantic love is part of sex, and exclusivity just goes with the territory. We want, maybe need, to be special to someone, to be chosen as someone's one and only.

Now fast-forward to the time between early adolescence and the midtwenties, when you were being flooded with sex hormones and your prefrontal cortex—the brain's judgment and decision-making center—was not quite fully developed. Of course, you didn't know this then.

Teenage Love

Recall your first romance, when your heart did a flip-flop and you got a warm pang of excitement or fear in your belly when you saw that special person. Could it have been seventh or eighth grade, when you were only twelve or thirteen? Maybe it was a bit later, when you were sixteen or older.

It was very likely a period characterized by a heady mix of pulling away from your family and being drawn toward unfamiliar and perhaps forbidden feelings. Maybe there was a sense that unknown possibilities and adventures lay ahead.

Typically, while new experiences are taking place outside the home, a different drama is taking place in the family. The teenager is beginning to assert his or her individuality and need for autonomy. According to University of Virginia psychologists Joseph Allen and Deborah Land, there are differences between secure and insecure family patterns during this difficult period of breaking away. In a secure family, the parents will attempt to resolve the issues in a way that preserves closeness. In contrast, insecure parents and their insecure teens typically have less confidence in each other or in successfully resolving their issues. They are more likely to get angry and yell and to grow more distant.

The same patterns of security or insecurity reemerge as working models of relationship during times of conflict in adult intimacies. The patterns that are at play can determine whether the partners know how to resolve issues to safeguard their closeness or whether they yell and grow distant.

Such is the backdrop to nascent romance and the intense emotions that drive up lusty desires. The need for autonomy, the dramas played out with the family, the violation of prohibitions, and the frustrations, thrills, and pleasures can all become part of our sexual programming and interfere with desire in a relationship.

Romance also seems to be associated with having a sense of freedom and an anticipation of new discoveries, even for a long-term couple. Power struggles or put-downs are romantic turnoffs, especially when they are reminiscent of old family struggles, and they suck the air out of any magic or playfulness.

It's well known that sexual behavior is largely learned and that our early history shapes our sexual beliefs, feelings, and expectations, but in terms of romance, some aspects of our behavior are also clearly innate.

Born to Love Romance

There is no doubt that romance is biologically tied to the human sex drive. All animals, including insects, have some sort of mating dance before the members of a pair clearly choose each other for sexual activity. Wooing and enticing is the human equivalent of the peacock using his extravagant tail to gain the admiration of the peahen and of the graceful intertwining neck dance of giraffes. It's playful and spontaneous. It's active and engaging. It's a sign of health and vitality.

It's also hardwired. Charles Darwin referred to these displays as "sexual selection" and considered them to play a key role in evolution. Only those male members of the species who best strutted their feathers were thought to have "reproductive fitness" and got to mate with the females and pass on their DNA.

The notion of human evolution itself has evolved past merely breeding and sustaining the species. Romance is as important to same-sex couples as it is to opposite-sex couples. Furthermore, romance is most likely a critical factor in maintaining sexual desire in any intimate relationship.

Courting is part of our erotic nature. Research shows that how two people look at each other, talk to each other, and even bob and sway with each other are all implicit triggers, intricately woven into the sex drive, that can stimulate erotic interest, focus, and arousal.

Courtship as the Body Language of Romance

We call courtship rituals the mating *dance* because the way human beings innately signal interest in each other is primarily nonverbal and governed by the shifting rhythms of bodily movements. Flirting is similar everywhere, from the way traditional Polynesian Islanders have been described in courtship to the behavior observed by researchers in pickup bars all over the world.

In fact, anthropologist David Givens and sex researcher Timothy Perper separately made studies of U.S. and Canadian cocktail lounges, college pubs, and singles' bars, and they essentially replicated each other's findings on courting signals. It starts with a look that lingers, a subtle smile, a look away, and then a look back. The next gaze becomes more deliberate, perhaps more inviting.

Anthropologist Helen Fisher called this the attention-getting phase, in which certain body movements are exaggerated. A woman might cock her head to one side and play with her hair—a gesture signaling vulnerability and invitation. A man may stick his chest out and lift his eyebrows as he moves closer to her—signaling male strength and confidence. These are mostly unconscious natural micromovements that are built into our biology and driven by the energy surge of the moment.

From there the two begin to engage in idle chatter, but what they're saying is not as important as their tone of voice, what scientists refer to as *prosody*. A melodious, mellow tone of voice signals interest, whereas a clipped tone of voice is typically a brush-off. If all continues to go well, the next stage for this winsome twosome is a casual touch, in which one of them "accidentally" grazes the other with a hand or a shoulder. The more the two continue to talk and touch, the more they move their bodies, swaying and bobbing to their own internal rhythms.

Givens and Perper both observed that at a certain point something fascinating begins to take place with the energized duo. Each person begins to mirror the other. He picks up his drink; she picks up her drink. She smooths her hair; he smooths his hair. Eventually, if their body movements reach total synchrony, the couple is soon likely to leave the place together.

The teenagers I see in therapy sometimes unconsciously mime for me how they act when they spend time with a cute boy or girl. Carla, a pretty seventeen-year-old, told me that she ran into a boy she liked at a friend's house. She felt very excited about the meeting and began to describe some of the details of how he sat down next to her on the couch and started to get "flirty" with her. As she was reliving the meeting, I saw her engage in some of the same movements described above. She threw back her head and began to comb her hair with her fingers as she talked about her experience. Her eyes sparkled as she remembered that he had lightly touched her shoulder and that it had turned her on. She put her hand to her mouth and giggled. She was clearly getting a little revved up just talking about the encounter.

Is Romantic Love Time-Limited?

The poets would have us believe that love is an intoxicant forever. The Victorian poet Elizabeth Barrett Browning ended her paean to her beloved Robert Browning, "How Do I Love Thee?" with the lines "I love thee with the breath, smiles, tears, of all my life! And, if God choose, I shall but love thee better after death."

These rapturous and articulate lovers began their romance with more than five hundred letters between them. Elizabeth was an invalid living in her father's house and forbidden by him to marry. When Elizabeth and Robert finally met, they immediately fell in love and soon eloped to Florence, Italy. Her father never spoke to her again. Elizabeth was forty years old; Robert was thirty-four. The marriage, which produced a son, lasted fifteen years, until Elizabeth's death at age fifty-five in 1861.

What a difference 150 years can make. Now most of us fall in and out of love a few times, at least. When we do finally commit to someone, we do so not just because it's the practical thing to do but because we are in love. Studies show that most Americans consider romantic love to be a critical basis for marriage.

Elizabeth and Robert had about sixteen years together. Can couples who commit in their twenties or thirties really sustain romance for a twenty-first-century lifetime?

What exactly are we talking about when we speak of romance? Is it a passionate feeling, a way of acting, a short-lived affair, or a lifelong adventure? Actually, it's all of the above and more!

The natural inclination toward romance starts early in childhood and can continue to stimulate arousal and erotic pleasures throughout a lifetime. It makes sense, then, to see what we can learn about romance: how it starts, what it does for us, what diminishes it, and how our experience of romance can evolve and develop throughout our lives.

Many scientific studies suggest that romantic love is most intense during the first months of a relationship and tapers off somewhere between three months and two and a half years. University of Minnesota social psychologist Ellen Berscheid, who has spent her career researching the intense emotions of romantic love and erotic longing, described romantic love as a jumble of contradictory emotions, from the positive experiences of exhilaration and love to painful episodes of depression, insecurity, and anger. She equated the condition of being "in love" with a heightened state of bodily alarm, which would be exhausting to maintain. Her verdict was that romantic love is "about 90 percent sexual desire as yet not sated."

Helen Fisher would mostly agree. To her, romantic love is one part of a three-part mating system, intertwined with yet distinct from lust and attachment. Lust is sexual craving, associated with high levels of dopamine and norepinephrine in the brain. Dopamine is a neurotransmitter associated with reward. Norepinephrine is a neurotransmitter and a hormone that keeps us alert and motivated. These two stimulants trigger testosterone, the hormone of sexual desire in both men and women. Although the biochemistry of lust is similar to romantic love, Fisher observes that lust can be satisfied by anyone reasonably attractive and willing. Romantic love can trigger lust, but in this case the desire is very specific to the particular individual who has captured your heart.

Romantic love has been shown to be lubricated by an additional brain chemical, phenylethylamine (PEA), a substance that has also been found in chocolate. This neurotransmitter is a natural amphetamine and generates positive feelings. However, under certain conditions and in combination with a low level of serotonin, PEA may also be responsible for the wild mood swings, fantasies, and obsessive thinking that are often characteristic of a highly impassioned phase of romance.

Yet once attachment enters the picture and romance turns into a commitment, a rather different biochemistry predominates. The bonding hormone oxytocin, which is associated with attachment in both males and females, and vasopressin, the hormone associated with monogamy in males, now prevail. The magic and spontaneity as well as the emotional highs and lows are replaced with a sense of calm and comfort. In other words, unlike the stimulants produced by lust and romance, commitment can act as a sedative, inhibiting testosterone and diminishing the sex drive.

However, more recent studies have shown that oxytocin has also been associated with sexual arousal, trust, reduction of anxiety, and orgasm in both men and women. Clearly, although this hormone has a relaxing and calming effect, its overall effect during sexual activity tends to be associated with greater emotional contentment and sexual satisfaction.

No one needs the uncertain, unrealized, anxiety-fueled early passion to last forever. But does a committed relationship really have to be sedating? Fighting is certainly one way to jack up the adrenaline, but that takes its toll, no matter how good the makeup sex is.

Romantic Love That Lasts a Lifetime

There is no doubt that feeling romantic about your partner adds vitality to sexual pleasure. We've come to accept the popular notion that over time in a good relationship, romantic love typically fades into companionate love: warm, platonic, and largely nonsexual. But is that the best anyone can realistically hope for? Is there any evidence that a romantic attraction that sparks emotional excitement and sexual desire can actually last for the long run?

We're in luck. In a series of studies at the State University of New York in Stony Brook, psychologists Bianca Acevedo and Arthur Aron showed that romantic love—defined as having intensity, engagement, and sexual liveliness—can last in long-term couples. What's more, for all couples, whether long-term or short-term, romantic love was strongly correlated with satisfaction in the relationship.

Subjects in a variety of studies were asked to respond to items on a relationship scale that rated various aspects of relationships. The researchers found that a substantial number of people in relationships of ten years and longer responded positively to items indicating that they continue to be in love with their partners, feel their bodies respond when their partners touch them, and feel "a powerful attraction" toward their partners.

In one study, seventeen men and women in marriages averaging about twenty-one years in length who scored high on passionate love agreed to undergo brain scans to identify what a brain in love looks like in a long-term relationship. The subjects were given photos of their spouses to look at. For comparison, they were also measured while gazing at photos of friends. The scans showed that looking at their mates activated the part of the brain associated with romance, the ventral tegmental area (VTA) in the midbrain, which produces dopamine and is active during intense feelings of love, just as it did when people who had recently fallen in love looked at pictures of their beloveds. For the long-term married subjects, however, something else showed up in their brain scans. The parts of the brain associated with attachment and contentment also lit up, the ventral pallidum linked to "liking" and bonding and the raphe nucleus, which produces calming serotonin. The study clearly demonstrated that passion and contentment can coexist in a long-lasting and loving relationship.

According to the researchers, in the past most of the studies on romantic love have looked at short-term passionate affairs that are often associated with obsessive thinking, jealousy, doubt, and mood swings tied to the lover's behavior. The difference between those early stages of a romance with the romantic love of older couples is that the mania and obsessiveness is gone but the attraction, excitement, and sexual interest have deepened.

When individuals in long-term romantic marriages were compared with those in companionate marriages—warm and affectionate but lacking in sexual engagement—Acevedo and Aron found that those in romantic relationships were the most satisfied with their relationships. People in the companionate relationships were satisfied, but more moderately so. Finally, the studies also showed a strong correlation between the enjoyment of romantic love and feelings of self-esteem, overall feelings of happiness, and even better physical health. The researchers hoped that their data might set a new standard for couples and marital therapists to aspire to in making the necessary changes to enhance the romance in long-term relationships. I couldn't agree more.

Most important, the critical difference between the highly satisfying romantic love relationships and the moderately satisfying companionate relationships was the presence of sexual liveliness. Clearly, the key to staying in love with your partner throughout the years is to stay sexually alive with each other.

Staying sexually alive together not only contributes to staying in love but also offers extraordinary benefits to both individuals' health and happiness.

What Makes Romantic Love So Powerful?

Research shows that when romantic love is lasting, it is a powerful influence on an individual's sense of personal power and his or her capacity for self-improvement. I think of it as breaking through your programming and becoming a self-made woman or a self-made man.

Stony Brook psychologists Arthur Aron and Elaine N. Aron amassed a good deal of evidence for what they called the "self-expansion model" and the central role played by romantic love. They observed that a core human motivation is to explore, be curious, and develop greater competence—in essence, "to expand the self." Their studies showed that falling in love with someone is one of life's most expansive experiences; it affects your resources on many levels, your perspectives on life, your sense of identity, and how you see yourself.

In one study, people were given a questionnaire to assess the degree to which they experienced their partners as being sources of knowledge, increasing their own skills, bringing new experiences, and facilitating positive life changes. They were asked such questions as "How much has knowing your partner made you a better person?" and "How much do you see your partner as a way to expand your own capabilities?" One finding was that people in love relationships who scored high on those items also consistently scored higher in feeling content with themselves.

Another illuminating finding was that the most satisfying relationships were those in which the other was experienced as part of oneself. Expanding the sense of self to include the other meant that one partner's loss or gain was experienced by the other partner as a personal loss or gain. The data showed that such a relationship was especially healing for individuals with insecure love styles, who were able to develop a sense of security through the love of a partner.

In other studies on romantic love, University of California, Davis professor Phillip R. Shaver and his associates found that caregiving, along with attachment and sex, is an essential part of a romantic relationship. Effective caregiving was defined as being sensitive and responsive to the partner's signals and needs as well as providing support and comfort. Their studies showed that a valued attribute of a romantic relationship is the partner's availability to be physically close and consoling when one is feeling troubled or upset. Most important, they found a clear association between love style and ability to respect a partner's needs, maintain closeness, and give physical comfort and reassurance.

Secure individuals are attentive to their partners' needs. They can tell when their partners are distressed, and they tend to move closer out of concern for their partners' welfare and development.

Anxious individuals tend to be compulsive caregivers, becoming excessively involved in the partner's distress and taking on the partner's upset. These people tend to be too attentive, even intrusive, and as such are actually less effective in giving support.

Avoidant people, as a result of their own neglect and lack of care, often have a limited ability to read a partner's signals of distress. These individuals tend to keep their distance from a partner who is stressed or upset, and they are controlling caregivers. They are apt to adopt a problem-solving stance to the partner's needs, and they offer limited opportunities for physical comfort. Ambivalent people are likely to be confused at how to respond to a partner's distress and are inconsistent as caregivers.

However, with the motivation to enhance the intimate connection and their partners, anxious, avoidant, and ambivalent people can learn to become better caregivers. That aspect of growth very likely takes place through learning to give and to accept the empathetic caring and comforting that was missed in childhood.

If we look for clues in St. Valentine's Day, the one day a year dedicated to romance, you might imagine that being romantic has to do with giving gifts of candy or jewelry or sharing a dinner in a candlelit restaurant. Of course, all that can be fun and romantic. Making a weekly date or spending a night or a weekend at a hotel can also be a welcome change to the routine and add a little romance.

But true romance between committed partners runs a lot deeper. Some of the relationship patterns that an individual transfers from the original family to the partner can seriously undermine the possibilities for romantic love.

Social Scripts and Romance

Psychologist and sociologists use the term *social scripts* to describe learned interactions that follow predictable sequences of behavior. These are beliefs and expectations that are taken for granted about what behaviors are considered correct or normal under what circumstances and are adhered to without questioning.

Some of the scripts that define the rules of a committed relationship dictate appropriate sexual behavior. There is ample evidence to show that a big reason for the loss of romance and eroticism between partners is the unexamined sexual scripts that they act out with each other.

Intimacy, Spontaneity, and Self-Disclosure

University of Georgia psychologists Steven Beach and Abraham Tesser offered their own analysis of what happens to romance and sexual passion once two people commit to a relationship. In studies that attempted to unravel the factors that lead to marital satisfaction, they showed that happiness in a relationship is particularly associated with an intimacy born of self-disclosure.

In psychological terms, the two individuals start out with unrehearsed scripts that set the stage for uncertainty and excitement. Even when two people have considerable trust, there is still the uncertainty of how the other will respond when one of them seeks to explore a personal concern not previously articulated— whether there will be censure or understanding.

When an individual expresses previously unexpressed feelings or acts in an unexpected way and the mate is accepting and understanding, a flood of warm feeling washes over the individual, reinforcing his or her love. But as the two grow closer, they're likely to develop more routine and predictable scripts, which in turn diminishes the possibility of sharing or discovering new emotional territory.

Beach and Tesser suggested that as a relationship develops, a couple's good feelings may be tied to a number of well-elaborated scripts. As a result, the couple is not likely to feel the passionate enthusiasm associated with exploring spontaneous and unrehearsed areas of interest or concern. Doing so would highlight each person's individuality, but it could also disrupt their cohesiveness as a couple.

Nonverbal Scripts

There are nonverbal as well as verbal scripts, such as the expectations associated with kissing. For example, in the beginning of a romance, kisses are likely to be spontaneous and playful. Yet as the relationship grows more familiar, what can replace that way of kissing is a predictable script of the closed-mouth little peck of a kiss we've already talked about—pleasant but nothing to get excited about.

Throughout the years, a couple is also likely to develop a well-established script for their sexual interactions. Although sex may still contribute to good feelings between the two of them, it is not likely to generate the intense passion of their earlier relationship. In other words, well-established scripts can keep the relationship running smoothly, but it doesn't make for interesting or exciting sex.

True Romance: Honoring Individuality and Otherness

The scripts that individuals are likely to play out with their partners can be generalizations and expectations about "all men" or "all women" that they learned from watching their own parents interact. Sometimes these are unquestioned notions about how we imagine we are supposed to be or act in a relationship. There may also be unfinished and unforgiven business from past relationships that each partner brings into the new relationship and automatically transfers to the partner. Scripts that require avoiding hot spots in order to get along undermine the likelihood of self-disclosure and discovery.

The working models of intimacy that are handed down from one generation to the next are expectations programmed in the brain. These old tapes come with their own distinct emotional patterns. I see couples playing out parent-child scripts that are right out of their childhood playbooks.

The "My Way Is Better Than Your Way" Script

I've encountered a number of relationships in which one person pushes his or her own scripts on the other person. Certain ways of doing something or saying something are deemed acceptable, "the right way of doing things," and other ways are not. Not only is this a kind of bullying, it completely stifles romantic feelings.

A woman named Stacy came to see me when she noticed that after six years of marriage she had lost her sex drive completely. She said she didn't know what was wrong with her. As we talked, what was really going on became more apparent.

Stacy and her husband, Jim, were still having some nice times together, she told me, but she had to be careful with him. He had very firm opinions about everything. He was continually correcting her language when she spoke and telling her how something she did should have been done differently. That continued into their sex play, with Jim giving Stacy a running commentary during their sexual activity on how to touch him. Stacy loved Jim and wanted to please him, so she was trying to learn his way of doing things, but she had completely lost her spontaneity in their relationship, and with it her desire for Jim.

Clearly, there was nothing wrong with Stacy. Her body was having a natural and genuine response to her partner's unappealing behavior. I suggested that it would be a good idea for Jim to come in with her, and to my delight he agreed. Their work in therapy then became not just an enhancement of their sexual life together but a great example of how a couple's patterns in sex can be a reflection of deeper emotional issues.

Stacy was used to placating her stern father and playing the role of the good daughter. Neurons remember. If a woman's early experience with her parents involved having to hide aspects of herself to be loved, she's likely to expect to have to do the same to keep love as an adult. Having your actions scrutinized and your language corrected doesn't do a thing for sexual desire.

Jim, who was very clear about what he wanted Stacy to do during lovemaking, came from a critical and unloving family. His father was particularly shaming toward him during adolescence. So here he was now, acting like his father toward his wife, who was doing her best to be a good girl. Not a very sexy scene.

It doesn't make sense to fall in love with an individual you see as rare and special and then turn around and try to make him or her over in your own image. Yet people do that all the time. Unfortunately, when one person dictates the scripts, what was once playful turns into a catechism—and there goes the romance and physical desire.

Free to Be Me

As I see it, the more a couple relies on well-established scripts to get along, the more that relationship is on its way to calcification. Naturally, the longer two people are together, the more likely they are to have established some routines that work. But there's a great personal loss when self-disclosure, and especially self-discovery, ceases to be an important part of a couple's intimacy.

Feeling free enough to express feelings that matter depends on trusting the other to listen without criticism. It allows people in a relationship to be individuals and not just part of a couple. Once you get past the stage of self-disclosure, a deeper intimacy comes not just by sharing what you already know but also by discovering new aspects of yourself in the company of the other.

Discovering yourself in the presence of the other is my definition of an intimate relationship.

The willingness to be spontaneous and uncensored, to explore your true thoughts and feelings with a trusted other, is also what makes for effective therapy. But a therapeutic relationship focuses on the discovery of only one person, the client. In a love relationship, it's a two-way discovery process.

Naturally, self-disclosure is unlikely in a relationship in which there are trust issues or real deception. If it has been your experience that your partner will use your disclosures against you in a power struggle, you're not likely to volunteer any new information. On the other hand, it is truly wonderful to be able to have cozy conversations with your mate in which you can explore your thoughts and feelings and feel safe.

Breaking Out of Old Scripts

The first step in breaking free of limiting old patterns is to recognize how you are bringing old family patterns into your relationship, whether by playing out mother-son, father-daughter, mother-daughter, or father-son roles. However, a male partner may be more like one's mother, or a female partner more like one's father. It's the personality of the partner and not just the gender that may trigger old parent-child dynamics between mates. Does one of you criticize, lecture, or scold the other? Do you answer criticism reflexively with the rudeness and disdain of a teenager? Does one of you set rules and threaten punishments? Or do you make the choice to take a moment to breathe and to respond as an adult and a peer?

The original script played out between a parent and a sexually blossoming child is typically one of conflict. The child needs to establish autonomy from the parent in order to assert his or her sexuality. Act like a mother or a father with your mate, and you are likely to get the same kinds of reactions your mate exhibited with his or her parents as an adolescent. Good luck squeezing any sexual juice out of that interaction.

In addition, we learned as adolescents to direct our sexual feelings and desires away from our family and toward the other, the outsider, someone who has to be wooed to be won. As we saw in an earlier chapter, the natural lure of the sexual outsider is a risk factor in sustaining a monogamous relationship. Let's face it, it's exciting to encounter someone new and different who wants to play with you. The question is, can that new and different personality be your partner?

When Stacy and Jim came for couples therapy, they both saw how they were playing out family patterns with each other. They hated to think of themselves as acting out roles they learned watching their own parents, and neither wanted to sacrifice their sex life. Stacy was just as motivated as Jim. Here again a sexual symptom was the inspiration to deepen an intimate connection by learning how to support each other's growth and to become more naturally playful with each other.

Differentiation

Is it possible to find someone new and different in one's mate? That depends on how free each individual is to be spontaneous without judgment, criticism, threat, or punishment. These are all forms of control.

If there are old patterns militating against openness in a relationship, it can take a while to build trust. Obviously, this does not happen overnight. The developmental challenge for maintaining a place for romance in a relationship is to appreciate your partner's uniqueness and to be respectful of how you are *not* carbon copies of each other. Psychologists call this *differentiation*, and it has to do with each of you maintaining a sense of self, with a right to your own opinions and preferences, apart from your commitment to the relationship. You and your partner were attracted to each other *because of*, not in spite of, your differences.

Another crucial aspect of differentiation is being capable of distinguishing your partner from the parent or sibling that you have unfinished business with. If you think your partner is just like your mother, your father, or a sibling, it may be because that's how you are treating him or her. Ask yourself if you are hiding things and feeling guilty the way you did with your parents or feeling competitive and jealous as you felt with your sister or brother. If the answer is yes, bingo! You have some stuff to work on.

Often the best way is to just "bust" yourself. If you let your partner know you're recognizing the patterns in yourself, your partner will be more likely to want to break his or her own patterns—especially if you talk nicely.

Finally, consider that dealing with these issues is part of what brought the two of you together. We are often attracted to those who can help us resolve some of our childhood issues and flourish as adults in a loving and sexual relationship. If there are no problems, there will be no growth. Another way of saying this is that if there is no challenge, there is no need to adapt, so there will be no evolution.

One of the best ways to break out of old scripts is to be playful with each other, especially romantically playful. Nothing undermines the tendency to equate your partner with family better than treating him or her as an attractive and sexually desirable individual to have fun with.

Romantic Play

We never outgrow our need for romance. Wooing the other person in a relationship fuels sexual interest in the same way that admiring the presentation of a lovely meal at a fine restaurant or sniffing a glass of quality wine whets the appetite. Appreciating your meal before ingesting it activates your taste buds and stimulates the secretion of saliva in the mouth, preparing you to enjoy your food. Flirting and being erotically playful can automatically stimulate the erotic imagination and mix up your favorite cocktail of dopamine and hormones to feed your sexual arousal.

The fun and playfulness of flirting can be one of the first things to go when two people commit to each other and move in together. For some couples, being sexy with each other ceases, the wooing game is over, and sex becomes expected. Before they moved in together, they enticed each other. They looked deep into each other's eyes and smiled; they caressed each other as they spoke sweetly and lovingly; they kissed and kissed. Now one of them "initiates" sex. It's like a trade deal.

When I hear a couple complain about who does or doesn't initiate sex, it sounds so boring. Typically, the initiator is the same person each time, and it's the other who gets to say yea or nay. Sometimes the initiator just asks hopefully, "Do you want to have sex?" and waits for a response. Then the other rapidly runs the calculus, taking into account the interruption to his or her schedule, how long this is likely to take, his or her energy level, and the forecast for a happy ending.

But the medium is the message. Enthusiasm begets enthusiasm. Nothing in this couple's initiation ritual whets the appetite and activates the taste buds for sex. A warm smile and a little focused attention on each other is much more likely to ignite a little spark.

Commitment doesn't have to be the end of flirting and being playful. We have a natural body-based ability to be responsive to romance.

How Can I Romance You?
Let Me Count the Ways

There are many kinds of romance. A romance can be a love story, a love affair, or a way of engaging and enticing a lover.

A Romance Is a Love Story

In classic fairy tales, lovers are kept apart by circumstances like crusades, wars, family feuds, and evil stepmothers. In the stories that end well, the lovers confront the obstacles, vanquish the dragons, and achieve everlasting happiness.

Every couple has its own love story: how the partners met, what their challenges were then, what their challenges are now, and how their love has, and will continue to conquer all. In all of the stories I've heard of how a couple met and fell in love, there's always a magic moment when the two people recognized each other as mates for life.

Keeping a relationship interesting involves invoking that magic from time to time. It helps to remind yourselves periodically of the special beauty of your own modern-day love story and to hold that vision dear.

A Romance Is a Love Affair

Typically short-lived and passionate, an affair is often a secret because one or both partners are married or they're breaking some rule by being together—like a company regulation against coworkers fraternizing. As a result, the two are in a bubble. Untainted by the real world, the lovers take respite from their mundane lives and responsibilities in their connection with each other. The tryst is a time set aside for love and pleasure.

A couple can also have a love affair. What it takes is the same motivation to steal away to create a bubble of time devoted to intimate pleasures. It's a romantic interlude, a time when all responsibilities are on hold and nothing else matters but enjoying each other and feeling good together. Ultimately, it's all about making the other person feel special and valued by making time for him or her.

To Romance Is a Verb

Lovers romance each other. They flirt with and tease each other. They take the time to entice each other playfully and erotically.

A couple can keep alive the quality of romantic love in the relationship if each person makes the other feel special and, at least occasionally, looks attractive just for him or her. To romance your lover, you want to draw him or her toward you to come play with you.

To Romance Is to Play

In my last book, *The Pleasure Zone*, I showed how play is one of life's core pleasures, and I cited studies indicating that playfulness and making time for play can actually enhance immunity and contribute to personal health and happy relationships. Sex researchers William Masters and Virginia Johnson themselves referred to the "pleasure bond" as one of the great values of maintaining an active and satisfying sex life for a couple.

When couples get stressed, their ability to play is one of the first things to go. But if something funny happens, and the partners are suddenly able to share some moments of laughter or enjoyment, their lightheartedness can inspire them to repair the damage and move on. To maximize your erotic possibilities you have to take full advantage of your ability to play.

The Powers of Play

When play is the medium, the body gets the message. Play is the life force in action. The opposite of play is not work, because work can be done in a spirit of play and be highly enjoyable. The opposite of play is forced labor: effortful, goal oriented, and nose to the grindstone.

Play is naturally relaxed and energetic at the same time. When you are at play, you are doing something just for the sake of doing it because it feels good and makes you glad to be alive.

Neurological studies show that the body at play confers the ultimate in neural integration: high sympathetic and parasympathetic arousal. This is the neural state associated with relaxed alertness. During play the brain secretes dopamine and acetylcholine, neurotransmitters that reward the activity, sharpen memory, and stimulate the brain's attention center.

In his studies with both human and animal subjects, Bowling Green University professor Jaak Panksepp found that play is a critical, inborn, and positively energizing motivational and emotional system. He observed that playful activity is also associated with the secretion of painkilling opioids that enhance memory and joyfulness. He suggested that if we are to become master of our own emotional dynamics, we are unlikely to find "any stronger therapeutic aid than that contained in the joyous potentials of *play*."

University of Illinois professor Steven Porges has highlighted the fact that playfulness creates a sense of safety between two people. During playful activity, people are more likely to touch, the muscles of the face relax, there are more instances of eye contact and smiles, and the voice softens. Each person's nervous system becomes mobilized, but without fear. Play engages us, regulates the nervous system, and inspires new learning and cooperative behavior.

Children are the great masters of play—they like to play at pretend, and once they get into it, they're spontaneous and very focused. A child at play is a happy child and is in the process of learning vital life skills. The child is still in us and as much in need of playtime as ever.

My dictionary defines *playful* as "said or done in a teasing way or in fun" and offers these synonyms: good-humored, light-hearted, teasing, joking, humorous, and mischievous. *Mischievous* is defined as being naughty or disobedient, but usually in fun and not meaning harm. This is one of the big reasons that romance can happen only between people who feel free to be themselves and not adhere to predetermined scripts.

Being romantic is a great way for partners to play. When one person is attentive to the other with a lighthearted and lively spirit and the other reciprocates in some way—laughs at the joke or smiles back and stays engaged—they've connected with their inner playmates.

Becoming a Charming Flirt

Flirting is not overtly sexual, although it can turn into something more erotic. Fundamentally, to flirt is to be attentive in a light-hearted manner, to have a sense of humor, and to acknowledge another as someone you like and want to play with.

The late Joyce Jillson, a television actress, an author, and the astrologer to Ronald and Nancy Reagan while they were in the White House, made some very perceptive observations on the fine art of flirting. Although she was mostly interested in how single men and women might attract each other, some of her tips ring true for couples. Jillson cautioned that flirting has to be subtle, or it's likely to be a turnoff. The basic characteristic of good flirting is simply to be warm and friendly. In fact, she suggested that just being warm and friendly toward anyone can be considered flirting, and she recounted that her female friends sometimes told her she was flirting with their grandsons when all she was doing was showing an interest in them. She called this aspect of flirting "old-world charm." For the modern man or woman that may be an anachronistic concept. But I think her observation is really insightful.

Being charming is almost synonymous with flirting. To *charm* someone is to delight or enchant that person, and maybe even to cast a spell on him or her. Charm is said to be the power to attract or persuade others. When someone is charmed by you, he or she is drawn to you. If you're charming, you are, by definition, a pleasure to be with.

According to Jillson, some flirtatious assets to hone in your personality include "having a sense of humor about yourself" and "being playful, whimsical and even prankish." Other qualities she highlighted are to "flirt without expectations of reward" so that you don't get fixated on any particular goal and to "show enthusiasm for the moment." I think she nailed it.

There's a myth that women are romantic and men are not. In fact, I sometimes think that men are more romantic than women. Both like to be told how special and how attractive they are. Both like to be the focus of undivided attention. Both feel warm and happy inside when their partners look into their eyes, stroke their cheeks silently, and smile.

It's true that a man with an extra measure of testosterone may tend to sexualize a romantic interaction faster than a woman might. But just because there is some sexual energy between them doesn't mean they have to stop everything and get prone. It's good energy, and both sexes benefit when eroticism morphs out of a spirit of playful romance and enthusiasm for more intimate connection.

Playing at Romance

While living in Paris during the 1930s, the American novelist Henry Miller was approached by a famous art dealer with a money-making offer. The dealer told Miller—whose books at the time were banned as pornography in the United States—that he represented a wealthy client who was interested in hiring him to write short erotic stories for the client's own enjoyment. The client wished to remain anonymous, and the exchange of money for the manuscripts would be undertaken by the dealer.

Miller could have used the extra funds, but he decided to stay focused on his own work, so he offered the assignment to his friend and fellow writer, Anaïs Nin. Nin started out writing stories for the client on her own, but as his appetite for more grew and she could not keep up with his demands, she called on a cadre of cash-strapped young artists to help with the writing and to split the income. They decided to write as a collective, so they sat together during the evenings and concocted tales, some of which were based on their own romances; others were pure fantasy. Each time the stories were received, however, the benefactor sent back the same message: "Cut the poetry, just write about sex."

The message infuriated them. Here they were, a group of young Parisian artists who had been given the opportunity to write about intensely arousing sex, and they were being stifled by some old man who was completely lacking in sexual sensibility and imagination. In her diary, Nin expressed this frustration in the form of a letter to the mystery client:

> The source of sexual power is curiosity, passion. You are watching its little flame die of asphyxiation. Sex does not thrive on monotony. Without feeling, inventions, moods, no surprises in bed. . . . We have sat around for hours and wondered how you look. If you have closed your senses upon silk, light, color, odor, character, temperament, you must be by now completely shriveled up.

Although she never called it by name, they are all the elements of romance. This great literary sensualist and doyenne of erotic imagination concluded, "There are so many minor senses, all running like tributaries into the mainstream of sex, nourishing it. Only the united beat of sex and heart together can create ecstasy."

Step four in the Loving Sex Program offers several experiments to do with a partner to stretch your pleasurable imagination and explore romantic play.

Step Four: Partners in Romance

Objective: To discover new ways to be romantic and playful with the one you love

Experiments in Romance

Romance has to be playful. If you play out a predictable script, it's not going to be romantic, because first, it's not genuine, and second, it's not unexpected. But you can play in fresh ways with old scripts, and you can also connect with each other in new ways. See what enlivens your playful connection.

The object of these exercises is to stimulate a pleasurable process between you and your partner that fosters spontaneous playful romantic engagement.

Gestalt Games for Couples

Based on embodied Gestalt therapy that teaches people to become more aware of ongoing moment-by moment experience, these are two-person, present-centered experiments done in the spirit of play. They are processes that can be enjoyed for themselves, and they can jiggle mental habits and lead to insight. They may also direct the way to new and better ways of doing things. These exercises require a willing partner to play with and may take anywhere from fifteen minutes to half an hour or more.

If you don't currently have a partner or your partner is not available, you can do these Gestalt games in your imagination. Picture the activity in your mind's eye with the partner of your choice. Watch how your body responds and be aware of any tension-relaxation shifts or emotions that bubble up. If you intend to pick and choose the games that most appeal to you, I recommend that you read through all of the games before you select any. That way you can still get some benefit out of exercises you don't do.

As always, all experiments start with embodied basics and breathing fully and deeply, focusing inward, and taking a felt-sense inventory.

1. SPEND A MINDFUL MINUTE IN A HUG

This experiment is meant to be just a few extra moments shared during a convenient time in the flow of the day. It does not require setting aside any structured time.

- Get your partner's consent to do this one. For the next few days, at some point in the day, maybe when saying hello in the morning or in the evening, greet each other with an extended hug and a few moments of breathing and relaxing together.

- Hold your bodies close. Feel each other's heartbeat, the warmth and smoothness of skin on skin. Breathe in each other's familiar scent, drawing a long deep inhalation through the nose and exhaling in a sigh. Then look into each other's eyes for a few moments, enjoy a little kiss, and go on with your day or evening.

2. SAY WHAT YOU MOST LOVE AND APPRECIATE ABOUT EACH OTHER

Invite your partner to do this with you. It may take no more than ten minutes.

- Sit comfortably facing each other and decide who will go first. The one who begins starts each sentence with "What I most love about you is" or "What I really appreciate is" and shares as many good qualities as he or she can think of in the moment. Look into each other's eyes as you talk. If you feel the need to look away, allow yourself to, and look back when it feels comfortable to do so.

- First one partner completes the exercise, and then the other partner does it. Do not interrupt each other. Just listen. After you both have expressed what you love and appreciate, thank each other with a hug and a kiss.

3. TELL THE STORY OF YOUR LOVE

Find a romantic spot in which to do this little exercise with
your partner. It could be at home with dimmed lights, soft
music, and a few lit candles. Or the two of you might be alone
in nature, walking on the beach at sunset or sitting outdoors
on a warm summer evening watching the stars appear in the
night sky.

- Each one tells the story of your first meeting in a new
  way. Share how you felt about the other at first, what
  first attracted you, and when you knew he or she was
  "the one."

- Reminisce together about any obstacles you had to overcome to stay together and say how you think those trials
  strengthened you and helped you to endure as a couple.

- Appreciate what you most treasure about the presence of
  the other in your life, what he or she means to you.

- Look ahead at some dreams you have for new experiences to share, places to travel to, and adventures to enjoy
  together.

- Say thanks for how the other has enriched your life.

4. HAVE A LOVE AFFAIR

Get out of the house. Take your love and your alone time
together outside the home you share.

- Meet after work for a drink, on a park bench, or at a nice
  place to walk. Take the time to greet each other warmly,
  making eye contact, smiling, touching, and kissing (discreetly, of course). Then just hang out together and share
  your day, especially the high points.

- Make a plan to go somewhere that would be special to
  you. If you can't agree on a place that has the same meaning to both of you, choose two special places and accompany each other to both. In either case, learn what makes
  the place so special to the other.

- Bring the other an inexpensive gift that you sense he or
  she will appreciate. Tell the story that goes along with the
  gift and what about it made you think of the other.

- Go to a hotel for a romantic night or weekend and plan to focus on each other. If it's a weekend, make sure you build in individual time alone as well so you can look forward to each other's return.

- Each of you plans a romantic evening at home. For each evening, make sure you will be alone all night. The host for the evening plans a light meal, selects the music, and creates an appealing environment. Each of you dresses to feel attractive, yet in comfortable, breathable clothing. Be an entertaining and attentive host and a gracious guest. Enjoy each other's company.

5. HAVE FUN TOGETHER

These are little games to play just for fun. They're meant to bring out your lightheartedness with each other. You don't have to do any of them more than once unless you want to.

- Make up some new pet names for each other. Be nice.

- Arm wrestle. The one who cares more about winning should always win.

- Groom each other. Comb or brush each other's hair, paint each other's toenails, rub lotion on each other's chest, shoulders, and back. Give him or her a footbath or a hand rub.

- Sit facing each other with knees touching. Take a few deep breaths and notice the distance between your noses. Remain seated exactly where you are, and very slowly and without any words, bend toward your partner, moving only your chest and waist. Keep moving closer and closer and see if you can get your noses to touch. If you don't succeed, do it again.

- Sit facing each other. Take a few deep breaths, hold both hands, and look each other in the eyes. Now take turns telling each other a joke. If your partner blows it, be comforting.

6. ROMANCE IS SELF-DISCLOSURE

The more openness there has been in your relationship, the easier these exercises will be. If you haven't shared much in the past, start with little revelations. Then move slowly, although perceptively, outside your comfort zone.

- Breathe. Reveal something new about yourself to your partner. It doesn't have to be something startling. Preferably, it's a feeling you haven't talked about before. If your partner doesn't respond as you had hoped, ask for what you want. Ask nicely.

- Breathe. When your partner reveals something new about himself or herself, pay attention to how that makes you feel. How are you responding, and how would you like to respond?

- Breathe. Reveal the ways your partner appreciates you more than you appreciate yourself. Tell him or her what that means to you and how that has affected your life.

- Breathe. Tell him or her "how you complete me." Share how he or she makes you more than you are without him or her.

- Breathe together. Lie in each other's arms. Feel blessed to have each other.

5

Body Talk

We live in a disembodied culture. We have air guitar contests and play tennis in the family room with imaginary balls on virtual courts. People kiss-kiss without touching. Kids can have hundreds of friends they've never laid eyes on. Women and men have hot sex with a throaty voice on the phone or with words scrolling across a computer screen. No wonder that even partners who love each other sometimes become physically disconnected.

When two people first get together, they can't stop touching. They walk holding hands or draped arm in arm. They sit leaning on each other. They talk to each other with their noses just inches apart. Think back to when you felt that way with someone: when you kissed hello or good-bye and really got into it; when you held a gaze, smiling into his or her eyes; when you held a hug, your body pressed against the other's, feeling utterly content.

Yet once partners live together, they may become increasingly cut off physically. They may take each other's presence for granted and quit taking the extra few seconds to look into each other's eyes and smile. They may hold grudges and punish by withholding physical contact. So they kiss on the run: good morning, sweetie; see ya later, hon; good night, dear. Eventually their interactions are more likely to be shoulder to shoulder than face-to-face—especially when raising kids or running a business.

In fact, the only face-to-face communication the partners may have is likely to be verbal, and even then they may not look each other in the eyes. Too often when I'm working with a couple, I'll notice that even though the two individuals are facing each other and one person is saying something really important, they aren't looking at each other. One is staring at the carpet while the other is looking out the window. That's a miscommunication in the making. In that moment, those two people are not connecting.

There is no doubt that we rely on words to feel loved and supported. We want to be understood. We want to be able to talk things over. We benefit from uncovering tacit expectations so they can be spelled out and negotiated. We feel valued when we hear "thank you" when we've been sweet and "I'm sorry" when we've been wronged.

"I love you" are the sweetest words in any language. Life is good when love is spoken here. But words can also do damage. When two people are having trouble getting along or getting it on, words are often part of the problem. Words can be wounding, shaming, inaccurate, and spoken in anger or fear. It can be harder for partners to recover from the words exchanged than from the problem they were hoping to talk through.

When a Body Meets a Body

It pays to take a closer look at why emotional balance cannot be achieved through words alone. Good words may be reassuring, but verbal reassurance is a quick fix, and it can even be counterproductive when a word triggers a fear or anger reflex in one or both partners.

It doesn't take much for individuals who are already primed for hurt to be offended by even an innocent comment. It doesn't matter who starts it. If the other person responds in kind, that completes the circuit, and the couple is off and running. Automatically, the old neural imbalance and insecurity return.

A major limitation of words is that when you're tense, the tension is present in the words you speak. Your face tightens and you look different. Even if you don't intend to judge, there's no way to avoid being read as condemning or blaming. If you lose it and yell, you've discharged your built-up pressure, but you've now infected your partner, who will have to expel it somehow. Then around and around it goes. When two people are in close physical proximity and one body radiates anger and fear, the other body will very likely catch the emotional infection.

Scientists have found that there's a close physiological connection between the positive quality of feeling empathy for another and the detrimental tendency to be contaminated by the other's feelings.

Empathy

We are born with the ability to read minds. Developmental researchers have discovered that one of the first interactions between mother and infant occurs when the infant opens his or her eyes, looks into the eyes of the mother, and reflexively begins to mimic the expression on the mother's face. This is the beginning of a primitive form of empathy activated in infancy that continues throughout life. It's a process in which individuals of all ages understand what another is feeling by reflexively and unconsciously mirroring the emotional expressions of the other.

Paul Ekman of the UCSF Medical Center did the classic research that showed the profound connection between facial expression and emotion. In one study, subjects whose facial muscles were wired to an electromyogram (EMG) were shown films of people displaying a variety of emotions, like happiness, sadness, anger, and disgust. While the EMG recorded the subjects' facial muscle movements, a camera was also trained on their faces and videotaped their facial expressions.

To the naked eye, no visible changes in the subjects' facial expressions were discernible. The subjects themselves reported no awareness at all of making any facial movements. Yet when the data were analyzed, the EMG recorded facial movements consistent with the emotions projected. When the videotapes were slowed down to microsecond slices, minute emotional expressions consistent with the ones displayed were completely visible. Although these emotional micro-expressions are clearly well below our conscious threshold, they have an enormous effect on us. In one study, people were asked to recall certain emotional experiences. Again, there were microsecond changes in facial expression, but the changes in the body were more than just facial.

Simply remembering an emotional experience triggered responses in the autonomic nervous system that would typically accompany the feelings of those experiences. The linkage between the face and the nervous system is so powerful that even when people were asked to make pretend facial expressions corresponding to different feelings, their nervous systems were still triggered to reflect those emotions.

The positive side of this is that we can actually feel another person's sadness and have compassion for what he or she is going through because it reverberates inside us, and our spirits can be lifted by an inspirational story and the warmth and caring of others. The downside is that we are capable of contaminating each other with fear and anger, escalating and intensifying painful emotions.

Emotional Contagion

Psychology professor Elaine Hatfield and her associates at the University of Hawaii in Honolulu have shown that it is not only through mimicking faces that we feel each other's feelings; we also automatically mimic and synchronize vocal tones, postures, and movements almost simultaneously with those we're observing. This is accomplished through a class of neurons that run alongside motor neurons that are called *mirror neurons*. Mirror neurons fire in response to observing movements in another that trigger the same muscles in the observer that are being activated by the person who is actually moving. Although there are no external discernible movements in the observer, internally his or her body is subtly replicating what the "mover" is experiencing. In addition, the right brain of the observer also picks up subtle cues from the mover that signify danger or safety. These microexpressions and microgestures either alert or calm the nervous system of the observer. Again, the underlying mechanism is automatic and unconscious.

Hatfield and her associates provided substantial evidence that it is through this process of unconsciously mimicking the facial expression, vocal tone, posture, and movements of someone close that one person can "catch" the anger, fear, or sadness of another. The observer's face tightens, the tone of voice and movements shift to match those of the mover, and the brain and the nervous system of the observer are triggered to experience the same emotion.

When Emotional Contagion Becomes a Habit

Janie and Theo were fighting too much over a lot of rather insignificant issues. They had been living together for three years, and they loved each other very much but were thinking of calling it quits. Most of the time they wouldn't even remember what started the fight but their communications would deteriorate into insults, name calling, and bad feelings. They knew they were in a power struggle, and they understood the childhood issues that had programmed each of them for conflict. They just couldn't control themselves. The constant combat particularly affected Theo, who had lost all interest in sex with Janie.

Janie was offended by a recent incident. They were supposed to meet friends for dinner, and Janie was running late. She was feeling insecure, probably because of a problem at the office, but she just couldn't decide on what to wear, so she was trying on several different outfits. Theo was getting anxious about not getting to the restaurant on time, so he went to the bedroom where Janie was dressing and tried to hustle her along. Janie lost it and screamed at Theo to leave her alone. He screamed back, and they ended up so enraged at each other that they made up an excuse and canceled their dinner date.

This is clearly an emotional infection that's being passed back and forth. It's like sneezing in someone's face when you have a cold, only with emotions, the effect is immediate.

I have a metaphor that seems to reach couples with a habit of this sort of contamination. If two people are walking together along a riverbank and one of them falls into quicksand, it makes no sense for the other to jump in, too. The solution is to throw the sinking person a lifeline and pull him or her out. Otherwise you're both going to go down—and as it is with quicksand, the more you struggle, the faster you'll sink.

How does one person in a couple resist getting infected when his or her body is naturally responding to contamination? The first step is to get into the habit of self-regulating stress independent of the partner. Self-soothing is a key aspect of emotional fitness: we have to take good care of ourselves. The second step is to help to regulate your partner's stress. If both of you are willing, you can learn to repair the relationship more quickly after an argument or a disagreement, soothe each other's hurt feelings, make nice, and move on.

Interactive Repair

Interactive repair is the term used by Harvard researcher Ed Tronick to describe the way that sensitive mothers calmed their babies' distress after being unresponsive to them for several minutes during a laboratory experiment. What has been discovered in real life is that repeated instances of parent-child distress that are followed by repair can have a very positive effect on a child. The child learns that painful experiences are temporary and to have confidence that relationship difficulties can be resolved with love. Perhaps most important, these experiences of interactive repair strengthen the bond between parent and child.

The same is true for adults. Interactive repair in a relationship is a way to alleviate the effects of emotional contagion. Without a doubt, the willingness and ability to soothe each other's distress strengthens the bond between lovers.

One couple I worked with came for a session after a nightmare weekend out of town. Cindy and Carl had been looking forward to a restful and romantic vacation, but when they arrived at the hotel there was no record of their reservation and they had to accept a less than desirable room. Cindy was feeling bad about it and was unpacking her suitcase in silence, banging drawers and tossing her shoes into the closet. Carl, also long-faced and silent, was getting more and more tense by the minute. Cindy broke the silence by looking at Carl and declaring emphatically, "We shouldn't have stayed." At that point, Carl totally lost it. He roared, "Then let's go" and flung a magazine he was holding toward the bed. It caught Cindy on the wrist, and she lifted her hands to her chest and cried out, "Why are you attacking me?" Carl felt bad and apologized but added that Cindy shouldn't have yelled at him. Cindy complained that he always blamed her.

They got it together enough to stay for the weekend, but they were edgy and cool toward each other the whole time. They had been looking forward to making love during their romantic getaway, but they never even kissed once. Cindy said that when Carl lost his temper like that, it ruined the whole weekend for her.

They had had a number of instances in the past in which Cindy would say something that would trigger Carl, and he would blow up. Eventually, he would go to her and say he was sorry, but he would explain how she had made him so angry. She would see his contrition as a manipulation rather than an apology and hold on to her resentment and disappointment.

In this instance, I told them it was obvious that they were both terribly disappointed. Yet instead of helping to soothe each other's heavy hearts, they just took it out on each other. I explained that they would benefit from honing their skills for dealing with disappointment by being generous and reassuring, feeling their pain, moving through it, and moving on. Then instead of staying fixed on what they *don't* have, they could both rally on enjoying what they *do* have. I told them that if this lost weekend helped them learn how to handle disappointments in the future, their loss would end up to be a big gain.

I asked Cindy and Carl to identify all the ways they contaminated each other and all their missed opportunities to put their disappointments behind them and have a great weekend. With hindsight and given the same circumstances, how might they handle such a disappointment in the future? Together they were able to identify all the critical choice points and what they could do instead.

The first thing they could do is to put off the unpacking, lie together on the bed, hold and comfort each other, and resolve to have a great time anyway. They each could breathe deeply and calm their stress. That way, when Cindy said they shouldn't stay, Carl might be able to reassure her that they could still have a wonderful weekend together. Cindy might recognize that Carl was feeling guilty about not getting them a better room and give him a hug. Carl might hold Cindy when he said he was sorry rather than embed his words in an explanation of how she had set him off. Finally, Cindy could accept Carl's apology and say something like, "Yes, let's not let this get in the way of a great weekend." They could kiss and make up. I reminded them that if one of them can self-regulate sufficiently to help the other, he or she becomes the "healer" in that moment, the one who can step out of the old routine and save the day.

New York psychoanalysts and researchers Beatrice Beebe and Frank Lachmann, who have developed a therapeutic approach based on the interactive regulation between mother and infant, have pointed out that in any adult interaction, each partner influences the other in different ways and to different degrees. Both partners don't have the same ability at any one time to regulate their stress. An important awareness is sensing how the partner's feelings and behavior are being influenced by one's own feelings and behavior. In other words, neither is at fault, but both are responsible. At any moment, one of them can turn things around, take the lead, and help to turn a difficult situation into a pleasant and even an enlightening one. In effect, this new way of dealing with things together can soothe hurt feelings and deepen their love.

Mutual Regulation

We've looked at the role of self-regulation, particularly in the early steps of the Loving Sex Program. If we don't regulate our own stress, our family programming can turn us into automatons, dictating how we react emotionally to the inevitable tensions in a relationship. If we weren't loved and reassured enough as a child, or if we got too much of the wrong kind of attention, we're more likely to misinterpret a partner's actions or overreact with an alarm reflex and become defensive. These reflexes are often old painful feelings that were never sufficiently soothed and resolved.

We can calm our nervous systems by breathing and reassuring ourselves. Ultimately, however, what it takes to enjoy a more long-term inner felt-sense of security and lovability is coming into attunement with another safe body. By sharing love and affection, two people can come into a neural as well as a physical attunement. This way of loving nourishes each other's felt-sense of well-being and deepens the ability to enjoy intimate pleasures together.

The ABCs of Primal Intimacy

Contrary to popular opinion, words are not the mainstay of intimacy. Scientific research tells us that the most profoundly fulfilling intimacies for adults are those that are rooted in the body and involve the same primal needs we were born with.

Data from developmental neuroscience, psychology, sexology, anecdotal evidence, and personal experience all converge to highlight three bottom-line essentials of primal intimacy—three basics for nurturing a more fully embodied, emotionally gratifying, inner felt-sense of closeness: empathic touch, eye contact, and intimate kissing. I think of these as the ABCs of a deep intimacy—a primal intimacy, the sine qua non of loving and sensual sex. They are more than simply activities. As we shall see, these primal pleasures provide the foundation for an attuned connection on which emotional, romantic, and sexual intimacies are built.

A. Empathic Touch: Mutual Stress Regulation

Everyday life has its everyday stress. Getting from one place to the next—geographically or metaphorically—is stressful. Some days are emotionally challenging. You may suffer a bout of self-doubt or have to stare down a dragon, and you come home carrying the day in your body. Your muscles are tense and achy.

We know that physical contact is a life-or-death factor in the health of babies and young children. There's now a great deal of evidence to indicate that this is true for adults as well. Studies show that physical touch balances the right and left hemispheres of the brain and coordinates the sympathetic and parasympathetic branches of the nervous system, creating greater integration and efficiency in the body. Touch can reduce stress, ease pain, slow the heart rate, lower blood pressure, and relax tense muscles. The result is an enhancement of attention, cognitive ability, and mood as well as a boost to the immune system.

Dr. Tiffany Field, director of the Touch Research Institute at the University of Miami Medical School, and her team of researchers have focused their efforts on examining the health benefits of touch and the effectiveness of touch in the treatment of disease. In one study, the staff and faculty of a medical school were given a fifteen-minute massage every day for a month, and their brain waves were recorded before, during, and after the session. They were also given a series of mathematical computations to do before and after the session. The results showed that the massage increased their alertness and greatly improved their performance on intellectual tasks.

Massage therapy has been shown to increase the production of serotonin and dopamine, the neurotransmitters in the brain that are associated with positive mood, and to reduce stress hormones like cortisol. Empathic touch stimulates the production of natural killer cells, which have been shown to protect us from illnesses such as autoimmune disease and cancer.

If a massage can do all this, then people who live together have the capacity to bestow greater health and well-being on each other every day just by holding and caressing each other.

Clearly, we never outgrow the need to be physically close to a warm, loving body. Unfortunately, people who were not held and touched enough when they were children typically remain touch-deprived as adults because they're not in the habit of reaching out for contact. That could have been my story.

Therapist, Heal Thyself

I have no doubt that I was a touch-deprived child. I don't remember my mother ever holding or cuddling me. I do remember her sitting between my grandmother and me in the backseat of a car on a trip to upstate New York when I was about eight. I recall going up a mountain road and squeezing toward the window to avoid her upper arm touching mine as the car shifted from side to side. I can still hear my mother saying to my grandmother, "Look. She can't stand my touching her." It was true—her touch actually disgusted me.

I learned a great deal about myself in the years I was in training as a therapist, and I was able to lift myself out of the constant undercurrent of anxiety and depression that had characterized the first twenty-eight years of my life. But I still didn't seem to be able to make a relationship work. I yearned for love and was jubilant whenever I found it, every three years or so. But invariably it came to no good. Either the love was missing or the sex was missing. And I wasn't capable of settling for less than both.

Finally, I met the man who would turn out to be my life partner. We fell in love one weekend riding our bikes along the beach in Santa Monica, bought a little house in a canyon, and moved in together. But instead of feeling loved, safe, and secure, I found myself becoming more and more anxious.

In those days he was doing a lot of traveling for his work, and it wasn't easy for me when he left for four or five days at a time. Many nights I couldn't sleep; I would panic at every creak that someone might be breaking in through a window to attack me.

One afternoon, as my sweetheart was leaving for a few days, I stood at the front gate with him as his taxi waited. I was sobbing, convinced that I would never see him again. It was hard for him to leave me like that, but I finally let him go.

I didn't recognize myself. Wasn't I a strong, capable woman—confident and tenacious? Who was this lily-livered whimpering fool crying because her man wasn't going to be around for a few days? Here I was with the love I had always wanted, but when I should have been stronger and happier than ever, I was totally losing it. I was determined to heal myself of this affliction. I was an embarrassment to myself.

A few days after he came home, I was once again filled with anxiety. This time, I approached him in tears, saying that I didn't know what was wrong with me because I was afraid all the time. When he sympathetically took my hand and told me not to cry, I got angry.

"Time out," I said. "How can you tell a therapist not to cry? We believe in tears. Tears are our stock-in-trade—tears are cathartic, cleansing."

Then *he* got angry and retorted, "Well, what *should* I say?"

Good question. I didn't know, either. I thought for a minute, and what came out was "Just hold me. And if you say anything, just say, 'There, there. Everything's going to be okay.'"

He said, "I can do that," and he did.

For several months after that, he held me silently or assured me that everything was going to be okay whenever I came to him with anxious feelings. I breathed into that sense of safety and let my trust in his love fill my heart.

I became aware that it was no wonder I suddenly felt this terror. This was the first time in my life that I felt safe enough to feel fear. When I was a child I had developed a bravado, a facade of imperturbability growing up in a tough neighborhood in Brooklyn with no one at home I could go to for comfort.

I was ashamed to show fear. I didn't face my fears, I barreled through them. Being held and comforted by my sweetheart finally gave me an inner felt-sense of safety that I had never felt before. I've now come to recognize this as an inner state of primal security. An individual has that sense of self-possession when he or she has been cherished as a child.

My husband was cherished when he was a child, and he has that sense. It's a body-based primal sense of love and safety. Just by holding me and loving me through my fear, he was able to pass that sense of love and safety on to me. In effect, he reset my nervous system.

Love Can Rewire Your Body's Default Settings

We know that a warm, empathic, nurturing parent balances a child's nervous system. The parent's ability to calm the child's stress and also to play and have fun with him or her sets the child up to become an adult who operates with efficiency energetically. The nervous system becomes wired that way. Essentially, less emotional energy is wasted on psychic "gas guzzlers" like worry, shame, and old unresolved resentments.

Through self-regulation, mutual regulation, and interactive repair, partners can do that for each other. Empathic touch is a critical part of the process.

Ilana Rubenfeld, the developer of a highly regarded system of touch therapy, has pointed out that touch is a nonverbal communication that has the power to heal. Some people touch with a great deal of intention that imposes on the other person. Rubenfeld proposes a way of touching with a "listening hand" that picks up on the messages sent through the muscles and the skin about where energy flows or is blocked. The listening hand listens, then speaks back through touch, communicating presence and caring.

We've already seen how empathic touch stimulates health and immunity. Other studies have shown that just *remembering* how it feels to touch or be touched by a loved one can boost anti-bodies in the immune system for more than an hour.

Loving touch is healing. Touch that senses the other is a silent way of speaking and listening to each other.

Practicing Empathic Touch: Holding and Breathing

As I became aware of the attachment research and the critical inter-action between the mother and the infant in her arms, it reminded me of an exercise I learned many years ago when I was studying Tantra, a spiritual approach to connecting with sexual energy.

Tantric yoga began in India thousands of years ago and has been developed today into a series of meditative practices for lov-ers. I adapted an exercise I learned as "breathing the one breath" or "matching breaths" to replicate what a warm, intuitive, attuned mother practices when she follows, rather than leads, the internal rhythms of her infant.

Whenever I see stressed-out partners who are out of phase with each other, one of the first homework exercises I suggest is holding and breathing together. It's my not-so-secret formula for success with couples.

I give some instruction in my office that starts with breath-ing and taking an emotional inventory. Then I ask one person to be the holder and the other to be held. The one being held is to lie comfortably, relax, and breathe. The one doing the holding is asked to match his or her breaths to the other. I tell them that it's not that easy to breathe the same way your partner does, but it's good to know how it feels to follow your partner's breathing rhythms. Then they switch, and the holder becomes the one held. Finally, I ask them to lie together and hold each other any way they like and for them to silently slow down their breathing, inhaling and exhaling deeply and in sync.

Here's an example. I gave this assignment to Janie and Theo, the couple who had explosive fights over insignificant issues. It took them two weeks to finally get to it, but once they did, practicing matching breaths had an amazing effect on them.

In their next session together they talked about the experience. Janie said that when Theo held her, he really got into just holding and being with her. He seemed to be totally patient and loving with her. She could feel her heart relax, and she just sobbed. Theo said there was nowhere in the world he wanted to be. He could feel Janie's sadness in his own chest and in the lump in his throat, and that made him feel protective of her.

When Janie held Theo, he said he felt complete contentment, as though he didn't have to do anything but receive. Janie held him and enjoyed feeling both her strength and his softness and vulnerability. She rocked him and even sang a soft lullaby to him. Theo said he loved it. They both laughed at that.

I was delighted to see how friendly they were toward each other. Theo added that holding and breathing together was especially helpful because it gave them something positive to do when one of them began to freak out, something each did periodically.

This was an especially effective tool for this couple because neither one of them had gotten much parental love, comfort, or attention as a child. It was as though they were both suffering from a vitamin deficiency. Vitamin L, maybe? It's probably why each had had such a low resistance to emotional infection.

B. Eye Contact: Mutual Attunement

Eye contact is the first point of intimate communication, whether for sweethearts or for mother and infant. We can learn a great deal about this very basic intimacy from what takes place in the brain during the earliest phase of nonverbal communication.

In the brain imaging studies in which both mother and infant wore electrode caps to compare the parts of their brains being stimulated, the results showed that when warm looks passed between mother and infant, the exact same part of the brain in each of them was stimulated at exactly the same time: the limbic area of the right brain.

The right hemisphere's limbic area is one of the first brain systems to be shaped by the parent-child interaction. It consists of a set of brain structures—the hypothalamus, the hippocampus, and the amygdala—associated with emotions and bonding, regulation of the autonomic nervous system, memory, motivation, sexuality, play, and pleasure. The limbic system also holds the ability to adjust to the inner state of another.

UCSF medical researcher Thomas Lewis and his associates, Fari Amini and Richard Lannon, used the term *limbic resonance* to describe how two individuals can become attuned to each other's inner states. One of the most powerful ways, which replicates the earliest intimacy of infancy, is simply by silently looking into each other's eyes.

Earlier we saw how empathy is directly associated with an inborn propensity to mimic the facial micro-expressions, vocalizations, postures, and movements of people in close physical proximity. Eye contact takes empathy even deeper.

Entrainment

The research consistently shows that eye gazing makes people feel more in touch with one another because they are actually becoming more physiologically entrained. They can read one another because their nervous systems come into what's called *neural synchrony*.

According to the Institute of HeartMath, a center in Boulder Creek, California, recognized for its valuable contributions in stress management and heart-brain research, entrainment can occur within an individual or between two individuals.

Within an individual, entrainment consists of achieving an increased synchronization between the heart and the rhythmic activity of other physiological systems—especially the respiration, hormonal, and immune systems. As a result, self-regulation encourages the body to function with a great deal of efficiency and harmony. Inner entrainment can be achieved through deep breathing and consciously generating loving thoughts that release tension in the heart, a process that enhances PNS activity and autonomic balance; reduces anger, anxiety, and depression; promotes a positive state of mind; and enhances health and healing.

Between two individuals, entrainment enables them to regulate each other's physiology in the same way that mother and infant regulate each other. In essence, two loving people can silently transmit information back and forth through eye contact as well as through touch that will adjust each other's heart rate, hormone levels, disease-fighting blood cells, and more.

Interpersonal Neurobiology

UCLA medical researcher Dan Siegel calls this kind of connection "interpersonal neurobiology." He identifies the experience as one in which the nonverbal signals unconsciously sent between two responsive people promote a sharing of mind and emotion and a quality of intimacy he calls "feeling felt" by the other.

The data show that it's this sense of connectedness that enables two attuned individuals to amplify positive emotions and reduce negative emotions. According to Siegel, this shared state is the foundation for the feelings of love. Even more, he asserts, this sense of attunement with another has healing properties in that it puts attuned people in touch with their authentic selves, enabling them to know and express their emotional truths. How can simply looking in the eyes of a beloved possibly accomplish all this?

There are obvious evolutionary advantages to being born hardwired to look into the eyes of the other and to see love and delight mirrored back. It stimulates the pleasure centers of both intimates, secreting dopamine, the stimulant associated with reward, and oxytocin, the bonding hormone that plays such a crucial role in physical health, emotional attachment, sexual desire, and orgasm. At best, when we look into the eyes of a beloved and see love reflected back, we feel lovable and worthy.

Limbic Rewiring

Unlike people who had a loving childhood and learned that love was protective and respectful, those with a difficult childhood may have learned that love is painful, suffocating, or unreliable. Lewis and his associates have suggested that when someone who suffers from a pattern of unfulfilling relationships comes for therapy, the therapist's task actually involves restructuring the client's limbic system through the therapist's ability to resonate warmth and understanding.

Loving partners who are willing to regulate each other with emotional warmth can also revise their individual brains' neural networks. These researchers consider loving intimate relatedness as a form of "simultaneous mutual regulation" that achieves a deeply gratifying physiological state.

When lovers tune in to each other's emotional states and calm each other's breath and heart rhythms, they are influencing each other's neural physiology, emotional stability, hormones, and immunity. Partners who can generate this state of limbic regulation together feel centered and energized and are more resilient to stress, particularly in their relationship.

Gut Feelings: We Know More Than We Think

I mentioned earlier that couples can get into the habit of not looking each other in the eyes when they talk. In fact, our right brains are continually in conversation when we are in close physical proximity. Even without looking directly, the eyes still pick up and send information to the brain. The brain receives and responds to the totality of implicit messages that include the other's grimaces or gestures, tone of voice, and posture, and it sends a message of comfort and security or tension. A soft and loving direct gaze between intimates reinforces a true meeting of the minds and hearts of equal partners.

There's no doubt that eye contact also imparts an added level of transparency between intimates. Although it is possible for a practiced liar to look someone in the eyes and maintain a complete fabrication, it's not easy for principled people to do so, especially with someone who is loved and valued. When I was a child, I remember trying to lie to my father, whom I adored, but whenever I did, I always ended up giggling uncontrollably and completely giving myself away.

This is called a *tell*. It can be a seemingly casual sniff, a shoulder shrug, or a quick glance away. It's the microgesture that professional poker players look for to detect if someone is bluffing.

Scientists call it *emotional leakage*, and when emotions are aroused, it's impossible to prevent it. We may not be aware of where the information is coming from, but our right brains can still pick up on it and send a twinge to the gut in warning.

In general, we're more likely to get a visceral sense of trust with someone when we make good eye contact. It's not a big leap to see that the more two people look each other in the eyes and have genuine smiles for each other, the healthier and happier they'll be together. It can be as simple as talking eye to eye or grabbing a glance, a smile, and a lingering little good-bye kiss before rushing out the door in the morning.

Practicing Eye Contact

When I notice that partners have a tendency to look away from each other when they talk, I give them a little experiment to try. I ask them to silently face each other, look into each other's eyes, and relax their faces, for just one minute. I say that I'll tell them when the time is up.

With some couples, I can see the partners' faces soften and their bodies relax and become less defensive. At the end of the exercise they say that looking in their partners' eyes brought up tremendous feelings of love and gratitude.

Other couples have more difficulty. I've seen some people with their faces frozen in a smile or a smirk. One woman who felt tense holding the gaze for a minute said she felt awkward because she realized that with two young children, she and her husband hardly ever looked at each other, especially when the kids were around.

Janie and Theo, the couple who had a bad case of emotional contagion, noticed that they hardly ever looked into each other's eyes when they fought. When one yelled and was nasty, the other usually looked away. Then the second one yelled and the first looked away. What they yelled at each other were the typical blaming and cutting remarks that each had come to expect, the standard claptrap that two people fling at each other in a fight: you're letting me down, this is not what I signed up for, you're so selfish, it's all your fault, and if you were different we wouldn't be having this problem.

I had Janie and Theo do several exercises in my office sitting opposite each other in silence. In one exercise, I asked them to recall a particularly pleasant memory of a time they shared together and then to hold on to the feeling as they looked into each other's eyes. The more these two people were able to comfort rather than intimidate each other, the easier it became for them to look into each other's eyes.

They also took it upon themselves to notice when they were talking about feelings without making eye contact and to stop talking until they were both looking at each other. That way, they weren't just on automatic, flinging insults; they could see the impact of their words or actions on each other's face. Really looking at each other enhanced their ability to feel empathy for each other.

C. Intimate Kissing: The Biochemistry of Affection

Whenever I see people who are dissatisfied with the quality of their sexual connections with their partners, there is one question

I have learned to ask that is the most informative of all: "Do you kiss?" It no longer surprises me when the answer is no. In fact, it's pretty standard.

One man, Chet, complained to me that he wasn't getting the strong erections he used to have before he and his wife were married just a year ago. When I asked Chet what he thought was going on, he said that his wife had a very specific way she liked to make love, and although he would prefer to be more spontaneous, he also wanted to please her.

Then I asked the magic question. "Do you kiss?"

He shook his head sadly. "Annie doesn't like to kiss. Or she doesn't like the way I kiss. I'm not sure which. But she usually just wants to get it on."

It's a commonly held belief that foreplay is what men do to accommodate women to get them in the mood. But I'm finding that it's increasingly the woman who is in a rush to get it on and get it off.

Recently, I heard a similar complaint from another young man. Brian had a problem of staying turned on with his live-in boyfriend, Ray. Ray was also impatient to get it on and didn't like to kiss. Yet like holding and breathing together or making eye contact, kissing is one of the essentials of primal intimacy that is at the foundation of emotionally gratifying sexual intimacy.

Primal Kissing

We're born with the primitive urge to suckle at the breast. There is no doubt that kissing is a more complex behavior that is built on early infant sucking and evolves from that basic reflex. Sigmund Freud wrote that the child sucking at the breast is the prototype of later love relations. Renowned psychologist Erik Erikson noted that it is during the oral stage, through sucking and stimulation of the mouth, that the individual first begins to build his or her basic sense of trust.

Child psychologists distinguish between the sucking behavior associated with food intake and nonnutritive sucking, which

reduces agitation and calms the baby. Whether it's through sucking a finger, a dry breast, or a pacifier, nonnutritive sucking triggers
the PNS and increases autonomic balance.

Anthropologist Helen Fisher pointed out that cross-cultural
studies have found that more than 90 percent of the world's population engage in kissing, and most involve the use of the tongue.
Even in the few societies where kissing was unknown prior to
contact with the West, lovers still licked, sucked, or nibbled at
each other's face.

Many animals kiss, such as "man's best friend," the dog.
Bonobos, the famously sexy chimps that have sexual contacts frequently throughout the day, also take obvious pleasure in kissing
and are the only other species besides humans who enjoy face-
to-face sex.

There are many kinds of kisses. There are social kisses, in
which the lips kiss the air or a cheek, and family kisses, which are
on the cheek and always with closed lips even if the lips briefly
touch.

Here we will focus primarily on the intimate kiss: lips, mouth,
and tongue to lips, mouth, and tongue. I call it the "wet kiss."

The Wet Kiss

This intimate lover's kiss starts with a drawing together of two
faces as their lips pucker and touch. Abundant nerve endings in
the lips, the mouth, and the tongue send signals to the brain that
cause an increase of blood flow to the lips, making them redder
and stimulating the secretion of saliva.

The mouth and the tongue are mucus membranes, like the
genitals—sensitive tissue that secretes moisture. The nose, another
mucus membrane, draws in pheromones and other chemical messages in the close encounter and adds to the internal sense of
arousal.

As two people share a wet kiss, hormones and neurotransmitters are exchanged in the saliva that arouse the body and
activate brain mechanisms associated with safety and security,

romantic love, and sexual desire. Adrenaline stimulates the heart. Endorphins and serotonin bring a sense of well-being. Dopamine stimulates feelings of reward. Oxytocin, the bonding hormone that plays such a key role in sexual arousal and orgasm, is also found in the saliva exchanged between lovers. Perhaps most important for lovers, kissing has the added value of causing a surge in the flow of testosterone, the hormone of desire, in both partners.

Laboratory studies also show that kissing can reduce cortisol, thereby lowering stress. At the same time, heart rate increases, blood vessels dilate, and respiration rate goes up—all signs of greater autonomic activation. Kissing has the effect of generating the most delightful and efficient internal event: being simultaneously energized yet relaxed.

I suspect that the unwillingness to kiss a partner is a control issue. That was certainly the case for Annie and Chet, I learned as I got to know them. Annie put up a good front, but she had a lot of fear and kept it under control with strong opinions about how things were supposed to be done. Chet was willing to go along with whatever made Annie happy, but it wasn't working for him. Nor, it turned out, was it really working for Annie, either.

Brian's boyfriend, Ray, wasn't willing to join him in couples therapy, and Brian was well aware that Ray was a control freak. With the encouragement he got from his therapy sessions, Brian was able to assert himself with Ray and to ask for the kind of physical intimacy that was most rewarding to him. For Brian, that included kissing.

One of the homework assignments I gave to Annie and Chet and to Brian to do with Ray was for each partner to give the other kissing lessons. I suggested they set aside ten minutes to kiss slowly and explore a variety of different ways of staying lip to lip and mouth to mouth and communicating with their tongues. It sometimes works best if at first one person leads and the other follows and then they switch. I suggested that they indicate nicely what they liked or didn't like, preferably without words, through gestures or facial expression. Ultimately they saw that they could arrive at a way of kissing that made each of them feel loved and cared for.

Body Attunement

To be in embodied attunement in all of these ways with another human being is a great gift. The ability to reduce each other's stress, resonate in harmony together, and share their biochemistry reaches deeply into both individuals. It's a present-centered, mutually shared, moment-by-moment interaction.

During intimate times with your partner, your hearts are entrained and actually begin to beat in rhythm. Your right brains are engaged in a wordless conversation of affection. Your nervous systems are in sync. At the level of your biorhythms, you are truly making beautiful music together.

A Poetic Take on Building Intimacy

One of my favorite books is Antoine de Saint Exupéry's *The Little Prince*. Published in 1943, it was written as a children's book, but it is recognized all over the world as an allegory for the deeper meanings of life and love.

The little prince lived above Earth on an asteroid that was no bigger than a single house, but he became unhappy and decided to leave home. He traveled to other little planets and learned many truths about life, but it was the encounter on Earth between the little prince and the fox that I have always cherished most.

The little prince was lying on the grass crying when a fox presented itself. The little prince told the fox that he was unhappy, and he invited the fox to play with him. The fox said, "I cannot play with you. I am not tamed." When the little prince asked what *tame* means, the fox replied, "It means to establish ties." The fox explained that at this point they were just a little boy and a fox, like any others. But if the boy tamed him, they would become unique to each other in all the world. The fox lamented that his life was boring and monotonous but explained that if the boy tamed him, "it will be as if the sun came to shine on my life."

The fox's instruction on taming was simple: "You must be very patient. First you will sit down at a little distance from me—like that—in the grass. I shall look at you out of the corner of my eye, and you will say nothing. Words are the source of misunderstandings. But you will sit a little closer to me every day." In this way the little prince tamed the fox, and they became friends.

Primal intimacy is like a mutual taming. When we start out together as strangers, we keep our distance and look at each other out of the corners of our eyes. As we come closer, we become more and more attuned to each other's rhythms. We can look each other in the eyes and feel safe. We build trust because we can actually feel each other inside ourselves. We touch and communicate affection through our eyes and smiles, through our hands and fingertips, and by pressing against each other's body.

Step five in the program offers several body-based exercises, games, and experiments holding and breathing together, looking into each other's eyes, and kissing.

Step Five: The ABCs of Primal Intimacy

Objective: To practice an empathic, personal, body-to-body, inner felt-sense of loving attunement

These explorations are for you to do with your intimate partner. If he or she is not available, you may try them in fantasy, imagining you and your partner doing them together. Breathe and focus on the images that come up in your mind's eye and on your feelings and see what you can learn on your own.

It's not through words that we allay each other's fears and calm and reassure each other. Rather, it's in the tone of the voice, the sensitivity of the touch, the softness of the eyes, and the steadiness of the gaze, and in how we hold each other and breathe together.

Nothing brings two people together into the present moment better than a lingering kiss. As your soft lips touch, you are breathing each other's air and commingling a bodily fluid that contains sex hormones, antibacterial agents, enzymes that heal wounds, and opiorphin, a painkilling opioid stronger than morphine. (It really does help to lick our wounds.)

The object of these exercises is to regulate each other's stress, come into mutual attunement, and bring your hearts and nervous systems into entrainment.

Holding and Breathing

Invite your partner to do this with you. Lie down together on a couch or a bed, and have some extra pillows nearby.

1. Lie on your back or on your side propped up by pillows. Have your partner lie facing you with his or her head on your chest and just under your shoulder. You're now the "holder," and your head remains higher than the other, who is the "held." The holder cradles the arms, back, and shoulders of the held as you might hold a baby. The held takes some deep sighs. The holder listens to the partner breathing and feels his or her breath expanding and relaxing the muscles of the torso with each inhalation and exhalation.

2. As the held continues to breathe deeply, the holder attempts to match his or her breaths to the held. It's not always easy to do, but see if you can speed up or slow down to inhale when your partner inhales and to exhale when he or she exhales.

3. Switch. The held now becomes the holder. As the holder, you get to listen to your partner's breath and feel the underlying muscles expand with each inhalation and relax with each exhalation. Then match your inhalations and exhalations to his or her rhythms.

4. Lie together comfortably in each other's arms and match your breath to each other. No one is leading; you're both following, attending to each other's breathing rhythm, matching breaths, and bringing your inhalations and exhalations into synchrony. See if whoever is breathing faster can slow the breath down to more closely correspond to the slower breathing partner.

5. When you feel ready to speak, share with each other what you most loved and appreciated about the experience.

Empathic Touch

With many partners I find that one is more likely to give massages and not as likely to receive any. The object of this exercise is to reciprocate massages. When it's your turn to give, see if you can "listen," with your hands, where and how your partner wants to be touched. If you're usually the one who would rather give than receive, this is an opportunity for you to give up control and relax.

1. *Hand massage.* Start by trading five- to ten-minute hand rubs. Decide who's going to be the "giver" and give the first massage. Sit opposite each other. The giver takes one hand of the "receiver" in both hands. Both of you close your eyes and take a few deep breaths.

2. *Giver.* With your eyes closed, hold your partner's hand, breathe, and relax. Notice what that hand feels like: big, little, soft, hard, warm, cold, or anything else you sense. Focus all your attention on this hand and how your partner is responding. Begin to massage and listen to how your partner is breathing. Feel how the hand responds. When your partner's breaths are full and relaxed, it's a good sign that you've hit a particularly enjoyable spot. After five to ten minutes, switch, and the receiver becomes the giver.

3. *Spot massage.* You can also gently knead each other's face and scalp, neck and shoulders, breast and chest, back, or butt.

4. *Sharing.* When you feel ready to speak, share with each other what you most loved and appreciated about the experience.

Eye Contact

This game requires consent from your partner to set aside some time to play. Sit comfortably facing each other with your knees touching. Set a timer for five minutes.

1. Close your eyes and silently take a few moments to yourself to breathe and relax and take a felt-sense inventory. When you're ready, open your eyes. When your partner's eyes open, hold the gaze. Keep breathing and relaxing as you look into each other's eyes. Keep your faces relaxed, without any fixed smiles or expressions. When you want to look away, look away for a few moments. Then come back to your partner's eyes. When five minutes are up, give each other a little kiss.

2. Both of you decide on a very pleasant memory: a place
   you visited together, a special event, or any other beautiful
   experience you shared. Sitting opposite each other with your
   knees touching, set a timer for five minutes and take a few
   deep breaths. Keep your eyes open and alternate between
   picturing the experience and watching the other's face. You
   alternate because while you are picturing something in your
   mind, you can't really see the other person.

3. When you feel like speaking, share with each other what you
   most loved and appreciated about the experience.

Kissing

Sometimes a couple doesn't kiss much because one partner doesn't
like the way the other kisses. Here's a good exercise to help your
partner kiss you the way you like. Since you want to maximize the
pleasantness of the experience, the two of you may want to brush
and floss your teeth before you embark on any kissing adventures.

This exercise can take from twenty minutes to longer, depending on how many of these kisses you try at one sitting. When you
finish, you may want to share with each other any interesting
observations or discoveries.

The object of this game is to expand your kissing repertoire by
practicing a variety of kisses. Take turns being the initiator and the
recipient. In each exercise, one person actively initiates the kiss and
the other meets the kiss and is responsive, both allowing and recip-
rocating. Then the recipient becomes the initiator. That means each
kiss in this list is done twice. No words, please, but soft sounds—
hums or moans of approval—are allowed.

1. *The little wet kiss.* Press your slightly parted and slightly
   puckered lips to your partner's lips and gently lick the space
   between your partner's lips with just the tip of your tongue.
   Pull away slowly, look your lover in the eyes, and smile.
   Switch; the recipient becomes the initiator.

2. *The around-the-world face kiss.* Press your slightly parted
   and slightly puckered lips to the center of your partner's
   forehead. Then kiss above each eyebrow and the right and
   left temples. Kiss the tip of the nose, the space between
   the nose and the upper lip, the right and left cheeks, along

the jawline and chin, and the space between the lower lip
and the chin. Finish with a little wet kiss on the lips and
switch.

3. *The ear kiss.* This kiss has to be very gentle, because there's
   nothing more annoying than a loud smacking kiss in the ear.
   Start by slowly kissing the outer rim of the ear from the top
   all the way around to the bottom and the soft fleshy earlobe.
   Your partner is also likely to enjoy your running the tip
   of your tongue in the creases of the ear and sucking gently
   on the earlobe. It never hurts to whisper something sweet
   and loving into his or her ear. Finish with a little wet kiss on
   the lips and switch.

4. *The neck kiss.* Starting just under the earlobe, and using just
   the tip of your tongue, softly kiss and lick your partner's neck
   and throat. Your partner may also enjoy a little sucking and
   nibbling on the neck—but don't get vampirish. Finish with a
   little wet kiss on the lips and switch.

5. *The around-the-world body kiss.* Every part of the body can
   be kissed with great enjoyment. Too often, people reserve
   their kisses just for the mouth and maybe the genitals and
   leave out everything in between, as an erotic wasteland.
   That's a great loss. Some of the less obvious places to plant
   loving kisses include the shoulders, the hands, along the arms
   (especially the crook of the arm), the chest and nipples, the
   belly, the legs and ankles, the back of the neck, the back, and
   the butt. Take some time to softly kiss your partner's body.
   Pick some places to kiss on your partner that you haven't
   kissed lately. Finish with a few little wet kisses on the lips and
   switch.

6. *The extended wet kiss.* Here you are both initiators and
   recipients. This starts out as a little wet kiss and grows. Once
   your lover has received your kiss and has reciprocated, and
   the two of you have given soft hums and moans of approval,
   your kisses may inspire more passionate kisses. Now you
   can introduce more tongue into your lover's mouth. If your
   lover welcomes your tongue and sucks on it, your desire for
   more is likely to grow. Typically, once you've accepted your
   partner's tongue inside your mouth, your partner is likely to

enjoy receiving your tongue inside his or her mouth. Finish with a few little wet kisses.

Be Silent Together

This experiment works best if you both firmly adhere to whatever time period you have agreed to remain silent. If one of you forgets and speaks, the other can offer a gentle reminder by touching your lips with an index finger. A smile always helps.

1. Set aside some time to be together in shared silence. It may be an opportunity to take a walk together somewhere pretty, listen to music together in candlelight, sit in a garden, dance at home, or visit a museum and walk together. What's important is that you enjoy each other's company without having to talk.

2. Communicate with your eyes and your smile, through touch and in gestures. Start by experimenting with being silent together for just fifteen minutes. (Another time you might experiment with half an hour or more.) Finish with a hug and a kiss.

3. When you feel like speaking, share what you most enjoyed about the experience.

PART II

Sexual Pleasure

6

Sexual Health
and the Body

I know some people question it, but there really was a worldwide youth-driven, birth control pill–fueled, liberation-minded, sexual revolution in the 1960s and 1970s. People everywhere sought to reclaim sexual exploration and playfulness, a phase of development that many believed they had missed.

That was the tenor of the time when I met the man who directly led to my becoming a sex therapist—a title I fought for years. He was the most exciting man I had ever been with. He was handsome and daring, a poet of sorts, a revolutionary, brilliant, and lots of fun. Unfortunately, the sex was terrible. We talked about it, but it just wasn't happening. I had heard about a new program on human sexuality being offered by UCSF at Langley Porter, where I had interned. Since this man and I were starting to work together, we signed ourselves up.

It was truly a startling experience while also very humbling. I had thought of myself as belonging to a special class of people who were hip and highly knowledgeable about sex. I was shocked to see the auditorium filled with all sorts of very unhip-looking people—doctors, nurses, social workers, teachers, priests, and nuns—and everyone was having a great time learning about sex.

With every topic we studied, from sexual development to masturbation to anatomy, my classmates surprised me with their candor and curiosity. Some shared poignant stories of repression in childhood; a few talked of abuse. Two very ordinary people— a man and a woman—actually volunteered to be models for sexological exams. Each was draped in a medical robe and lay on an examination table on the stage of the auditorium, genitals exposed, as the entire class filed by, one by one. I myself would never have done it.

My mate and I learned a great deal about sex, and our relationship lasted another couple of years. In the end, it wasn't the sex that drove us apart. We just fought too much. But the course we took in sex changed the direction of my work and shaped my life.

I was already an embodied Gestalt therapist, practicing a method of psychotherapy that emphasized awareness of moment-by-moment experience. I had also studied and worked with a range of body-oriented therapies, including Reichian, bioenergetics, sensory awareness, breath work, dance workshops, Feldenkrais, Rolfing, yoga, and Vipassana meditation. All of these methods reinforced in me the value of tuning in to the body. I liked Fritz Perls's admonition to "lose your mind and come to your senses."

At the same time, a powerful trend in personal development known as the Human Potential Movement had gained momentum. Growing out of Abraham Maslow's humanistic psychology, Carl Rogers's client-centered therapy, and embodied Gestalt, it was fed by the rising popularity of Zen Buddhism and other Eastern philosophies. The movement spread the philosophy that human beings are innately good and that with greater self-awareness we can heal ourselves and access our full potential for health, happiness, creativity, longevity, and spirituality. We were giddy with the possibilities.

Growth centers sprang up everywhere, offering weekend seminars modeled on those developed at the Esalen Institute in Big Sur, California. For me, Esalen became a horn of plenty: a place of personal healing, an unparalleled training center, and an opportunity to develop my work.

By most accounts, the emphasis on human potential has now become mainstream and integrated in today's society. Self-help books, motivational and management training seminars, holistic medicine, and the trend in research psychology to study happiness and well-being have all become widely accepted. Yet when I was involved in those early days, they were all novel and exciting ideas.

I was very interested in sex because I saw it as the core of life, the juncture that connected everything, especially if one ever hoped to have a lasting love relationship, which I very much did. I completely resonated with the Reichian view that the ability to allow pleasure is intimately connected to emotional well-being and physical health.

My interest in human potential naturally led me to wonder about sexual potential. How good can sex be, especially if you choose to partner with someone for life primarily on the basis of the love you share and not on how great the sex is?

Sexual Science after 1980

When I started attending sexology seminars and sex therapy conferences in the early 1980s, I was disappointed to discover how much these psychologists, biologists, professors, therapists, and educators were focused on dysfunction and all of the problems associated with sex. The sexual freedoms and excesses of the 1960s and 1970s, along with the newly emerging horrors of AIDS and HIV and a whole crop of other sexually transmitted diseases, had clearly created an antisex backlash.

Much of what was being discussed among these professionals and researchers was about the dangers of sex: abuse, pedophilia, addiction, teenage pregnancy, and infections with dire consequences. It was not the time to say anything good about sex.

The times have changed. A major inspiration came from President Bill Clinton's surgeon general, Dr. David Satcher, in reaction to what he observed as a significant public health challenges regarding sexuality.

Sexual Health

Dr. Satcher was responding to the high incidence of sexually transmitted diseases as well as other concerns about sex in the United States: that nearly half of all pregnancies were unintended, the highest rate among the developed countries; that almost one in four women and one in five men have been victims of forced sex; and that more than a hundred thousand children a year are victims of sexual abuse.

Noting that each of these problems has lifelong consequences not just for the individuals but also for their families, their communities, and the entire nation, Satcher was prompted to seek out scientific research and to explore public health strategies to address these issues. The result was a thin booklet, published in 2001 as *The Surgeon General's Call to Action to Promote Sexual Health and Responsible Sexual Behavior.* In it he wrote,

> Sexual health is inextricably bound to both physical and mental health. . . . Sexual health is not limited to the absence of disease or dysfunction, nor is its importance confined to just the reproductive years. . . . It includes freedom from sexual abuse and discrimination and the ability of individuals to integrate their sexuality into their lives, derive pleasure from it, and to reproduce if they so choose.

This call to action was one of several reports Satcher wrote during his tenure in office; the others included a study of the health risks of long-term tobacco use and a study of suicide. Like these other reports, the one on sexuality did not make much of a splash in the general population. Yet it produced a tsunami in the inter-disciplinary fields of sexual science, sex therapy, and sex education because of its emphasis on sexual health rather than disturbance.

Satcher created a new, more positive focus on sex by high-lighting the interconnectedness of sexual health, physical health, and emotional well-being. He recognized sexuality as spanning the lifetime from childhood to old age. His recommendations encouraged more public dialogue about sex that was honest and mature, respectful of diversity, and seeking common ground.

In effect, the good doctor wrote a prescription: "Talk about sex." Talk about sex in the privacy of your home with your children and your spouse. Talk about sex in community-based programs, schools, and clinics. He asked that physicians, teachers, health-care workers, and others who work with the public become more informed about sex and more comfortable discussing sexuality.

Talking honestly about sex, however, is not always so easy to do. We don't even have a good vocabulary for sex. Polite lan-guage can feel stuffy and clinical, whereas slang sometimes sounds juvenile, silly, or offensive. When feelings are involved, it can be difficult to put those feelings into words, and people don't always know how they really feel.

Talking about sex with your partner or with friends can help, but many people are in fact misinformed about what is normal and natural. Even just a few sessions with a licensed and certified sex therapist, someone who is knowledgeable and comfortable dealing with sexual issues, can be highly informative.

When you finish this book, you will surely be well informed about sex and, should you choose to talk about it, highly conver-sant on the topic.

Sex and Overall Health

There is an overwhelming abundance of data that show that com-fort and satisfaction with one's sexuality have myriad blessings.

The benefits of sexual activity begin with solitary sex. In 2002, Planned Parenthood published a report on masturbation. It compiled a detailed history of how the practice went from acceptance in ancient times to condemnation by the church and general stigma. It included a diverse collection of studies that made a good case for the value of masturbation in sexual health.

The research showed that healthy infants naturally engage in genital play by the third to fourth month of life and that the way parents respond to their children's masturbation often affects how the children feel about themselves. Studies even showed a strong link for individuals between a lack of sexual satisfaction as adults and the experience of parental disdain upon having been discovered masturbating when they were children.

Arousal and orgasm from solitary sex is shown to be effective at reducing stress, alleviating physical and sexual tension, and providing a soothing outlet for people without partners—especially the elderly. Masturbation can induce sleep on a restless night. Self-stimulation and pleasure can strengthen muscle tone in the pelvic and anal areas, particularly when those muscles have been compromised through childbirth, illness, or surgery.

Developing skill in masturbation has consistently been an effective way for women to overcome an inability to achieve orgasm. Masturbation skill can also help men to learn effective methods for maintaining erection and ejaculatory control.

A second Planned Parenthood report, issued in cooperation with the Society for the Scientific Study of Sexuality, looked at the research on the physical, emotional, and spiritual health benefits of sexual satisfaction. Findings from multiple peer-reviewed studies showed that an increased incidence of sexual expression was correlated with a boost in the immune system, a reduced risk of breast cancer, relief from migraines, and management of chronic pain. The mental health benefits of satisfying sex included a lower likelihood of depression and suicide and an increase in self-esteem. Sexual satisfaction was also shown to correlate highly with stability and satisfaction in long-term relationships.

In one study, data collected from more than thirty-five hundred American and European women for ten years showed a correlation between having an active sex life and a youthful appearance. A panel of judges looked at each subject through a one-way mirror and guessed her age. The data indicated that the sexually active women were consistently underestimated by as much as seven to twelve years.

Men benefit greatly from an active sex life. A ten-year study of men found that the incidence of death during this time was 50 percent lower among men who had at least two orgasms a week compared to men of the same age, health, and lifestyle who had orgasms less than once a month. The more orgasms, the lower the incidence of death. Frequency of male ejaculation also correlated with a significantly lower risk of developing prostate cancer.

In both men and women, frequency of orgasm was associated with a less frequent occurrence of heart disease.

Sexual Satisfaction and Subjective Well-Being

Studies consistently show that sexual satisfaction is strongly predictive of relationship satisfaction. Recent studies, however, clearly demonstrate that the inner felt-sense of satisfaction extends well beyond the relationship.

Canadian psychologist Diane Holmberg and her colleagues were interested in studying whether sexual satisfaction positively correlated with satisfaction in other areas of a woman's life, particularly with physical health and mental well-being. The researchers used several scales to assess the level of sexual satisfaction, including types of activities for women in same-sex and opposite-sex relationships. Relationship satisfaction was tested through indicators for love and trust; mental well-being was assessed through indicators for the presence of depression, anxiety, and stress; and physical health was assessed through indications of being bothered or distressed by minor symptoms like a stuffy nose, headaches, or stomach pain.

The study showed a high degree of correlation between a woman's sexual satisfaction and emotional, physical, and relationship well-being regardless of her sexual orientation. Of course, this doesn't necessarily mean that sexual satisfaction makes people healthier. The researchers acknowledged that it works the other way, too. Having a good relationship and being emotionally content and physically fit also makes people more interested in sex and more invested in their physicality. The researchers concluded that it is most likely that all aspects of well-being feed into one another and create a reciprocally reinforcing, self-sustaining loop.

What Makes Good Sex So Good for Us

Good sex is playful and lightens the spirit. The senses become activated and engaged. Aerobic spouts of activity induce deep panting, work the chest and lungs, and get the heart pumping. Sexual activity can also take on a slow and easy rhythm, bringing every organ of the body into entrainment—an equilibrium that imparts a visceral sense of inner harmony.

Fulfilling sexual experience floods the bloodstream with a host of biochemicals that have been shown to boost the immune system. Dopamine and norepinephrine activate the reward and pleasure centers in the brain and stimulate the nervous system. Endorphins, the body's own opiates, reduce pain and stimulate exuberance. Oxytocin, the bonding hormone, bestows a calm sense of deep satisfaction. The latter two are released at orgasm, triggering the feelings associated with the afterglow.

The entire body is infused with streams of energy that make us feel happy, alive, and energetic while also peaceful, loved, and loving.

What Makes Stress So Bad for Sex

When a person feels insecure in a sexual situation, his or her stress level goes up. Feelings of anxiety, guilt, or shame may be triggered. Instead of deep breathing, the breath is held and the belly tightens. Under these circumstances, the blood flow is reduced, the pelvic tissue becomes anaesthetized, and maintaining arousal or achieving orgasm becomes physiologically impossible.

Bodily attunement with a loving partner can, with practice, replace these stress reactions with feelings of safety, love, and confidence in a loving sexual situation. The same embodied experiences that work for self-regulation and mutual regulation also enhance sexual experience: holding each other and breathing together, making eye contact, touching empathically, and kissing.

Sharing these primal intimacies can bring two bodies into greater inner resonance with each other. To take it to the next level of sexual resonance with a partner, however, it's important to learn more about your own and your partner's male or female body.

Male and Female Sexuality

I once heard someone suggest that maybe the difference between a man's orgasm and a woman's orgasm is like the difference between a sneeze and a yawn. Either way, an orgasm for all of us is like an underground earthquake of sweet pleasure with three epicenters—the genitals and pelvic floor, the spinal cord, and the brain—with ripples of seismic activity that spread throughout the body.

William Masters and Virginia Johnson, the first researchers to observe and record physiological measures of subjects having sex in a laboratory, found that both men and women go through the same four phases of sexual response. In the first two, the *excitement* and *plateau* phases, there's an increase of blood flow into the genitalia, resulting in erection and flattening of the testes in men and vaginal lubrication and swelling in women. *Orgasm* for both involves genital contractions at intervals of four-fifths of a second for several seconds while all of the muscles of the body contract and then relax. Finally, there's a *resolution* phase, in which the body returns to its resting state.

In a carefully controlled study, men and women were asked to write descriptions of the orgasm. The descriptions were edited to replace gender-specific terms with gender-neutral ones and then given to another group of people to judge whether the descriptions were written by women or by men. The results showed that even though all of the descriptions were vivid, the judges were unable to decipher whether men or women had written the descriptions.

This suggests that the psychological, emotional, and physiological microsecond-by-microsecond experiences and sensations of orgasm are very similar for both sexes. Yet what happens in the body, given our different anatomy, is somewhat different, and the comparison of sneezes versus yawns—albeit intensely pleasurable varieties of these—may in fact be a good one.

A Man's Body

As far as is known to date, male orgasm occurs when semen fills up in the ducts of the penis and is held in place by a system of sphincters, probably creating a kind of pressure chamber. As the pressure builds, at the point of orgasm, the sphincters suddenly release, shoot a spurt of semen, rapidly fill up again to shoot another spurt of semen, and so on, continuing several more times in rapid succession.

According to sex researchers Barry Komisaruk, Carlos Beyer-Flores, and Beverly Whipple, at least two separate sympathetic nerves, the pudendal and the hypogastric, which exit the spinal cord, are involved. They trigger involuntary contractions of the smooth muscles in the penis and the pelvic floor, including the perineal muscles and the anal sphincter.

Timing is supposedly everything, and that certainly is the case for two of men's biggest problems with orgasms: early (often called *premature*) ejaculation and delayed ejaculation.

Early Ejaculation: What's Too Soon?

When a man complains of ejaculating too quickly, the underlying goal is usually extending the sex play during penetration. Surveys have shown that men who feel in control of their ejaculation look forward to sex and feel capable of attending to activities in sex that can add to their own and their partners' pleasure. Men who expect to ejaculate before they wish to tend to focus on feelings associated with failure, like embarrassment and guilt, and as a result they are less able to attend to activities that bring greater pleasure.

Sex educator Paul Joannides, who has authored a definitive and, at almost a thousand pages, the largest guidebook to "getting it on," has provided a great deal of data to show that there are many possible reasons a man may ejaculate quickly. Some men have had this issue all of their lives; others acquire it as a result of a medical problem. It might be learned, or there could be a genetic propensity.

Joannides reported on neurological findings that there is one thing premature ejaculators have in common. When men who can control ejaculation get an erection, their heart rates speed up at first and then slow down. For men with difficulty controlling ejaculation, their heart rates speed up once they get an erection and *stay elevated*. This means that the nervous system of the man who is quick to ejaculate stays dominated by the sympathetic nervous system (SNS), the part of the nervous system that signals ejaculation. When men who control ejaculation get an erection, their heart rates slow down and their arousal becomes dominated by the parasympathetic nervous system (PNS), which means they relax. Only when they are ready to come do they start to rev up, and the SNS takes over. In other words, in order to stay up you have to calm down.

Delayed Ejaculation

At the other end of the spectrum is the man who can't seem to come no matter what he does. It becomes a problem when his flagging partner has been around the track three or four times and he's nowhere near the finish line. Under these circumstances, having an orgasm can feel like work. Joannides pointed out that the research shows that most men with this issue can bring themselves to orgasm easily through masturbation, and there's no reason to dismiss this as a suitable alternative. Although difficulty reaching orgasm may be a possible side effect of drugs like antidepressants, analgesics, or nicotine, there are also some emotional avenues for insight and release that are worth exploring.

In therapy, I have found that a number of men with this issue knew that they were holding themselves back in other ways from their partners. Many became aware that once they got hard, they could feel themselves emotionally restraining themselves, cutting off more vulnerable and tender feelings.

Some men also manage to separate themselves from any sensation in their penises and to stay focused on performance, not allowing themselves the pleasure of surrender. When they're ready to come, they remain goal-oriented and focused on performance, like a horse heading for the stable. Yet what's more likely to allow release is to give up the goal and get into the sensuality and emotional connection of the present moment.

The Erratic Erection

There's an old joke about a man having two heads, a big one and a little one. When he gets into trouble, it's usually because he's thinking with the smaller head, the one without a brain. It's usually the big head, however, that interferes with a man's ability to be on the same wavelength as his penis. Here's an example.

Chris was a twenty-six-year-old markedly handsome and fit young man who confessed sadly that he had a history of not being able to sustain an erection with a woman. He was just starting a relationship with Peggy, a young woman he really cared about, and his penis wasn't working at all. He said he got better erections when he was home alone and just thought about her than when he was with her at her place.

Peggy had begun to notice that Chris was restrained when they made out, and she took it personally. She told Chris that she thought he wasn't turned on to her and that he didn't like her body. He reassured her that it was because he cared about her that this happened, but he wasn't even sure that was true.

When Chris gave his family and sexual histories, it became apparent how Chris's erection difficulties had begun. He described his big family as very competitive. His two older brothers were natural athletes like his father, and a younger sister was bright and bookish and kept to herself. Chris's mother always felt overworked and hassled. She wasn't very affectionate, but he liked being with her. He helped her in the kitchen whenever he could, just to be close to her. His older brothers called him a mama's boy.

Chris's troubles began when he turned sixteen. His brothers decided he was ready to "lose his cherry" and surprised him with a trip to a prostitute in a downtown hotel room. They delivered him to the room and told him they would sit in the lobby and wait for him.

Chris was horrified. He wasn't attracted to the woman; she was much older than he was and wore too much makeup. He didn't like the smell in the room or the strange furniture, and he felt affronted by the liberties she took opening his pants and handling his penis. Chris never got erect with her, no matter what she did. When the woman walked him back to the lobby, she shrugged her shoulders and told the brothers that she had tried everything but nothing had happened. They paid the woman but complained to Chris that he had wasted their money. Chris felt humiliated by the entire experience, and it alienated him from his brothers even more.

This sounds like something that could have happened fifty years ago, but it happened in the United States in the 1990s. Surely this is a form of sexual abuse: coercing a young person into cold, impersonal sex as his first sexual experience. To Chris, it was a test of his masculinity, and he had flunked it.

Naturally, Chris felt inadequate and completely confused about himself as a man. Much of our work together focused on helping him to become more skilled at reading his body and processing the emotions that kept parts of his torso and pelvis tight and not breathing. When he breathed more fully and took a felt-sense inventory, he could feel his tension patterns, particularly in his chest, gut, genitals, and rectum.

We processed the images that spontaneously came to him from his childhood, such as feelings of abandonment by his mother and his sister and of not measuring up to the men in the family. We also worked on helping him to heal his own wounded relationship with his penis. He seemed to have a medicinal view of masturbation, and much of his masturbating was a quickie in the shower or in the bathroom to relieve his stress. Instead, I encouraged him to masturbate in a more relaxed way, lying down in a candlelit room, listening to music, and fantasizing about sexy scenarios.

We also talked about getting his mind off his penis and focusing on Peggy when he was with her. He was a bit obsessed with what was going on between his legs, and he needed to raise his consciousness. When he and Peggy were together, he practiced being present with her sensually by putting his full attention on how she looked, sounded, smelled, and tasted. He reminded himself to exhale and to take slow, relaxing inhalations.

One evening, Chris caught himself holding back from passionate kissing because he didn't want to disappoint Peggy when she wanted more. He decided instead to just let himself melt into Peggy's soft body. To his surprise, he had an immediate result: the strongest, "happiest" erection he had ever had. Peggy felt it, too. The evening resulted in their most satisfying lovemaking to date.

Chris talked about it with me several days later. He said he was going through a sexual awakening and getting a chance at a do-over. The notion of having sex for love and pleasure, and not as a test, was a major game changer.

The Wisdom of the Penis, a Delicate Organ

The old term for erection difficulties is *impotence*, which means weak and powerless. That's completely inaccurate, because nothing is more powerful than a penis that won't perform when it really doesn't want to. A penis has feelings, too.

Here are two examples of other men who conquered their difficulties by attending to the emotional needs—yes, *emotional* needs—of their penises.

Some men can do terrible violence with a hard penis, so divorced are they from the loving side of sex. Men who rape often can't get an erection without violence. But good, decent men are more sensitive.

Unfortunately, Stan was a little too good and too decent. He had trouble maintaining an erection with Karen, his wife of five years. He seemed hesitant to complain about her, but he did admit that he was bothered by her aggressiveness with him. He described instances that suggested that her style, when she wasn't getting what she wanted from him, was to berate and shame him.

Karen was going through a lot of job-related stress. Stan felt sorry for her in the same way he felt sorry for his mother's struggles. His father had left his mother when Stan was five, and she had raised him as a single parent by working at a department store. She would often come home cranky and feeling sorry for herself, and she continually complained and put him down. Stan just swallowed his anger when his mother was verbally abusive with him. Now as a man, he was still swallowing his anger. In his heart he was able to excuse Karen's bad behavior. His penis, however, was less forgiving.

When Stan recounted tales of the mean things Karen said to him, especially when they were unsuccessful at intercourse, I was amazed at her insensitivity. She told him that he wasn't a man and that she didn't find him as attractive as she once had. Stan wasn't helping by taking her abuse. I kept telling him that he wouldn't stand up *for* her until he stood up *to* her. That's exactly what happened.

As Stan breathed and accessed the feelings in his body, he was able to feel his anger toward Karen and also, through imagery, toward his mother. One evening, as Karen was giving him a particularly hard time at the dinner table, he felt his anger rise, and instead of pushing it down he jumped to his feet and yelled, "Stop!" That got the attention of them both.

Stan apologized for his outburst but told Karen he was tired of her coming home from work and taking her frustrations out on him. Karen was stunned; she got up, walked away, and refused to talk about it. That lasted about a day, but then things began to change. Stan let Karen know that she couldn't unload her office resentments on him, and he firmly disallowed her verbal abuse.

It also helped that Stan became better at hugging and comforting Karen when she was stressed out; this enabled both of them to regulate their stress. Stan recognized that his tendency to withdraw and hide might have contributed to Karen's misguided way of trying to get a reaction out of him. During our work together, as Stan became able to hold and comfort Karen and to speak openly to her, she stopped acting like his mother and became more like the woman he had fallen in love with. The whole shift in their relationship enabled both of them to feel safer and more aroused when they made love.

The Penis Reveals What the Heart Keeps Hidden

Here's an example of a man's erection difficulties that were motivated by an entirely different set of feelings and circumstances.

Max was a successful businessman who was referred to me by his physician. He told me he didn't need psychotherapy and was interested only in learning skills for getting his penis to perform better. Max's first wife had died of cancer about four years earlier, and he had just married Rita, a woman who was about ten years his junior. They had a great relationship except that once they were married, he began to lose his erection just as they were about to make love.

Max was very clear that he was not interested in breathing or getting in touch with feelings. He was fine; it was just his penis that wasn't working that well.

I told him that I could certainly suggest exercises for masturbating in a way that could help, but unless he was willing to do some breathing and to read his body to see what feelings *might* be blocking him, I didn't really think I could help him. Since his physician had recommended me so highly, he wasn't ready to give me up yet, so he reluctantly agreed to give my methods a chance.

When Max breathed, I could see that while his entire torso was tight, his rib cage and belly were particularly tense and unmoving. I asked him what he was feeling, and he said, "Nothing." I told him that tension in that area may signal feelings of guilt, responsibility, and obligation, and I asked if that's what he felt. Max shrugged it off, saying that as head of his company he had lots of responsibilities and obligations. Could be, I acknowledged. Then again, it could be something more.

In a subsequent session, when Max was halfheartedly willing to experiment, I suggested that he close his eyes, focus on breathing into and expanding his tight rib cage, and see if any images appeared before his mind's eye. To his utter amazement, he saw his first wife on her deathbed, and it brought tears to his eyes. Although Max may have been over the grief of his first wife's death, he revealed that he wasn't over the guilt he had felt from having cheated on a woman he regarded as a saint. He had described his mother in saintly terms as well.

As our work unfolded, what emerged was that after their early years together, Max hadn't been able to make love with his first wife, either. He had ongoing affairs throughout their long marriage, and even though she suspected as much, she had never confronted him on it. That's what made her a saint.

Max saw that he was about to canonize yet another woman, but this time he was determined not to let that happen. Through our work together, he was able to see how so much of his libido was tied up in conquest. Once he won a woman over, he lost interest in her sexually.

Max was now convinced of the value of conscious breathing and processing emotions through the body. He worked on his feelings of guilt and love for his first wife. He said that he was ashamed of himself, and he wept for how he had taken advantage of his first wife's steadfast loyalty and quiet anguish.

Eventually Max was ready to forgive himself, but he was clear that he never wanted to be ashamed of himself again. He knew he needed help in that department, so he invited Rita to join him in couples therapy. She gladly accepted, delighted that what had started out as sex therapy was uncovering a truer, more emotionally available Max.

Sexual Hydraulics

Why should withheld, unprocessed emotion have such a profound impact on a man's erection? To get a more intuitive sense of it, we need to look closer at what actually takes place in the body when a penis gets hard. Thanks to researchers like Komisaruk and his colleagues, we now know a lot more about the science of orgasm in both men and women.

As a man becomes sexually stimulated, hormones originating in the brain activate nerve fibers that run down the spinal cord. These in turn activate the PNS nerves that run from the pelvic area of the spinal cord to the spongy tissue in the penis. The PNS nerves release nitric oxide and other neurotransmitters that relax the smooth muscles and blood vessels in the penis. In essence, it is the relaxing of the muscles of the penis that allows the spongy tissue to be engorged with blood, expanding and becoming rigid. The resulting compression closes off the veins that drain the blood, trapping the blood in the penis.

When implicit memories and withheld feelings are aroused by subtle environmental or relational cues, even though they are not consciously perceived, the brain triggers the SNS and a reflexive holding of the breath and muscular tension. Without the PNS activation and relaxation, there can be no erection.

Men and women who have experienced sexual abuse or any emotional sexual injury often hold tension in the belly and in the pelvic muscles. But in a sense, most of us have been sexually mistreated. Because this society typically fails to acknowledge and guide children's healthy eroticism, shame and insecurity can become associated with sex. Sex-negative programming and a lack of accurate information about sex in childhood may also be considered forms of sexual injury.

A Woman's Body

During the Victorian era (the 1840s to the beginning of the twentieth century), it was believed that sexual desire in women was a sign of disease or immorality and that women—at least, the "respectable" ones—weren't capable of orgasm. In the 1960s, Masters and Johnson found not only that women are capable of orgasm but that some of their female subjects could have as many as fifty orgasms in an hour. The researchers had advertised for easily orgasmic subjects, and clearly they found a few.

No one really needs fifty orgasms an hour—and counting them could be very distracting—but there is now a wealth of data to show that many women do have multiple orgasms. That's one orgasm followed by another, followed by another, and so on— each with its own buildup and explosive release.

Besides that, research has determined that different parts of female anatomy can provide different kinds of orgasms, and each kind feels different. Since a woman's pleasure anatomy is complex, with many different parts, it pays to know where the opportunities are and what to zone in on.

The Intricate Female Anatomy

A woman's genitals consist of three areas: (1) the vulva includes all of the external female sex organ, the mons veneris—a pad of fatty tissue over the pubic bone, usually covered with hair—the outer and inner labia, and the hooded glans of the clitoris; (2) the vulva also includes the area known as the vestibule, which consists of the area inside the inner labia and around the introitus, or entrance to the vagina, and the opening to the urethra; and (3) the internal area, which includes the vagina—a flattened tube that ends at the cervix (the neck of the womb)—and the inner structures of the clitoris. Sensitive touching, squeezing, pressing down on, or stroking any of the three areas can be pleasurable.

The clitoris has the densest supply of nerves in the human body and is the only organ with no other function than to give pleasure. The clitoris is a much larger organ than most people suppose; it is often thought of as merely a little pea at the top of the vaginal opening.

In fact, the clitoris is like a small penis with a shaft and a head, called the glans, that sticks out from under the hood. The shaft of the clitoris runs under the pubic bone. Emanating from either side of the glans like a wishbone are the two legs of the clitoris, or *crura*. The entire clitoris, laid out end to end, could be seven to eight inches long.

As a woman becomes aroused, blood rushes into the pelvic area, swelling and lubricating the vagina and causing the clitoris to become erect. At least three different nerves stimulate orgasm in women: the *hypogastric* nerves convey sensory activity from the uterus and the cervix to the spinal cord; the *pelvic* nerves bring sensory activity from the cervix and the vagina; and the *pudendal* nerves convey stimulation from the clitoris.

There is some controversy about vaginal orgasms versus clitoral orgasms. Most women who have orgasms have clitoral orgasms, and Masters and Johnson believed that all female orgasms were clitoral, even when an orgasm is experienced as coming from the inside of the vagina during penetration.

Women who do have vaginal orgasms say, "No way!" Some of these women identify their vaginal orgasms as originating at the G spot, a sensitive area along the front wall of the vagina. Others say they feel it coming from the cervix or the back wall of the vagina. Wherever it's coming from, a vaginal orgasm feels very different from a clitoral one.

One big difference is that after a clitoral orgasm, there's often a refractory period, much like what a man has, during which time the clitoris can feel too sensitive to touch. Yet at that point the vagina can still feel primed for action.

With penetration (whether with a penis, a dildo, or a finger) and slow, deep pushing and grinding movements, some women may be able to have a series of orgasms. Deep thrusting also works for some women. As long as sensitive stimulation is maintained, she may continue to have waves of orgasms until she's exhausted—or her lover is.

Women who have vaginal orgasms may also find that they experience female ejaculation, a gush of fluid from the vagina that accompanies orgasmic contractions. Secreting copious amounts of fluid can be embarrassing for women if they think they've lost bladder control. But according to sex researchers Milan Zaviacic and Beverly Whipple, female ejaculate whose chemical composition has been tested in a laboratory has typically shown not urine but something more akin to the fluid found in the male prostate.

Women who gush are hot women. And that's nothing anyone has to apologize for—not in this millennium.

The Elusive Female Orgasm

By adulthood, most women have downloaded into their brains and nervous systems centuries of female sexual repression. It's a process that automatically bestows a patina of shame over their female anatomy and an array of misconceptions and anxieties about sex. Until very recently, women were led to believe that a man, through his wink-wink experience, knew more about her body than she did.

Lena is the woman who was contemplating having an affair with a coworker whom she had endowed with special powers to bring her to orgasm. She was appalled at the thought of having her first orgasm with her husband, Al.

Lena loved Al—he was a good provider and a good father to their two girls—but he wasn't sexy to her. At night when they went to bed, Al would sometimes roll toward her and start to caress her. Usually she'd give him a quick-and-final goodnight kiss and roll away. Sometimes, if he persisted and didn't try to kiss her, she would feel sorry for him and allow him to enter her vagina from behind and get himself off.

I told Lena that offering herself to be used as a vessel for Al was not doing her or Al any favors. I wondered how their sex life had come to this.

Lena's history shed some light on what was going on. Her parents divorced when she was twelve, and she lived with her mother and her sister, who was three years younger. She was very critical of her mother's dating other men soon after the divorce, and she was especially disgusted at her mother when her future stepfather began to sleep over and she could hear the two of them having sex.

Lena was particularly offended at how oblivious her mother was about her "noises." She seemed totally insensitive to the effect her moaning would have on Lena and her little sister and how disrespectful it was toward their father, who never got back on his feet after their divorce.

As Lena got into breathing into her belly and scanning her body on the inside, feeling for tension, she became aware of holding tension in her vagina. She traced this tension pattern back to when she would lie in bed at night hearing her mother make love and feeling disgusted with her. She went through a gamut of emotions in that bed: disgust, anger, pity for her father, and concern for her sister. I told her, hoping she wouldn't take offense, that sometimes hearing people make love can stimulate sexual feelings in a young girl. She said the thought nauseated her.

Lena bemoaned the fact that she could not bring herself to orgasm. All of her girlfriends were capable of masturbating to orgasm and bragged about having multiple orgasms with the men in their lives. Why couldn't she? When I asked her how she masturbated, she told me she used a vibrator, sometimes until she got numb. It felt good—at least, at first—but nothing major ever happened.

We did some process work on Lena's body-held feelings toward her mother and father and how that was connected to keeping her husband at a distance. In the meantime, I gave Lena two exercises for homework. The first was to put aside her vibrator for a while and to practice masturbating with her hands. I gave her some instruction on how to do that. The second was to exercise the genital muscle known as the pubococcygeus (PC) muscle by tensing and relaxing it a few times a day.

Lena practiced her exercises and masturbated for a week, still occasionally feeling almost there but never quite making it. In her next session, when I asked her what it felt like to almost be there, she said, "It feels like I have to pee."

"What do you do then?" I asked.

She said, "I get up and pee. By the time I get back, the feeling's gone."

Aha! I told Lena that it's not uncommon for a woman to confuse the sensation of orgasm with the need to urinate. I suggested for the next week that she pee before she masturbates, then put an absorbent towel under her bottom. When she gets the feeling of the need to pee, I told her, she should let herself pee.

"In bed?" she screamed, shocked but with a smile.

"Go ahead," I told her. "You're worth it."

Something in that thought struck her funny bone. Lena started to laugh so hard I thought she might pee on my couch.

A week later, there was success at last! Lena finally had her orgasm. How did she do it? She masturbated slowly and breathed. She consciously tensed and relaxed her vaginal muscles. When she came to the point at which she felt the need to urinate, she could feel her vaginal muscles start to close up. This time, however, she breathed into the feeling and had her first earth-rocking orgasm.

No question about it, it was the real thing. To Lena's surprise, she peed only a little. I told her that the next time she probably wouldn't pee at all—but so what if she did?

Between her success in having an orgasm and her recognition that she had transferred her pity for her father to her husband, Lena was able to consider being more available for sex with Al. To her surprise, only a few weeks after her first orgasm by herself, Lena had her first orgasm in face-to-face sex with her husband.

Kegel Exercises for Women and Men

The exercises I recommended to Lena for contracting and relaxing the PC muscle, and that I recommend to all the men and women who have difficulty with orgasm, are commonly known as the Kegels. Named for Dr. Arnold Kegel, a California gynecologist who developed them in the 1940s as a method for controlling incontinence in women after childbirth, they have been found to have a host of other benefits for both women and men.

The PC muscle, present in both sexes, is shaped like a hammock and stretches along the pelvic floor from the pubic bone to the tailbone, or coccyx. It controls the flow of urine and is activated during orgasmic contractions. One way to find your PC muscle is to stop the flow of urine while you are peeing.

For women, the Kegels are recommended for bladder control, as an aid to vaginal tone, and for achieving fuller and more consistent orgasms. For men, practicing the Kegels aids bladder control and also helps in achieving more consistent and stronger erections and control over early ejaculation. Strengthening the muscles of the pelvic floor can also help a man to learn to orgasm without ejaculation, potentially enabling him to achieve multiple orgasms during sexual activity.

To do the Kegels, inhale deeply, squeeze and hold your PC muscle, and count to three. Then let everything go: exhale as you release the squeezed muscles. Feel them opening; breathe and relax. Then do it again. You may be able to squeeze and hold up to a count of five or more.

Another helpful exercise is to simply pulse your genital muscles, tensing and relaxing quickly, to a count of ten. The nice thing about pulsing your PC muscle this way is that you can practice doing it anywhere, because no one knows you're exercising. You can do it while waiting in line at the supermarket or riding an elevator to the top floor.

Vaginal Pain: Vulvadynia, Vulvar Vestibulitis, and Vaginismus

The Kegel exercises can also be an important part of the treatment for women who suffer from any condition that results in painful intercourse or in a vaginal spasm that may make penetration, even with a finger or a Q-tip, impossible. The pain has often been described as a burning or stinging sensation that may also flare up during physical exercise or normal daily activities. There are many possible causes of these conditions, and it's very likely to result from an interaction between several factors, both psychological and physiological.

As a result, treating these conditions entails a multilevel approach that begins with a gynecological exam to check for infections that may be treatable with medication. When there's no evidence of infection, effective treatment may involve psychotherapy to explore underlying feelings about sex, sex therapy, changes in diet, and some solitary genital exercises that include breath awareness and gentle Kegels. An understanding, patient, noncomplaining partner can be enormously helpful, especially one who is willing to follow directions and do very light empathic touching and breathing exercises in sync with the partner in distress. Naturally, as long as the pain persists, women with these conditions should not have intercourse.

Your Sexual History

As we have seen, your earliest experiences with your sexual body, both pleasant and unpleasant—and the emotions that accompanied those events—can have long-term consequences. We can get stuck in certain emotions and then stick with tried-and-true pleasures that work, but the lack of growth can be stifling.

Sexual evolution in the context of a loving relationship involves coming to terms with the pain of the past and the disappointments of the present and broadening loving sexual pleasures.

It involves recognizing and coming to terms with any unresolved feelings about yourself as a sexual being.

Naturally, it takes time to process the emotions and replace old habits and reflexes with loving and playful choices. Think of it as building new sensory-neural pathways. It's certainly a worthwhile endeavor, however long it takes.

The philosopher George Santayana is often quoted as saying, "Those who cannot remember the past are condemned to repeat it." Santayana was known as a pragmatist who placed a high social value on human happiness. Learning from our past frees us to reinvent ourselves in a way that supports personal well-being and happy relationships.

Each of us has a past that has shaped his or her body and that promotes fulfillment or blocks it in some ways. In the same way that we have looked at family history to learn about our patterns of attachments and enhance how we love, we also need to study and accept our sexual histories to move forward and expand ourselves sexually. Step six offers you an opportunity to study how your sexual history is influencing your sexual present.

Step Six: The Sexual History Profile

Objectives: To explore early emotional influences on your sexual arousal and to understand and appreciate your sexual self

This profile is designed to make it easier for you to take your own history without bias and to see yourself in a new light. It may take a while to get through it—probably more than one sitting—and you are likely to find that all sorts of feelings arise as you recall past events.

Copy this grid to a notebook or to your personal computer (if your privacy is completely secure) so that you have plenty of space to fill in the blanks. Once you have your history in print, you may want to share it with someone else.

If you are in an intimate relationship, it would be valuable for each of you to do the profile separately. Then you can share with each other some selected discoveries and insights.

As always, begin this exercise in a private place where you are unlikely to be disturbed. Begin with some basic embodiment exercises: do a few complete breaths, deep sighs, and a felt-sense inventory; stretch, relax, get into your body. Then take a few mindful minutes and come to a place of presence and focused attention.

This is essentially an exercise in memory, including both mental imagery and emotional awareness. You want to see what images spontaneously arise and the feelings that accompany them as you recall these periods of your life. Be aware of any buildup of tension in your face, throat, chest, diaphragm, belly, genitals, thighs, rectum, and butt.

Age	Event	Emotions	Rating	Present Emotions
1 to 6				
7 to 12				
13 to 17				
18 to 25				

Event. Take each of the age blocks, one at a time and starting at the top, and in this column write down any sensual or sexual memories that pop up in your mind's eye—whether they were wanted or unwanted. Just give it a quick title, like: "tore pants," "touched Jackie," or "played doctor."

Emotions. For each event, see if you can recall the emotions you felt at the time. This is not how you feel about it now, but how you felt about it then. You might write *happy*, *scared*, *excited*, or *ashamed*—whatever was true for you as you remember it.

Rating. In the next column, rate each emotional event as you felt it then on a five-point scale: positive (5); mostly positive (4); don't know (3); mostly negative (2); negative (1).

Present emotions. In the last column, note the feelings that come up for you now as you recall these singular events. What unfinished business do you have? Can you complete it on your own through your own awareness, self-acceptance, and compassion, or would you do well to talk it through with someone, like your partner, a friend, or a therapist?

Include in the appropriate age category the first time you did the following:

- Felt genital sensations
- Engaged in genital self-touching
- Learned about sex
- Engaged in childhood sex play with a playmate
- Had a crush
- Kissed
- Made out
- Fell in love
- Had an orgasm
- Had intercourse
- Experienced sexual disappointment
- Experienced unwanted sexual touching
- Experienced sexual trauma
- Had an outstandingly wonderful experience

Pay particular attention to the "Rating" column. A lot of 1's and 2's suggest that it would be helpful to go over some of these early experiences and see how you can make sense of them in a way that derives value from them.

Also pay attention to the "Present Emotions" column. See which memories still have the power to arouse emotions and where in your body you feel these emotions. Pleasant emotions are energizing; unpleasant emotions create tension. Tension and holding in the area of the diaphragm and belly are often signs of guilt. Tension and holding in the genitals, rectum, thighs, and butt are often signs of shame.

Most of us have been raised to feel guilty for youthful sex play and to be ashamed of our sexual anatomy and desires. See what's true for you.

If some emotion arises while either you or your partner are doing the profile, take some time to hold each other, breathe together, and give each other some love.

7

The Evolving Orgasm

When an orgasm is simply a reflexive discharge, it's likely to be the same each time or to diminish in intensity as one gets older—particularly if the sex is routine or nonexistent. In contrast, for women and men who value their orgasmic experiences alone and/or with a partner, skilled practice can help their orgasms to get better and better.

What I mean by *better* is more reliable, perhaps, but more intense would also certainly be part of it. The ability to enjoy a full body orgasm is another. This is what Wilhelm Reich called "orgastic potency" or the capacity to surrender to the flow of biological energy, free of any inhibitions.

Evolving one's orgasmic experience may also involve having more than one kind of orgasm sequentially. For women, that may include clitoral, vaginal, or multiple orgasms. For men, that may involve learning to contain the ejaculate and having multiple mini-orgasms before the final discharge and release.

Another quality worth evolving is what I call a *heartgasm*. This is the powerful sensation of opening in the chest and heart that is experienced as intense love for your mate at the same time that you orgasm.

Just as we can become wiser and more skilled in our work as we age, so too can our orgasms get better. Wherever we are in our own sexual evolution, there's always a next step. That's what evolution is about.

The critical next steps in the process of evolving your orgasm are (1) to develop a more loving and pleasurable relationship with your genitalia, and (2) to learn to build arousal by relaxing and containing your excitement.

First things first: your relationship with your sexual parts.

Loving Your Genitals

Why are our privates so major? Is it because when we were children they defined us as male and female, dictating our lives, yet no one was allowed to talk about them? Is it because they have made us feel such pleasure yet also such guilt and doubt? Is it that they can be so contrary, so unruly, with such a mind of their own? It's all that and more.

It's become apparent to me that a lot of people don't like their genitalia. I have heard too many women say they don't want to look at their vulvas in a mirror because they think that part of the body is ugly. When men are questioned on anonymous surveys about their degree of comfort in locker rooms, many respond in ways that indicate sensitivity about penis size.

In the body, the emotion associated with rejecting a fundamental part of oneself is shame. Nothing is more inhibiting of the body's natural responses than feelings of shame. It's as though the whole pelvic floor tightens, shrinks, and tries to hide.

Tensing the thighs, genitals, anal sphincter, or butt prevents blood flow, automatically limiting arousal purely on a physiological basis. In a sexual situation, a person with a tendency to feel ashamed of his or her body is likely to avoid being looked at nude and more likely to pull away from a lover's touch rather than melt into it. Right there, two potentially rich sources of erotic stimulation are eliminated.

Whatever reason people have for not loving their genitals, the emotion stirred up is shame. They may have been brought up to feel their genitals are unclean, defective, embarrassing, or unreliable. Even if they no longer believe it, the motivational component of shame makes people want to cover up and hide.

The opposite of shame is self-love and respect for one's body. What does genital self-respect, or pride, look like?

Genital Self-Love

A man who feels good about his penis is comfortable with its size. Whether it's big or small, he values the pleasure he receives and can give to another with his penis. He enjoys his erections and enjoys masturbating yet doesn't feel driven to do so. He feels good about sharing his penis with his lover as a gift for their mutual sexual pleasure.

A woman who takes pride in her body feels good about her vulva—the outer and inner labia, the clitoris, and the vagina—and the distinctive pleasures each part gives her when it is stimulated. She enjoys masturbating with or without orgasm. She can enjoy the touch of a sensitive lover and can relax and allow her vagina to open and surrender to sexual pleasure.

For men and women who suffer from sexual shame but are determined to overcome this programming, there are some excellent ways to deprogram this limiting feeling.

Overcoming Chronic Shame

It has been said that sunshine is the best antiseptic. In general, chronic shame is a persistent hurt feeling of oneself as flawed and defective in body or character and of wanting to hide from judging eyes. Obviously, the antidote to chronic shame, assuming that a person wants to get rid of it, entails some kind of emotional exposure. Naturally, it has to be in the company of someone warm and reassuring so that the feeling can be experienced and released in the presence of love.

It's not easy to confess shameful feelings because doing so involves speaking up about a part of yourself you've always wanted to hide. When the emotion starts to well up, you may feel like running away and never showing your face again. That's why people are more likely to work on their shame in therapy, relying on a trusted therapist to create a safe space for exploring feelings of self-judgment.

People who have suffered sexual abuse as children may carry feelings of shame in their bodies. They may feel defiled or power-less when it comes to a sexual situation and automatically tense their bodies and split off mentally from what is taking place with a partner. A victim of abuse may feel especially ashamed if he or she felt any pleasure during the molestation, which is not uncom-mon. Talking about it in therapy, or with a loving, compassionate partner can help enormously. Doing the breathing and holding exercise with a partner, especially during an intimate encounter, while practicing to stay present—by talking, making eye contact, kissing, or focusing on the senses—can be a very healing process.

In order to free your body of shame, exposure doesn't neces-sarily mean you have to strip naked. You don't have to grin and bare it, so to speak. Yet with an intimate partner, it could help. If you've been dressing and undressing in the bathroom to avoid being seen, then baring your body is like baring your soul. In fact, it may be exactly what is needed to shake the habit of shame that is so self-diminishing, causing you to shrink from view.

One aspect of genital shame is the feeling that one doesn't measure up. Most of us grow up wanting to be just like everyone else, especially the attractive ones. But as we move along in life, we often discover that the most interesting people are not the ones who are like everyone else.

Diversity is critical to evolution; it creates infinite possibilities in the evolution of an individual as well as in a species. Women who have surgery to shorten their inner labia want to look the way they imagine all other women look. They're willing to sacrifice *feeling* as good as they can for *looking* as good as they can—or at least what they *imagine* to be looking good. By doing so, however, they give up their individuality and risk loss of sensation.

The truth is that everybody is different. Labia, clitorises, and vaginas are as distinctive as faces or hands. Every penis is a work of nature's art. That's what makes our bodies interesting. They look different, feel different, smell and taste different from one another, and each has its own personality, preferences, and quirks.

It can be very freeing to appreciate yourself for your uniqueness and who you really are. Tall, short, fat, or thin, everyone can be beautiful in the eyes of a loving beholder.

Overcoming Chronic Guilt

There is a difference between *guilt* and *shame*. When you feel guilty, you feel bad about something you've done, should have done, or shouldn't have done. When you feel shame, you feel bad about who or what you *are*.

Chronic guilt is often felt as a persistent knot in the diaphragm. Chronic shame tends to affect us a little lower, limiting sexual arousal by generating chronic tension in the pelvic area.

Some people feel so guilty about something they've done— or something that *was* done to them—that they are ashamed of themselves. When the behavior was sexual, it can have a major effect on their sexuality.

Confessing to someone you trust and respect that you feel inadequate or that you think you did something terrible and feel guilty about it can be very emotionally freeing. Men and women have confessed things to me that they did as children that still brought up feelings of guilt and/or shame decades later.

One woman who had difficulty achieving orgasm began to see how she typically carried tension in her genital and pelvic muscles, particularly when she made love with her female partner. As we looked into her childhood experiences, Jean admitted to me, with a great deal of pain and self-loathing, that she had molested her sister when she was ten and her sister was eight.

Jean was so condemning of herself that she resisted talking about it. Eventually, she opened up and described those early experiences. As she did, she said that her heart was pounding and that she felt shame all over her body. She could feel her pelvis getting tight and going numb. I encouraged her to breathe and pulse her PC muscle to relax it. She did this as best she could.

I told her that it was not uncommon for siblings to explore sexual feelings together and that as a child herself, only two years older than her sister, she was not a child molester. She protested that she shouldn't have done it, that she was forcing her "gayness" on her little sister. That was complete nonsense. It's quite common for children to engage in sex play with children of the same sex before exploring it with the opposite sex.

Forcing someone to do something he or she doesn't want to do, of course, is never right, but Jean acknowledged that she did not threaten or physically overpower her sister, who did seem more than willing to play with her like that. Still, she felt that she was the older one and her sister may have felt forced.

I suggested that she take a few breaths, imagine her sister, and apologize out loud if she had felt forced to do things she really didn't want to do. It felt good to Jean to give voice to some feelings, but she still had a hard time forgiving herself.

The amazing thing about the whole situation was that after all those years, she and her sister had never discussed it. After our session Jean decided to talk to her sister about it. When they talked, it turned out that her sister had in fact been holding on to some resentment—but not about the sex play. Apparently, Jean had forced her to do other things that she resented. The two of them had a good talk, wept together, laughed together, and declared their undying love for each other. For Jean that was the beginning of a process of self-love and acceptance that ultimately led to her becoming more accepting of intimate pleasures with her partner.

Eroticizing Shame

For some people, shame itself can be eroticized. In one study, sex researcher Jack Morin compiled stories of peak erotic experiences from a diverse group of respondents. He found one aspect of eroticism continually alluded to, what he called "the naughtiness factor": an excitement that comes with violating prohibitions.

Even just the hint of naughtiness carries the excitement of breaking the tether of respectability and being a "bad" boy or girl. Morin observed that some of the typical fantasies people enjoy have to do with being forced into sex or engaging in activity they would never want to do in reality.

Some men and women also find it arousing to act out fantasy scenes that involve humiliation. Studies suggest that there's no harm in it as long as the scenes are played in the spirit of sexual adventure with a mutually inclined partner and that they spur passion without causing physical injury, emotional distress, or self-hate. That's a big order, but apparently many people can fill that bill and distinguish fantasy and role-playing from reality.

The Paradox of the Orgasm

You may want to feel more aroused, let go more, or become more sensuous, spontaneous, and free. You may want sex to last longer and to enjoy more frequent and more intense orgasms. There are some excellent and pleasurable ways to practice building skill at arousal and orgasm.

The paradox is that in the moment it's happening, you can't be too goal-oriented, because that's trying to make something happen. Orgasm is all about letting go. You can be deliberate about your movements and do what feels good, but you can't strive to let go. They're contradictory actions, like trying hard to relax. If you try for something, you'll limit your possibilities to what's typical. You'll be firing your left brain and linear thought, turning up your SNS stress circuits, and triggering old reflexes.

Once again, maximizing your experience is all about breathing, relaxing tense muscles, and letting the energy flow. As you take deep sighs and move into your senses, you activate your PNS and get the right brain firing. Now you have entered the realm of imagination and eroticism, body language, pleasure, and presence. All that exists is this sensuous present moment, this wonderful feeling, this aliveness in your body, and, when you're with a partner, this special time together.

What you'll want to avoid is getting into a frenzy of activity that is over before it fully begins—before intensely pleasurable excitement can fill every pore in your body.

Containment and Sexual Arousal

In the early days of psychotherapy, therapists firmly believed in the value of clients' explosive emotional outbursts during the session, signaling a genuine release of blocked feelings. It's called a *catharsis*, a word derived from the ancient Greek meaning "cleansing" and "purification." Freud saw it as an instinctive and involuntary body process.

Without a doubt, there is great value to providing a protected place where a person can break through years of withheld grief, guilt, and hurt by sobbing at a memory or yelling at a violator seen in the mind's eye. Unexpressed sadness or rage are kept locked in the muscles and organs of the body and can cause damage. It's healthy and freeing to get them out of there.

But therapists and clients alike began to see that we could get hooked on the dramatic displays of sobbing and screaming. People were starting to show up at workshops covering the same emotional territory, beating pillows, and venting a seemingly inexhaustible supply of rage or tears. Catharsis didn't seem to be helping. We began to see that simply discharging the emotion might be temporarily relieving, but without fully processing the underlying unresolved issues, the frustration and outrage would simply build back up.

Around that time, social psychologist Carol Tavris came out with a book challenging the current trend in psychotherapy that embraced what she called a "ventilationist" position, the notion that releasing pent-up emotions gets rid of them. In fact, she suggested, you are teaching a "cathartic habit" and missing the nuances of the situation. Tavris advocated cognitive approaches that essentially sought to contain the behavior. She suggested taking the time to reduce the rush of adrenaline through reappraisal and humor, and if you must vent anger, decide on an effective course of action that will bring a useful result.

Psychologists Jack Rosenberg and Marjorie Rand also took issue with the traditional emphasis on catharsis, but instead of containing the *behavior*, as body-based psychotherapists they focused on containing the *emotion*. They suggested using breathing methods to stay with the anger or fear sensations without releasing them and to simply watch the flow of feelings and the holding patterns in the body.

They observed that when people breathe into their tense muscles and relax, the body—essentially a physical container—can expand to make room for the increased emotional activation. The energy can then spread and circulate throughout the body without being discharged in catharsis. The person can face the feelings more clearly and do what's necessary to come to terms with the issues.

What does this have to do with sexual arousal? The way many people "do" sex resembles a kind of cathartic habit. Rather than allowing the energy to build and containing it, they go for a quick explosive discharge and are finished. But when you breathe into the sensations, the chest, the rib cage, the belly, and the pelvic muscles relax and allow the sensations to intensify.

There's certainly nothing wrong with a good orgasm, but an orgasm often ends the sex play. It is possible to have a new experience in sex by playing with the sexual energy and the intensity of the sensation rather than discharging it at the first opportunity. That way, the first orgasm can be the beginning of a stream of orgasmic pleasures.

Containment Is Not Suppression

With emotion, when you are containing rather than suppressing yourself, you are feeling it in the body, breathing into it—not tensing, but relaxing. You don't deny your feelings as you do when you suppress yourself. You feel where in the body you feel them. You keep breathing into the muscles of the torso activated by the emotion, expanding with each inhalation and relaxing with each exhalation. In this way, you can feel your feelings and still be in command of how you interpret or express them.

It's the same with sex. Containment is essential for building and sustaining sexual arousal, desire, and pleasure. It's another paradox. To enhance your capacity for sexual abandonment, you have to learn to relax and contain yourself.

Containment and Sexual Freedom

Some people are afraid to look at what turns them on because they're concerned that if they do get aroused, they'll have to act on it—with a sense of urgency. In fact, muscular contraction does generate pressure to do something to get rid of the feeling.

But when you keep breathing and relaxing, regulating any stress or emotion, you can tolerate the growing excitement. Containing sexual feelings allows you to sustain and enjoy them, letting them develop gradually over time rather than having to discharge them immediately.

People who notice that they have a tendency to squeeze their thighs, genitals, or butt can get anxious when they start to let go, because they feel exposed and unprotected. That's natural at first. It's worth recognizing that you actually have greater control and more choice when you're relaxed. You can feel sexy *and* do nothing but enjoy it. That's true sexual freedom. You can notice an attractive woman or a handsome, well-built man on the street and get turned on. Enjoy the rush. It doesn't mean you have to get a room together. Nor does it mean you're cheating on your partner. It's a private moment you've had for yourself.

Whatever contributes to being in touch with your sexual self during the day sends a shot of warm blood and good energy into the pelvis. That keeps the region alive and vibrant, which is good for your committed partner.

The Essential Role of Masturbation

Masturbation is the most prevalent sexual activity. Some statistics show that more than 90 percent of the male population and 65 percent of the female population in the United States masturbate.

In "Sex in America," the highly regarded 1994 University of Chicago survey of nearly thirty-five hundred participants, the researchers made some interesting discoveries about the practice of masturbation. Among Americans between eighteen and fifty-nine years of age, more than 60 percent of men and 40 percent of women admitted to it; especially surprising was that most of those who masturbated frequently had regular sex partners.

This contradicted the widely held belief that masturbation is a substitute for sex with a partner, necessary for releasing sexual tension but not something that people with partners need to do. In fact, the researchers found that the most satisfied people masturbated the most, indicating that masturbation "is not an outlet so much as a component of an active sex life."

It makes sense. Sexual appetite is not like a desire for food or water. If you're hungry or thirsty and you eat or drink, you feel sated and you're done eating or drinking. In contrast, good sex makes you want more. Masturbation stimulates erotic fantasies, responsiveness to sexual stimuli, and thoughts of sex—all of which maintain sexual interest.

For both women and men, practicing the Kegel exercises to strengthen and relax the PC muscle and developing a greater proficiency at masturbation are the most effective methods for maximizing the pleasures of orgasm (see chapter 6).

Erotic Self-Attunement

Studies show that virtually all males begin to masturbate early in their development and certainly by puberty. Many women, however, did not masturbate as girls. Among those who masturbate as adults, a majority started only after they had had sex with a partner. It's been speculated that the low incidence of masturbation in many adolescent girls may have a limiting effect, developmentally, on their ability to enjoy sexual pleasure and achieve orgasm with a partner.

Honing your skills at stimulating yourself to orgasm is an important developmental step for both men and women in shaping how you orgasm with a partner. Beyond orgasm, self-pleasuring is also an opportunity to sensitize and eroticize the whole body.

Slowing down, breathing and relaxing, and building and containing excitement are critical skills for women and men who want to get the most out of their love lives.

Skillful Self-Pleasuring for Women

For some women, the lack of familiarity with their own bodies operates against knowing what turns them on or, as you will see in the next chapter, makes them unaware that they even *are* turned on.

With practice, women can learn to masturbate in ways that stimulate different kinds of orgasms: vaginal, clitoral, or both simultaneously, and genuine multiple orgasms, one right after the other. The critical factor is to try a variety of ways to stimulate yourself and not just to rely on a vibrator.

Women can learn to stimulate the clitoris with one hand while they have inserted one or two well-lubricated fingers into the vagina. They can also explore different dildos and perhaps experiment with a dildo that's specifically designed to stimulate the G spot.

Some women bring themselves to orgasm by squeezing their thighs together, but that method may not be conducive to being able to orgasm with a partner. These women may want to experiment with bringing themselves to orgasm by opening and relaxing their thighs—skills that would have more positive transfer with a partner.

Skillful Self-Pleasuring for Men

All boys masturbate, and adult men typically achieve orgasm more easily than women do. However, most boys learn to masturbate as quickly as possible in the bathroom or behind the closed doors of their bedrooms. The fear of getting caught is likely to ratchet up the excitement. But the habit of a quick, secretive "jerk-off" can operate against a man when he wants to sustain his pleasure with a partner.

Although ejaculation and orgasm generally occur together, a number of men have discovered that they can separate the two, withholding their ejaculate while allowing themselves the pleasure of orgasm. California sex researchers Bill Hartman and Marilyn Fithian found that men who were capable of separating orgasm from ejaculation could also learn to have what might be considered multiple orgasms. Practicing the Kegel exercises proved to be very helpful in learning this skill.

Also, by practicing self-stimulation to the point just prior to ejaculatory inevitability and then relaxing, some men are able to train themselves to enjoy mini-orgasms during sexually stimulating activity. Doing so gives them better control over the final and full-bodied orgasm, choosing when to release it to maximize their sex play with their partners. For men who want to withhold their ejaculate until their partner orgasms first, this is a highly valuable skill.

Sexually Explicit Material: Pornography, Erotica, and Fantasy

It's common knowledge that sperm banks hand out sexually explicit magazines along with a container to the men who are there to make a deposit. Most males grow up using pictures of naked people to stimulate themselves during masturbation.

Today a big concern about pornography is that the women typically depicted in it (whether in magazines, on the Internet, or in videos) don't look or act genuine. A steady diet of porn stars can desensitize the male libido toward real women.

Erotica is "women's porn"; it typically consists of stories or novels that focus on building desire through romantic obstacles to consummation. Some women also enjoy watching sexually explicit videos, particularly those like Femme videos made especially for women, and they may masturbate to what they see there. They also might masturbate to a favorite fantasy about a romantic crush or even a sexual encounter they would not consent to in real life.

One frustrated woman who couldn't have an orgasm with the man she was falling in love with told me that when he left in the morning, she was able to orgasm by herself by picturing him making love with her. But she couldn't do it when he was actually there. "How sick is that?" she cried. I understood completely. When she was with him, she was too busy worrying about what he thought of her to relax and enjoy him.

One question I am often asked is whether it's okay to mentally fantasize during sex with a partner about someone else. For some people, doing so increases the likelihood of having an orgasm with the partner. However, it does keep them from being fully present. I suggest alternating between brief fantasies and making contact with the lover.

I encourage people to stop working so hard for an orgasm. If they open their eyes and interact erotically with their lovers, it is very likely to enhance their enjoyment of each other.

I've also been asked whether a repetitive fantasy can indicate a desire for it in real life, like fantasies of being raped or being a voyeur or an exhibitionist. For most people, fantasies do not translate into activities a person wants to act on. If you can enjoy having a fantasy about a naughty or even illicit activity without feeling compelled to act on it in real life, you're safe. If you feel pressure to act on a fantasy that may be criminal or cause you or another some harm, then clearly you're in danger. See a therapist before you hurt someone or yourself.

Relaxed Excitement: The Key to Building and Containing Arousal

An orgasm is the ultimate experience of intense excitation and complete abandonment simultaneously. Once again, relaxed excitement is the key.

Loving sex completely depends on being able to enjoy high levels of physiological activation coupled with deep relaxation—in the heart and chest certainly, and particularly in the diaphragm, the belly, the genitals, and the pelvic muscles. If you feel yourself tensing your pelvic muscles, you can experiment with pulsing your muscles, vacillating between gripping and letting go. As you breathe deeply and pulse your muscles, tensing and relaxing on purpose, that action is likely to build excitement until you're ready to release control and abandon yourself to pleasure.

A person who can enjoy the sensations of arousal and desire without having to discharge the excitement can boost the intensity of all aspects of libido and sexual experience. Allowing sexual pleasure is like tuning the nervous system to run at a more intense level of activation while also letting go and enjoying the sensation of increased energy flow.

Masturbation as Art

In the early 1970s I attended the opening of the Erotic Art Museum in San Francisco, and in the idiom of the time, my mind was blown. I wandered through the exhibit, viewing paintings, detailed drawings, and sculptures of genitalia and men and women in various sex acts. I was enthralled by the beauty of the works displayed.

Betty Dodson's drawings particularly appealed to me, especially the ones depicting female genitals spread open and stylized as flowers. Georgia O'Keeffe had also painted lush flowers that appeared to be inspired by vaginal imagery, but she denied it. Dodson's drawings were clearly intended.

A few years later, I enjoyed the first exhibit of *The Dinner Party* by feminist artist Judy Chicago. Chicago also used the theme of female genitals in her monumental piece of mixed media using embroidered textiles, weavings and ceramics commemorating historical and mythical women. Each place setting at the table featured plates shaped as open vulvas in beautiful flowing designs.

Betty was my earliest inspiration, however, and I sent away for her self-published booklet, *Liberating Masturbation*, which included a series of pen-and-ink drawings of female genitals held open in artful designs. She called it "designing an aesthetic for the female genitalia." In her newer books she has included male genitals.

I still show those original drawings to female clients who have no idea what the inside of the vulva looks like. I also find them useful with couples and with men who want information on how to please a woman. I like that I'm showing artwork and not an anatomy chart.

In her "Bodysex" workshops, Betty introduced me to the notion of masturbation as an art form to do for yourself, like dancing or playing the piano when you're alone. Her notion of masturbation as a meditation on self-love further casts a warm and relaxed tone to solo sex.

Step seven offers some new methods for solitary pleasures.

Step Seven: Erotic Basics

Objectives: To discover new ways to pleasure yourself and to allow excitement to build and flow throughout your body

Most people have some reliable methods for bringing themselves to orgasm. These exercises are meant to offer an opportunity to do things a little differently and try something new. For that reason, none of these exercises starts with the use of vibrators or sexually explicit photos or videos. It's not that I'm against them; I'm just encouraging you to try something different so you can add to your repertoire.

Once again, the trick is to stimulate your excitement while becoming more relaxed. That's containment. Containment is an erotic asset that can be practiced at every stage of sexual arousal. The basic principle of containment is to feel the charge of energy and to breathe into it and relax rather than tense, suppress, or discharge the excitement. Breathing and relaxing allows the energy to build and become a reservoir you can dip into when and how you choose in order to become sexually engaged or enjoy release. Orgasm that follows containment is more intensely pleasurable than an orgasm that pops out.

Each exercise can be done for just a few minutes or for an hour or longer.

Solo Eroticism

Naturally, you can enjoy solo sex anytime the mood strikes, as long as you have privacy. The following suggestions are meant as opportunities to enjoy more extended periods of exploration.

1. To fully enjoy your sensual and erotic play, go to a private space where you won't be disturbed. Turn off the phone. Spread a thick towel on the bed, a yoga mat, or the carpeted floor—wherever you intend to experiment. Put out whatever lotions, toys, or other sensuous items you might like to include. Be sure to have at least one or two pillows around to use under or between your legs. You may also want a light blanket to use part of the time.

2. Dim the lights, light a candle, and put on some soft music. Sit on the towel and take some deep breaths and a few sighs, and check in with yourself. You may want to do a few stretches to relax your body and blow out any tension. You can begin this exploration with or without your clothes on.

3. Lie on the towel with a pillow under your knees and take deep inhalations that begin in your belly, widen the rib cage, and lift your chest. Blow out slowly and steadily on the

exhalation, and keep blowing until you run out of air. You'll feel your abdominal muscles pull in as you push out the last bit of air from your lungs.

4. Begin your sensuous self-massage with your head, face, back of the neck, and throat. Just feel your own skin, muscles, and bones with care and consciousness. You may want to use lotion. Move your hands down slowly and smoothly along the muscles of the arms, chest, and rib cage. Use your fingertips to massage tense intercostals (the spaces and muscles between the ribs).

5. Most women don't get their breasts touched and massaged enough, so if you're a woman, take this opportunity to squeeze and massage your breasts. Both women and men may enjoy lightly touching and stimulating the nipples. Breathe slowly and deeply, sighing and relaxing.

6. Now is a good time to remove your clothing if you haven't done so already. But instead of touching yourself with the goal of bringing on an orgasm, massage yourself slowly and sensuously. Stroke your belly with both hands and breathe so that the belly grows round and full with each inhalation. Massage your thighs and work your way to your genitals.

7. If you are a woman, tug and squeeze the outside of your vulva and see how much of the inside you can stimulate just by squeezing and massaging yourself on the outside. Press down on the pelvic bone and feel how that can stimulate your clitoris without actually touching it on the inside. Take some deep sighs and relax. If you have never seen the inside of your vulva, place a mirror between your thighs and take a look.

8. If you are a man, put lotion on you scrotum and lightly massage your testes, drawing them up toward your belly. Then move your hands to your penis as you gently slide up the shaft and tug on the head. Massage your penis slowly and deliberately. See if you can discover some new strokes.

9. Feel yourself becoming more excited. Make some deep sighs and relax into it.

Sexual Imagery

Sexual fantasy keeps your mind focused on the erotic and helps to fan your passion. Most of us have our favorite fantasies: mental pictures and scenes that can come from early childhood or adolescent associations or from hot real-life experiences.

1. Play out a favorite scenario in your mind's eye, but this time embellish it by using all five ordinary senses in your imagination. For example, if you are imagining yourself with a partner who is nude, add some visual details to the image of your partner's nude body. Imagine the sound of your partner's heavy breaths in your "mind's ear."

2. Imagine yourself stroking your partner. Imagine the sensation of gliding your hand along his or her smooth skin. See if you can conjure up the pleasing smell of his or her body and the taste of his or her kisses.

Change the Routine

Since the purpose of these exercises is to slow down and experiment with pleasuring yourself differently, change your position at least once or twice.

1. If you usually lie flat on your back, try bending your knees or lying on your side with a pillow between your thighs. You could also sit, get up on your knees, or stand up and see how it feels to stimulate yourself that way. Some men and women may enjoy putting a firm pillow between their thighs to squeeze against.

2. You might also enjoy pulsing your PC muscle as you stroke your genitals, tightening and releasing, tightening and releasing as you breathe and relax.

Orgasm for Women

Remember that sometimes the beginning of an orgasm feels like the urge to urinate. To avoid having to get up to go, it's always good to urinate before you start. Also, make sure you have something absorbent underneath you so you won't be afraid to let your PC muscle go.

For women who enjoy using a vibrator to orgasm, it's reliable and I have no quarrel with using one. Nevertheless, to broaden your erotic repertoire, I encourage you to discover the pleasures to be had with your own sensual, sexy hands.

1. Explore two-handed masturbation. Use one or two well-lubricated fingers of one hand to stimulate the clitoris while one or two well-lubricated fingers of the other hand are inserted into the vagina. Saliva is a great lubricant because it's handy and organic, but anything you like is good. Press down on your pubic bone and squeeze the outer lips together to stimulate the internal parts of the clitoris.

2. Fantasize and practice slow, deep erotic sighs. If you get tense in your groin, pulse and relax. Change your position at least once. As your excitement increases, notice how your breath naturally quickens.

3. Women can also practice containment by relaxing the PC muscle and other pelvic muscles and letting the sexual energy spread. You can stimulate yourself and build excitement, then stop, breathe and relax, and start again. Do that once or twice before allowing yourself to orgasm. See how extending your orgasmic experience affects the sensation of release throughout your body.

4. Some women also enjoy inserting a dildo inside the vagina, slowly and rhythmically pulling it out and sliding it back in while stimulating the clitoris. Once a woman has enjoyed a clitoral orgasm, a dildo may help in reaching a vaginal orgasm.

Orgasm for Men

For many men, the big challenge is to slow down and change your boyhood patterns. If you typically use sexually explicit materials, try doing without any, relying more on your imagination. Be sure to take the time to create a sensuous environment with low lights and music where you won't be interrupted.

1. Explore two-handed masturbation. Apply lotion or oil to your genital area and use both hands to stimulate your

scrotum and testes, gently pulling upward. Use both hands to slowly squeeze along the shaft of your penis.

2. Between the shaft and the head of your penis is the coronal ridge, a rim of tissue at the bottom of the glans that is one of the most sensitive areas in the male genitalia. Pay particular attention to stimulating that ridge as well as the glans.

3. Take slow, deep erotic sighs. Many men have learned to masturbate or make love without making a sound, and that can inhibit their enjoyment. When you begin to feel your excitement increase, try vocalizing your sighs and see if that adds to your pleasure.

4. Fantasize and practice deep sighs. If you get tense in your groin, pulse and relax. Some men enjoy inserting a finger or a dildo inside their rectum. Change your position at least once. As your excitement increases, notice how your breath naturally quickens.

5. Practice containment. Learn to recognize the point just prior to inevitability, when you won't be able to stop from coming. When you recognize the sensation, stop stimulating yourself, slow your breath, and relax the diaphragm, the belly, and the pelvic muscles. When you're ready, let yourself come.

You are now very likely to know your sensual and sexual body better than you did before.

8

The Nuances of Sexual Pleasure

U p to now, I've been using the terms *desire*, *lust*, and *libido* interchangeably, but they're really not synonymous. What is more accurate is to see them as phases, ranging from mild to most intense, of sexual excitement and abandonment. In effect, the entire erotic spectrum represents all aspects of libido, the sex drive.

Without a sex drive, it is still possible to enjoy physical contact and the ability to please a partner. But to truly enjoy emotionally gratifying sexual pleasure, libido is an essential motivator, and as such it's an important aspect of sexual health. Just as cooking a good meal takes skill and reading an inspirational menu at a restaurant can make you hungrier, erotic skills and an expanded erotic menu can enhance libido.

The Erotic Spectrum

What is erotic is anything that arouses and intensifies sexual feelings. The spectrum begins with *sexual interest*, which with more sensual and erotic stimulation becomes *desire*, which with more imagination becomes *lust*, which with greater abandon gives way to *passion*, *orgasm*, and occasionally *ecstasy*.

Sexual Interest

Sexual excitement starts when something piques your interest. If you have a strong libido, you may be walking around with a tiger in your tank all the time. If that's not the case, where does the first erotic prod come from? Is it a spontaneous fantasy? Does it happen when a partner shows interest? What about recalling an attractive stranger who caught your eye?

For a woman, context is everything. Research shows a big gender difference here. Sexual interest for her has a lot to do with the larger situation and, if she's with a partner, the quality of their connection.

For a man, context is not as critical. For some men, a willing partner is quite enough. The research on male libido may be confounded, however, by a common male belief that a "real" man is always available for sex, especially if the woman is offering. In truth, it's natural for men's sexual interest to ebb and flow in response to what's going on in their lives.

Women, on the other hand, may be more available than they give themselves credit for. A good deal of evidence is accumulating to indicate that many women may be unaware of their own physiological sexual arousal.

In one intriguing set of experiments psychology professors Meredith Chivers, currently at Queen's University in Ontario, and J. Michael Bailey of Northwestern University set up a laboratory to test male and female arousal patterns. Subjects who had self-identified as heterosexual, lesbian, or gay were shown a series of video clips: a man and a woman engaged in sexual activity, two men together, two women together, a man masturbating, and a woman masturbating. Also shown were clips of male and female bonobos mating, a well-toned man walking nude along a beach, and a woman doing calisthenics in the nude. All of the subjects were fitted with devices on their genitals: a penile cuff that measured swelling and a small plastic probe in the vagina that measured vaginal blood flow and lubrication. The subjects were also given keypads to rate how aroused they felt.

The results showed that men tended to respond in what the researchers called "category-specific" ways. Heterosexual men responded to the man and woman having sex, the lesbian clip, the woman masturbating, and the exercising woman; they did not respond to anything strictly male. Gay men were responsive to the two men having sex, the masturbating man, and the man on the beach; they were unresponsive to anything female. For both groups of men, their subjective responses closely matched their physiological responses.

Women responded quite differently. They showed a strong genital response to *all* of the sexual stimuli. Yet they also appeared to be unaware of much of it. Their subjective responses seemed completely out of touch with their physiological responses.

Straight women looking at lesbian sex reported less excitement than their vaginas showed. They reported a lot less excitement than their vaginas showed while they were watching two men. They reported a lot more excitement than their vaginas indicated while they were watching a man and a woman. They also had a stronger physiological response to the exercising woman than to the man on the beach. Again, however, they didn't report it that way.

As expected, the lesbians were turned on watching sex between women. In that case alone did the subjective and objective responses match for women. Lesbians also reported much less arousal than vaginally recorded while they were watching two men or a man and a woman.

None of the women, straight or lesbian, seemed to notice that their bodies were becoming aroused while watching the bonobos getting it on.

It's not surprising that men are more in touch with being turned on than women are, since their physiological response is external and pretty obvious. But it's likely that a lot of women could be more in touch with their bodies, especially their vaginas. These findings also reinforce the data showing that context is essential for women. Women aren't automatically turned on to sex just because their vaginas are.

Chivers and Bailey weren't sure what to make of their finding that women respond to a wider range of sexual stimuli than men. It does seem to suggest that women's sexuality may be more flexible than men's.

What does all of this mean? Are women born with a wider erotic spectrum than men? Does this make women more sexually adaptive with a wider assortment of possible mates, as evolutionary psychologists might suggest? These are interesting speculations.

On a more pragmatic—and possibly therapeutic—note, does this mean that a woman's sex drive could increase just by tuning in to her vaginal responsiveness? This is certainly a possibility.

Are men so categorical because the male ethos—the standard notion of manhood—looks down upon sexual fluidity in men? Even for male homosexuals, there's a strong pressure to be exclusively gay. Bisexual men are often disparaged as unwilling to come out all the way.

Is it possible for a man with a low libido to become more sexually interested in his partner by giving himself permission to enjoy a wider range of erotic stimulation? Maybe so.

Desire

A woman I know once confided candidly that she didn't miss sex. What she missed was missing sex. Desire is a turn-on.

Sexual desire is an appetite or a hunger for sex—a pleasurable craving that grows more urgent as it builds. Arousal is the physiological response to erotic stimulation. It involves erection in a male and vaginal wetness and swelling of the vulva, clitoris, and labia in a female.

It's commonly assumed that you have to feel desire to become aroused. But if you think about it, you'll see that it's usually the other way around. First you get turned on, and *then* you begin to feel desire.

People in a relationship who wait until they feel desire to be sexually playful are missing the point: you have to be sexually playful to get turned on. Then, the more turned on you are, the more your appetite grows.

Just as eyeing a favorite cupcake, hearing the sizzle of a steak on the grill, or smelling the aroma of a freshly baked pie can make you suddenly salivate, what whets your sexual appetite has a lot to do with your senses. Desire requires some focused attention. Interest and appetite build as you focus on sexy sights, sounds, smells, tastes, and touches, especially when you relax into the sensuality of the experience. Everything depends on your ability to stay present and be attentive to the sensuous experience.

Another crucial aspect of enabling desire to build is hanging out with it. It takes time to tune in visually to your partner's sexiness, to attend to the sounds of his or her breath, to taste your kisses and breathe in the scent of his or her body. Taking deep breaths in close physical proximity also confers the added benefit of breathing in each other's pheromones: hormones released in the sweat glands of one person that can affect sexual desire in someone close by.

To touch and be touched is, of course, the sexual sense par excellence. When else can we be held so close, be caressed in places not ordinarily touched, squeeze and be squeezed, and feel silky skin upon skin?

Again, the critical element is taking in the experience and staying focused on the pleasures of the present moment.

Lust

Lust has a bad reputation. One of Christianity's seven deadly sins, lust by definition is immoderate and possibly dangerous. It's often thought of as a realm visited by people who push the limits sexually, who engage in fetishistic sex play, or who may be sexually compulsive, needing a constant sexual outlet. That may very well be true.

Fantasy and imaginative sex play feed lustful feelings. There's no doubt that violating moral codes, such as in exhibitionism or engaging in an extramarital affair, can ratchet up the lust factor. Lust can become so driven that there is an absence of love, of empathy for the other, or of good judgment. Yet none of that has to be the case. Taking a wider perspective, we can find aspects of lust to admire.

We appreciate people who have a lust for life or a lusty quality. My dictionary defines *lusty* as (1) in extremely good physical health, possessing great stamina and strength, (2) full of energy, vitality, and enthusiasm, and (3) strongly desiring sex. Synonyms for lusty include *hearty*, *healthy*, *vigorous*, *forceful*, *robust*, and *strong*. The antonym is *feeble*. Who wouldn't want this kind of lust?

Sexologist Jack Morin sided with this view of lust. He suggested that "our erotic health requires that we make room for lust, for it provides much of the zest that makes sex fun and self-affirming." He also acknowledged, however, that what arouses lust is to objectify the other and to use the other for your own gratification.

Isn't that something we actually want with the person we love and who loves us: to be seen as a sex object and to be a source of his or her gratification, as he or she is for us? Morin solved the problem saying that lust can be a positive experience "when lusty objectification is balanced by your capacities to empathize and respect others."

Cambridge University philosophy professor Simon Blackburn found great value in lust after making a thorough incursion into its cultural and philosophical aspects, examining everything from ancient Greek culture to religious thought, biology, science, and art.

To Blackburn, the major value of lust is abandonment. He wrote that "we should not want to persecute lust simply because of its issue in extremes of abandon. Indeed, such experiences are usually thought to provide one of life's greatest goods . . . ecstatic communion with God."

Lustful feelings may not be everybody's cup of tea, and they are certainly a challenge to maintain with one person for the rest of your life. But if both people are on board—and I emphasize *both*—new explorations can have an invigorating effect on a relationship.

To get into it, you would most likely focus on some of the playful aspects of lust, like playing dress-up and doing some role-playing. Some people hone their lust by narrowing their attention and affection to a particular body part. Others may push their erotic envelope by trying something new—and maybe even a little naughty.

Passion

We can be passionate about anything: passionately in love, passionately in a rage. It is an expression of intensity. The "passion of the Christ" refers to the intense suffering of Jesus. Sexual passion is all about being swept up uncontrollably, physiologically, in the power of the moment. Feelings of love, anger, guilt, shame, and suffering may add rather than detract, as long as they don't compete with the eroticism. The whole body lets go, allowing a buildup of energy that feels highly charged and exhilarating. In *The Pleasure Zone*, I described it this way: "Whereas lust can frequently be mental and even verbal, in passion it seems as though all thought ceases and the body is shot full of electricity. There is no holding back, no boundaries to hold on to. The only thing possible to do is to completely and utterly surrender to the flood of excitement overpowering the mind and the senses."

Heavy breathing, a rapid heartbeat, increased sweating, sounds escaping from the throat, and moaning and groaning are some of the signs of a mounting passion. All of it is stoked by the thrilling sensations of the genitals and the entire pelvic area preparing for sexual surrender.

Orgasm

The Big O, for a lot of men and women, is the major attraction of sex, and the sooner they get there, the happier they are. But it's like everything else: the more you put into it, the more you get out of it.

An orgasm typically lasts about six seconds, involves three or four intense contractions of the muscles in the genitals, and can include the entire pelvic floor, the anal sphincter, and, in women, the uterus.

With some added attention, orgasms can become even more satisfying. With continued stimulation, some women and men are capable of multiple orgasms: a series of orgasms occurring within seconds that can grow more and more intense. Multiple orgasms may be spontaneously discovered or develop as a learned skill.

There are also blended orgasms. In a man, that might involve stimulation of the anus and the prostate as well as the penis. In a woman, intense orgasms may be triggered from simultaneous stimulation of the clitoris and the vagina, or deep penetration of the vagina and brushing the cervix, or including the anus in the sex play.

According to sex researcher Barry Komisaruk and his colleagues, the parasympathetic nervous system (PNS) is critical for achieving orgasm. They report that the bonding hormone oxytocin plays a major role for both women and men during sexual excitement and orgasm. Secreted into the bloodstream by the pituitary gland, oxytocin surges just prior to and during orgasm. This hormone acts as a PNS neurotransmitter, triggering the contraction of smooth muscles in the genital area, including in the uterus. These contractions increase the perceived intensity of the orgasm and the subjective experience of pleasure.

Studies also show that this release of oxytocin, along with the release of vasopressin in men, accounts for the feelings of contentment and affection after sex and contributes to feeling emotionally bonded with your partner. In chapter 9, we'll take a more in-depth view of orgasm and the skills that can be practiced to enhance and evolve the orgasm.

Ecstasy

Ecstatic sex is not an everyday occurrence. Occasionally, the conditions are just right. You and your lover are feeling particularly close. Maybe you've shared a celebration together and each of you is more in touch with feeling blessed to have the other. Maybe you haven't seen each other in a while and you've missed each other.

You start to make love, and your kisses are more tender than usual; your body movements are more rhythmically in sync. You feel like you're in a fluid sensual dance together. After the first orgasm, you may find yourselves flowing from orgasm to orgasm. You may reach a point where you feel merged into one body, soaring through space.

Ecstatic sex is a transcendent experience that lifts you out of ordinary reality. Spiritual traditions for thousands of years have celebrated sexuality as a vehicle for personal transformation.

In Western religions, sexuality is dealt with cautiously and with many restrictions. Yogic scholar Georg Feuerstein, however, describes a wide range of spiritual disciplines, including Tantrism, Hinduism, Chinese Taoism, and even some forms of Jewish and Christian mysticism that teach erotic practices as a gateway to the spiritual dimension. All of these practices share a focus on developing the ability to achieve relaxed excitement: staying serene as you reach and maintain high states of sexual arousal.

Erotic Play

As we have seen, the process of play is generating a great deal of interest among neuroscientists as a major factor in fostering resilience, flexibility, new learning, and positive emotions in people. To Bowling Green neuroscientist Jaak Panksepp, the best place to look for happiness is in play. He observed that play triggers a flood of dopamine, making you feel engaged, happy, and optimistic. Playful activity affects the neural circuitry of the brain, reducing negative thoughts and feelings and enhancing *neuroplasticity*, the ability of the brain to become rewired and evolve. Just as romance is a playful way of expressing your love, eroticism is a playful way to arouse desire and sexual pleasure.

Erotic Play versus Married Sex

So far we've looked at a vast number of issues that can interfere with maintaining desire and becoming aroused in the context of an intimate love relationship. Now we are going to tackle one of the biggest issues to overcome: the tendency to give up sexual playfulness. A big contributor to the loss of desire in a committed relationship is what I call "married sex."

You don't have to be married to have married sex. You just have to be living together and following what sex researcher Shere Hite identified as "formula sex": foreplay, penetration, male ejaculation, and occasional female orgasm.

It's not just how sex is performed, but where and when. Typically, married sex occurs in bed just before going to sleep at night. If both people are into it, I'm not knocking it—on an occasional basis. But if that's the only way two people make love, it's understandable that one or both will lose interest. I think of this kind of sex as the last weary act of a long weary day.

The other aspect of married sex is that it's all or none. There's no time for real play. When people live together, they typically get into a pattern in which they are not sexually playful with each other except when they are available for intercourse. Then they engage in foreplay, a brief scripted pattern that occurs once they've agreed to intercourse. The contract is for an orgasm for at least one of them. The goal is to get it on, get it off, and get to sleep.

As a result, such a couple is likely to have no reserve of sexual energy. At the point at which the partners agree to "have sex," they are likely to have intercourse before they're fully aroused.

Erotic Playfulness

Erotic playfulness involves acting in lighthearted ways that maintain a sexual aliveness in the relationship. The time invested may be very brief, perhaps only a few seconds when a quick good-bye kiss becomes one partner's inspiration for a longer, wetter kiss and a smile. Ten seconds here or ten minutes there is like money in a special bank—one that actually builds interest.

Erotic Play and Arousal

Arousal is the number one requirement for great sex. Oddly, I've heard both women and men say that they're waiting for the feeling of desire to motivate them to be sexually playful. To me that's putting the cart before the horse.

Sexy is as sexy does. Erotic playfulness evokes feelings of desire and not the other way around. It takes a long time to warm a cold engine. It makes more sense to run the motor once in a while.

After adolescence, most people require regular stimulation to keep up sexual interest. Even the most fleeting erotic play contributes energy toward staying sexually motivated.

Being a Sex Object

I know some people have a knee-jerk reaction to being objectified, as though it means your partner doesn't appreciate your many good qualities and wants you only for sex. But if you want to feel sexy, then that's not the time to be appreciated for your mind or for all the good you do in the world. It's only about feeling good in your body. If you and your partner love and respect each other, it's not a debasement to be a sex object for him or her. It's a tribute.

Body Image

A major hindrance to allowing oneself to be a sex object is a negative body image, also known as body dysphoria. Thanks to a multitude of cultural factors—magazines, television, movies, and the fashion, cosmetic, and diet industries, women in particular are barraged with unrealistic images of what they're supposed to look like to be sexually attractive.

One survey led by Pennsylvania State University professor Patricia Barthalow Koch found that the emphasis in American culture on being young and thin has a more damaging influence than menopause on sexual functioning and satisfaction. Almost a fourth of the survey respondents reported feeling dissatisfied with their bodies, in particular their belly, hips, and thighs.

In some studies, a woman's weight gain after marriage was shown to result in a decrease in sexual interest in the woman by her husband. But that could also be an effect of how weight gain changed the woman's behavior toward her husband.

Sexologist and sex coach Patti Britton considers body dysphoria to be the greatest block to sexual self-acceptance and fulfillment, particularly for women, suggesting that a woman who does not see herself as desirable is very likely to lose her desire for sex. She reports that many women she has worked with have a misguided image not only of the female body but also of female genitalia, thinking that their clitoris is too small or their labia too big. That has been my clinical experience as well.

Men are also affected by negative body image, with their discomfort typically focused on the size of their genitals. Men with body dysphoria may think of themselves as scrawny or out of proportion and, like body-dysphoric women, are typically very critical of their mirror image. Gay men are subject to anxieties about remaining physically buff to keep their partners attracted.

In my experience, some of the most attractive people are the most insecure about their appearance. Good-looking people don't necessarily enjoy sex any more than plain-looking people do. Rita Hayworth, the stunning Hollywood star and sex symbol of the 1940s, became very discouraged by her lovers. She was reported to have lamented that they went to bed with Gilda—the sultry erotic dancer in the film of the same name—but they woke up to just Rita.

Body image is just that: an image. If you have a rigid standard, like a template by which you measure yourself, and a fierce inner judge, you are going to hide your body and shrink inside, no matter how you really look.

Highly self-critical people are missing the point. It's not how you look that counts, but *how it feels to be with you*. It's your personality, liveliness, and dynamism that make your imperfect body attractive and sexy. Your enthusiasm in the moment is your best quality.

Evolving an Erotic Body Image

To fully allow yourself to be somebody's sex object, you have to be willing to be playful and to get over how you look. Here's my prescription for making peace with physical imperfection and embracing an erotic spirit. I have used it myself throughout the years.

Take a good look at yourself naked in the mirror—the living and vibrant creature that you are—and focus your attention on what you *do* like about your body. Savor your good points. Then look honestly at the rest of it and practice shrugging off whatever you don't particularly like. Depending on your mood, tell yourself, "Looking go-o-od!" or "So what! This is it—get over it!" Those are the only two choices. It has worked for me.

For clients with unrealistic images about real female and male bodies, I like to show them drawings by erotic artist and sex educator Betty Dodson. Her portraits of female and male genitalia show the beauty to be seen in the great variety of shapes and sizes of the vulva, clitoris, and inner labia of different women and of the penis and testicles of different men.

I also appreciate television series like HBO's *Real Sex* or some of the shows on Showtime that challenge people's images of who and what is sexy. In a Variety.com review, *Real Sex* was described as "exploring the modern sexual world and its fetishes in a provocative, entertaining and informative manner, without ever becoming sleazy. . . . Segments highlight individuals and groups whose occupations and leisure activities revolve around sexual adventures."

Whatever these randy explorers are up to, whether they are sitting naked in a class on how to masturbate or how to give oral sex or are in costume attending the Erotic Masquerade Ball, they are all having a nonjudgmental good time acting sexy. There are thin people and heavy people, people in their twenties and older folks. It's quirky and silly and depicts some activities that to me look decidedly unappealing. But it challenges old images about sex, and for that it's illuminating.

For people ill at ease in their bodies, one suggestion I make for enhancing bodily self-acceptance is to practice walking or dancing around the house naked when no one else is home.

Your Partner as an Object of Desire

Thinking of your partner as a sex object is the other half of the sexual equation. That may be really easy for people whose partners are attractive to them but more challenging for those whose sweeties are not in great shape.

To get more turned on to your partner, you may have to become more forgiving, probably toward both of you. You also want to enjoy your partner not just for looks but also for his or her manner, playful personality, warmth, smell, sensitivity, and especially enthusiasm for you.

I once saw a T-shirt that read "I may not be perfect but parts of me are excellent." I found it inspirational. It's certainly less daunting to think in terms of perfecting parts rather than achieving perfection, particularly as you get older. The body does change with the years, and that's the reality of the situation.

No-Strings Erotic Play

If lovers get away from the notion that sexual activity, once begun, should proceed straightaway to a finish, then they can really develop their creativity. I suggest to the couples I work with that a good guiding principle is to be erotically playful, especially when they aren't available for intercourse.

I think of it as having sex more often than having intercourse. That way, when partners do have the time and inclination to devote to fully making love, they're starting up warm.

Before we look at how lovers can intensify their sexual experience, let's look at just a sampling of the different kinds of erotic play and anticipation two people can get into. Each of these can be pleasurable in itself without it having to lead to anything more.

Developing Your Erotic Personality

Some people have a way of dressing or a way of acting that makes them feel sexy. It's like having an erotic alter ego. For a woman it might be wearing dangling earrings or spike heels that she wouldn't wear outside the house. For a man, feeling sexy may entail putting on silk Lycra bikini briefs, or a revealing thong or just unbuttoning his shirt and showing some chest.

I've heard women complain that their partners are too eager and that it doesn't give them an opportunity to get into their alluring temptress persona. One woman told me that she even asked her husband to please hold back when she started to come on to him because it turned her on to seduce him.

Erotic Focus

Distractibility is the enemy of sexual passion. To get into your playful erotic personality, you have to hone your ability to be attentive to the moment.

For most of us busy people who do five things at once, a big part of that skill depends on learning to compartmentalize. To tap into the body's natural sexual reservoir of energy, you can do only this one thing: pay attention to your lover. This means that barring emergencies, you put aside all other concerns so you can be present with him or her in the spirit of the moment.

Getting sexy, even for just a few minutes, is a playful time-out. Whether you get into it for a moment, the next ten minutes, or the next hour, you are nowhere else but right here. Sexual pleasure is a great way to learn how to focus and be attentive to an ongoing experience.

A Sexy Come-On

An often overlooked element of the lovemaking experience is the come-on. The best come-ons are simply a declaration of appreciation of the other's fine qualities without demands or expectations.

When the recipient of a come-on responds warmly and moves forward, the two people are engaged in erotic playfulness. But even then the erotic energy may simply be a brief pleasurable connection that is delightful in its own right. It could be a kiss that lingers, a deep gaze into each other's eyes, a sensuous hug, a cute comment uttered in a soft tone of voice, or an invitation to dance. A playful come-on is a shot of erotic energy.

Pleasurable come-ons draw your partner to you. The responsive partner picks up on the sensuous connection and adds his or her own playful seductiveness.

Making Out to Music

An extended period of erotic play may or may not lead to something more. One example of this is making out to music. Kissing and caressing each other with mellow music in the background is a time-honored ritual, for good reason. It brings two bodies into a sensuous rhythm with each other. You're sharing your biochemistry, breathing in each other's pheromones, and caressing sensitive nerve endings on the skin to playfully awaken each other's bodies to pleasure. It's even better when you light a few candles.

Some partners also enjoy taking a hot bath in candlelight, soaking quietly while listening to soft music. They may give each other foot rubs or soap each other up on different parts of their bodies. Taking into account the constraints of the tub, they may be able to find different ways to sit or lie together in the water, bodies pressed up against each other.

Erotic Touching and Massage

Another possibility for an extended period of erotic play is erotic massage. One of the great joys of lovemaking is the touching: being squeezed, hugged, fondled, and caressed. Taking turns gently kneading the tense muscles in each other's back and butt can be highly erotic, especially when accompanied by kisses, little licks, or nibbles in different places on each other's body.

Not everybody likes to keep things gentle. One woman who had lost interest in having sex told me that she would enjoy her husband spanking her but that he refused because he considered spanking abusive. When they came in together as a couple, we talked about how spanking could be an act of playfulness rather than punishment. Furthermore, for people who carry tension in the butt, some sweet slaps on the rear can release holding in the entire pelvic area. He finally got it. She became more turned on to him, not just because of the butt slaps that loosened up her pelvis but also because he listened to her.

Notable Sexual Manuals

The *Kama Sutra*, first published in English in 1883, is an ancient Hindu text that is considered the classic work on how to make love. It is believed to have been written in the second century as a guide to *kama*, love. According to Hindu teaching, *kama*, *dharma* (right conduct), *artha* (wealth), and *moksha* (liberation, or salvation) are the four main goals and critical achievements of life. The book is best known for its detailed descriptions of sexual positions.

Most sex manuals today continue to emphasize sexual positions or behaviors. Alex Comfort's *The Joy of Sex* is probably the most notable manual of modern times for its influence during the sexual revolution of the seventies. It was the first illustrated sex manual to be published in the United States and remained on the *New York Times* best-seller list for two years between 1972 and 1974.

The Joy of Sex was illustrated with Asian erotica and pencil drawings of a modern couple engaging in a variety of practices, including oral sex, decidedly nonmissionary positions, and ways to enjoy sexual bondage. In doing so, it sought to allay feelings of sexual shame and to promote the notion that sex was fun.

Since that time, there have been numerous sex manuals on how to make love. Some of the most recent and best include *The Great Sex Weekend* by Pepper Schwartz and Janet Lever, *The Great Lover Playbook* by Lou Paget, and *Loving Sex* by Laura Berman.

Unlike a sex manual, step eight in our program aims to expand your erotic repertoire without emphasizing techniques for pleasing a lover.

Step Eight: Erotic Play

Objectives: To widen your range of erotic pleasures with your lover and to experiment with new ways of doing familiar activities

A body-mind approach to emotionally gratifying sexual pleasure is not so much about positions or what you're doing, but more about how present you are in your body as you're doing it. In essence, it's about how mindful and tuned in you are to yourself and to your lover.

Erotic play is completely dependent on your ability to play. If sex is serious business to you and something to get to right away, you won't be expanding your repertoire. You'll be impatient to get on with it, and *it* will be the same old *it*.

Everyday Eroticism

Romantic play is the precursor to erotic play. You can't expect your partner to be able to make the switch from friend, roommate, or parent to lover on a dime. Erotic play is something you cozy up to, and romantic play is the intro.

What works best is to weave romantic, sensuous, and erotic play into the fabric of your everyday life. An appreciative comment, a warm appreciative look and a smile, a lingering kiss, and a full body hug all keep two people physically attuned to each other.

A few minutes of erotic play here and there when your partner is available or can be enticed can build up a store of sexual energy, especially if you walk away from each other while you're turned on. It keeps the engine warm and the battery charged.

Make a Date for Erotic Play

Some couples have a date night to make love, but they don't leave much time for erotic play, and that keeps their sexual repertoire very limited. They may end up making love at the low end of the erotic spectrum, at *sexual interest*, and never get to *desire* or *passion*.

Set aside some time with your partner to have an erotic date that doesn't necessarily have to end in intercourse. You might start briefly in the morning if you have to leave each other for the day.

See how many of the elements of eroticism detailed below you can include when you and your lover have set aside time to play:

- Come on to your lover. Play at being sexy. Talk sexy and act sexy. Don't take yourself too seriously. Just do it for fun.

- Show your erotic personality. How does your erotic self dress and play?

- Make out to music. Dim the lights, cuddle, kiss, fondle, and stroke each other.

- Touch and massage each other sensuously. Give pleasure.

- Play dress-up. If you both like role-playing games, see if you can expand your repertoire of roles to entice each other.

- Stay erotically and empathically attuned. Breathe fully, kiss deeply, make sweet talk, and take turns giving each other pleasure.

9

Ultimate Pleasures

Suppose we have two people who—aside from everything else that's going on in their lives—repair their upsets sooner rather than later, are sensitive to each other's bodily rhythms, and have maintained an ongoing physical intimacy with special moments of romantic and erotic playfulness.

They breathe and hold each other for a few minutes every day. They make eye contact when they talk. They sometimes disagree or get angry with each other, but they also get over it. They help each other to calm down, and they make each other laugh. They like to kiss.

What, then, can turn a comfortable moment into the "right moment"? And what can make the right moment absolutely wonderful? We're now ready to talk about sex.

Hot and Loving Sex

First of all, what's *hot*? If you take your cues from the movies or from pornographic videos, much of it does not represent the best of genuinely hot sex.

Sex on film is an actor's performance of a director's fantasy. It's a pretense of hot that may be pretty good and arousing to watch, but it's acting. It's also usually a depiction of a cultural stereotype in a bed, against a wall, or the highly unlikely and overworked kitchen table.

Real hot is less of a show. Real hot is more internal and is unchoreographed: breathing, moving, shifting energies, fast, slow, motionless, panting, holding your breath, feeling. One partner is active, the other is allowing. Top becomes bottom and bottom becomes top. It's energized yet relaxed. More and more excitement builds internally, like rivulets of warmth spreading through the body as the muscles relax, let go, and surrender.

But we're getting ahead of ourselves.

We are about to take an unabashed view of lovemaking skills. Making love is a series of activities, each of which depends on the focused involvement, graceful movements, empathy, and generosity of the participants.

Lovemaking is probably one of the most complex human processes we ever engage in. We don't give ourselves enough credit for being able to accomplish this complicated series of actions and feelings as well as we do. Just think about it. Making love involves a sequence of highly unique behaviors, usually accompanied by an array of mixed emotions, in order to reach a greatly valued goal that we may judge ourselves by, which may or may not be achieved. What's worse, we generally learn to do it by trial and error, without much guidance or good information.

The Expanded Erotic Repertoire

So here we are, adults who are capable of regaining our authentic erotic nature and directing our own sexual evolution. How can body-mindfulness energize the erotic life of a committed couple?

Erotic Attunement

Just as holding, breathing, and looking into each other's eyes bring two people into *emotional* attunement, kissing and caressing eroticizes those activities and brings them into *erotic* attunement. The two are communicating through nature's own formidable martini, the biochemical cocktail in their saliva, passing varying levels of adrenaline, dopamine, oxytocin, estrogen, and testosterone back and forth. Pheromones released in their sweat are like microscopic stimulants sent through the air and drawn into the nose and passed to the brain with each breath.

As they hold and stroke each other, the partners' breathing patterns come into sync, and their brains and their nervous systems, both the sympathetic and the parasympathetic branches, are getting charged. They are hooking up into an interactive wireless and wordless communication.

Even when the partners are talking, it's what their bodies are saying that counts. There's a kind of positive emotional contagion going on: two people catching each other's breathing rhythms and heartbeats in a sensuous, pleasurable dance that both soothes and excites. They don't need verbal feedback to know how the other enjoys being touched in this moment, because they are in resonance and can feel it empathically. Each one is reading it in the lover's breathing, in his or her movements and sounds, and feeling the same way.

Intensifying Erotic Pleasures

For any activity to be erotically stimulating, it has to be experienced as genitally arousing, even if the activity is nowhere near the genitals. It may start off as a kind of bioelectric buzz in the pelvic area. A man may notice his scrotum tighten as his penis stiffens. As studies show, a woman may not be as aware of her genital signals as a man is. But with bodily awareness and mindfulness, a woman will feel her clitoris throbbing or her vagina getting wet, or even her uterus tugging at her cervix.

Erotic energy naturally ebbs and flows as the energy shifts between partners, but excitation is cumulative. After a short rest, sensations of excitement build back up quickly and grow more intensely pleasurable.

The more the excitement builds and spreads throughout the body, the greater the intensity of sensation. The more fully embodied the sexual experience, the more fulfilling the orgasms. A person can feel turned on from the top of the head through the belly and down to the toes. Then orgasm becomes a total body release.

Building Anticipation

Sex therapist and researcher Jack Morin, in his studies of peak erotic experiences, considered longing and anticipation to be erotic intensifiers, because each emotional state can maximize arousal and contribute to memorable sexual experiences. Both are fueled by the space between the arousal of desire and the possibility of fulfillment.

Longing is typically more long-term, such as when the lover is absent or unavailable, and leads to prolonged and sometimes painful yearning. Anticipation is more short-term and hopeful, and the longer the feeling of eager anticipation builds, such as through flirting or teasing, the more powerful the desire will be.

Pleasurable Wanting

The late psychologist Abraham Maslow, the founder of humanistic psychology, a school of thought derived from studying people who are productive and happy in their lives, would have concurred. Maslow discovered that these "self-actualizers," as he called them, consistently enjoyed the state of need. He called it "pleasurable wanting."

He noted that, whereas insecure or unfulfilled individuals were more likely to feel frustration when a challenge delayed reward, individuals motivated by growth more typically welcomed the postponement of gratification. It's like solving a puzzle or developing a skill: the greater the effort expended in making it happen, the greater the pleasure at its achievement.

Pleasurable wanting during lovemaking involves the same kind of ability: allowing a need to grow stronger and stronger and relishing the craving. The higher the arousal, the more intense and prolonged the pleasure.

Pleasurable Containment

Enjoying pleasurable wanting is an aspect of containment: holding on to sexy feelings rather than aiming for a quick climax. You hold on to the excitement not by holding the breath and tensing the muscles of the torso, but by breathing into them and opening them. Imagine the way a balloon expands to accommodate the air you blow into it. That's how the breath expands the body to allow the flow of blood and the felt-sense awareness of sexual desire.

You breathe deeply and feel the movement in the chest and the rib cage, expanding the back and the torso, filling and releasing the belly, relaxing and warming the pelvis and the genitalia. Breathing into the sensations of arousal intensifies the arousal.

Nongenital Stimulation

Taking the time to stimulate and make love to the whole body is one of the most reliable ways of intensifying sexual pleasure and increasing the likelihood of fully embodied arousal and orgasms. The best way for partners to awaken each other's body to pleasure is to kiss and stroke unexpected areas. Loving attention may start at the face, the ears, the neck, and the shoulders. The crooks of the arms, the wrists, the hands and the fingers, the small of the back, behind the knees, and the ankles—areas where the blood flows close to the surface of the skin—are particularly sensitive to warm tender kisses and licking. The inner thighs, the butt, the calves, the feet, and the toes can also be highly sensitive to gentle stimulation and when given some loving treatment, can contribute enormously to each other's excitement. Here are some more obvious examples of nongenital eroticism.

Breast and Nipple Eroticism

Some of the most intimate places to touch on the human body are the breasts and nipples. Most of us grew up knowing how important "second base" was. When you "pet," this is where sex really starts.

It's sexually thrilling to be an adolescent girl of fifteen and to be kissing and getting felt up by a boy. It's thrilling for the boy as well, who is playing with her soft nubile breasts and responsive nipples and feeling his erection.

How soon we forget. When we're blinded by the light of hitting a "home run," "second base" often gets a perfunctory fly-by. But this area can be a trove of erotic passions. Many women regularly incorporate nipple stimulation in their masturbation. Some have reported that they can bring themselves to orgasm just by stimulating their nipples.

A woman's breasts, along with the muscles of the chest, can be massaged delicately and with sensitivity. They can be kissed. Nipples can be licked and sucked. Many men enjoy sensitive and sensual stimulation of their nipples and also appreciate their lovers' attention to their chests.

Anal Eroticism

The anus has a high concentration of nerve endings, shares pelvic muscles with the genitals, and contracts with the genitals during orgasm. According to the University of Chicago "Sex in America" survey, about 25 percent of men and women indicated that they had had anal intercourse in their lifetimes and more than 10 percent indicated that it was a significant part of their erotic repertoire.

Sex researcher and therapist Jack Morin, who has researched anal pleasure and health, has pointed out that anal intercourse is the least practiced form of anal eroticism. More commonly, the anal opening may be stroked during masturbation or during times of oral sex.

Some men and women enjoy having a finger or a small dildo inserted during various sexual activities. Once a finger or dildo has been in contact with the anus, however, it should be kept out of contact with the vagina.

Morin advises that anal stimulation should be discontinued if it's at all painful. He also suggests that the best time to explore anal pleasure is often immediately after a bath or a shower.

Naughty Fantasy and Role-Playing

If both partners are into it, lovers can enjoy talking sexy or making up erotic stories to tell each other that turn up the heat. They may also create dominance and submission games to act out. There's nothing wrong with that if both people enjoy playing this way. It doesn't diminish your love for each other, and it's not abnormal.

One couple came to see me when they realized that as much as they loved each other and got along, neither of them had any interest in sex. They hadn't had sex in more than a year, and they both missed it.

When we got into talking about some of their most erotic early experiences together, each independently came up with a scenario they had acted out in a hotel room one time when they were traveling. She had gotten into acting tough and ordering him around and making him do things to her. They both had incredible orgasms. Then they never did it again.

What stopped them was that they both felt it was "sick" to act like that, and they had felt guilty about enjoying it. As we worked together in therapy, they saw how seriously they took a lot of things and how judgmental they were of themselves. They had both come from strict religious backgrounds and strove to be good people. As I came to know them, I saw that they *were* good people, not only being kind and generous to their friends and family but also donating their time to good causes.

No wonder they stopped having sex. They scared themselves. We talked about their fears, their shame, and their interpretations and how they did that in the rest of their lives as well.

We also talked about how acting out sexy scenarios, when two people agree to play and trust each other, is just a game—an adult erotic game. It was a way in which they could lose their familiar personas and lighten up. I suggested that they make up some rules about how to play safely and then to experiment with making sex more fun. It seems to have worked wonders.

On Being a Top *and* a Bottom

The biggest complaint I hear from heterosexual men who have lost interest in sex is that the women are passive. One man complained that he was always the one to come on to his wife, and when they made love, she didn't do much to touch or pleasure him. He thought that she took a lot more than she gave.

Some men complain that their wives or girlfriends think it's up to the man to turn the woman on and to give her an orgasm, as though she has nothing to do with it. I've also heard women voice that belief.

One man told me that his girlfriend was so passive with him that he felt utterly bored with their sex. Nothing happened between them sexually that he didn't initiate. When he told her that he would like her to be more active, she felt criticized and hurt.

Straight women also sometimes complain that the men take too much charge over what is happening sexually and there's no room for the women. One woman told me that her husband completely takes over when they make love, and she typically feels left out. It's as though he goes into a trance. "He can't even seem to remember what I like," she growled in frustration. "And we've been together twelve years!"

The terms *top* and *bottom* are often used to describe the more active and more passive sex partner, respectively. Sex educators Simon LeVay and Sharon Valente attribute the terms to the gay and lesbian community, in which tops are considered to be the partners who assume the dominant role and bottoms are submissive. This typecasting can be very limiting. One gay man came to see me after he and his partner broke up after four years together. He was mournful, but he said they never had sex. They were both tops.

A woman in a ten-year relationship with another woman described her partner as a perpetual bottom, and she was getting tired of doing all of the work in sex. "I'm not as butch as I look," she said, "and sometimes I'd love to lie back and play femme."

LeVay and Valente cite evidence to show that since the 1970s and the early years of the gay liberation movement, gays and lesbians have been discovering the limitations of those terms. The researchers suggest that it was a way for the community to conform to traditional gender roles. Although some may still refer to themselves with these terms, surveys show that gay sex is, in reality, more versatile and that compatible partners typically switch between being dominant and being receptive.

With my gay male client, the fact that he and his partner were both tops was actually just a small part of why they broke up after four years. As he reflected on their relationship, he saw that they were inflexible with each other in many other ways as well.

Heterosexual partners also benefit from diversifying. The most exciting sexual activity occurs between partners who take turns being active and passive. In that way, the one on the bottom gets to relax and surrender to the pleasures of receiving. Then, infused with energy, he or she rolls on top and gets to be the giver.

For the man who was disappointed in the routine male-dominant sex with his passive girlfriend, we looked at how he had approached her. He was angry, he said, and he let her know it. I could hear the resentment in his voice, so I understood how she might feel criticized and hurt. I suggested that he try a more playful approach.

A week later he had some good news. One night when they were kissing he pulled her on top of him and whispered in her ear, "Come on, gorgeous, show me who's boss." He said she looked at him in surprise. But when he smiled and whispered the words again while gently sucking her earlobe, she began to bounce on him, and they both laughed. It was a great moment, he said, that turned very hot soon after that. Once again, sweet and friendly is the best message.

Masterful Lovemaking

Those who take pride in their lovemaking know that direct genital stimulation is best left for last. It's only when other parts of the body have been fully aroused that skilled lovers turn their attention to maximizing genital pleasures. Studies have shown that building anticipation and longing for genital touch is one of the most effective ways to intensify sexual excitement and orgasmic release.

We're now ready to go for the ultimate pleasures two people can experience with each other.

Genital Stimulation

Genitals are like snowflakes: no two are alike. What turns us on and gets us off is completely subjective and individualistic. The best sex expert on how to stimulate your partner's genitals is your partner.

During lovemaking is generally not a good time to be giving or taking verbal instructions—unless, of course, it's done in a sexy and appreciative way that can make the moment even hotter. Otherwise, I tell people to talk it over later.

Even better, I recommend doing a "dry run": get sexy together in a playful way specifically for the purpose of sharing favorite hot spots on the body and your preferred ways of moving and being touched. You never know—some dry runs have pleasantly unintended consequences.

The major practices of direct genital stimulation are *frottage*, *hand skills*, *oral skills*, and *penetration*. All of these natural sexual activities can be developed and refined for maximum pleasure and emotional connection. All it takes is consistent practice.

Frottage

Frottage, or dry humping, is essentially two people rubbing genitals together, with or without clothing, as a way to build sexual excitement or to achieve orgasm without penetration. It's an early favorite of adolescents and a popular form of arousal and release among lesbians and gay men.

According to Urbandictionary.com, frottage has become more prevalent among singles due to the increased awareness of sexually transmitted diseases. Subtle forms of frottage between dancing partners are reported to be occurring more frequently at music concerts and nightclubs.

Frottage can be very hot, even for long-term couples. Like everything else, nuanced frotting involves skill and improves with practice.

Hand Skills

Developing skills during solo eroticism can help in learning to give your partner pleasure. With empathic attunement to a partner's response, skilled hands and fingers can be especially adept at intensifying sexual pleasure without aiming for release.

Oral Skills

Cunnilingus and fellatio as part of the erotic repertoire apparently go way back in history. Despite the typical nonsexual translation of the biblical book Song of Songs (also called Song of Solomon), some references suggest that the tenth-century poem's lines that describe the princess's navel as a rounded "goblet that never lacks blended wine" is more likely an allusion to sipping at her vagina. Fellatio has been depicted in scenes on ancient Greek and Peruvian ceramics and in erotic temples in India that go as far back as 1200 BC.

The Egyptian goddess of magic and fertility, Isis, is said to have restored the god-king Osiris back to life by gathering up his body parts, which had been strewn throughout the land of Egypt after a battle. Failing to find his penis, which had been swallowed by a fish, she fashioned one out of clay, and putting it to her lips, she blew life into it. Could this be an ancient derivation of the term *blow job*?

Nowadays, oral sex has been reported to be prevalent among young teenagers. Ironically, many don't consider it to be sex, and therefore they see it as an act that can be performed without sacrificing virginity.

Giving and receiving "head" or going down on each other is probably one of the most enjoyable sexual activities for both men and women.

Penetrating Options

There are many different kinds of penetration. Both a man and a woman may be penetrated with fingers, a tongue, or a dildo and experience intense orgasms and emotional connection with a partner.

The term *penetration* can refer to heterosexual intercourse as well as gay and lesbian sex. Although this discussion at times specifically addresses penis-vagina intercourse, much of it also holds for the sexual activities of same-sex lovers.

Whether you call it coitus, intercourse, fucking, banging, balling, or getting lucky, penetration is what most people really think of when they talk about making love. Much has already been written about how to do it and the variety of positions to maneuver, replete with drawings or photographs.

From a body-mind perspective, three aspects of penetration bear emphasis: *entry, internal movements,* and *tempo.*

Entry. For lovers, entry is a defining moment. When to insert the penis takes physiological readiness, signs of assent, and physical cooperation on both sides. At its best, it is a moment of high erotic attunement, communicating through breath and sighs, eye contact, vocal sounds, kisses, responsiveness to touch, and rhythmic movements of the torso and pelvis.

I've heard women say that how their lovers enter them is a turnoff. If a man is too forceful, pushes too hard, or pinches her skin, it can be a painful or anxious moment for both. That's why relaxing and taking your time to be erotically attuned at that moment is so important.

Lubrication is crucial for smooth entry, and if the body doesn't lubricate sufficiently, there's nothing wrong with adding a lubricant. A number of commercial and healthy products are available; however, if you use condoms, choose carefully, because oil-based lubricants can weaken latex and cause the condom to tear. I think saliva is the best lubricant because it's always handy wherever you are and can be easily applied with a tongue or moistened fingers.

Internal movements. These are the movements made once you have achieved entry. The emphasis in the literature on sexual position is related to the fact that different positions stimulate different sensations and orgasms of different intensities or qualities. Two people who breathe, relax, and stay engaged can explore different movements together that can generate a high degree of passion and thrilling sensations. They can hold a deep penetration and make grinding movements, point the penis up, to one side and then the other, and slide along the bottom wall of the vagina. Each angle feels distinctive and special.

Tempo. Rhythm is another critical factor for changing the variety of orgasmic sensations. Sometimes intercourse is deliberate, with both partners focused as the well-lubricated penis glides millimeter by millimeter along the walls of the vagina. In the spirit of fitness, I think of this as full range of motion or *slow-and-easy* sex. Other times intercourse is fast and hard—what might be considered *cardio* sex. Studies have shown multiple fitness benefits from the exercise in an athletic style of lovemaking.

Mutual Orgasms

Like every other aspect of our growing selves, with skill and mindfulness, orgasms with a partner can also evolve.

When most people think of orgasm, they think of it as the pinnacle of sex and the end of the lovemaking. It's followed by the proverbial slow draw of success on a cigarette, or maybe the "afterglow," lying bonded in mutual exhaustion in each other's arms.

Still, that doesn't have to be the end of sex. The most intense pleasures can come after the first orgasm. Orgasms can come in multiples and, with proficiency, one orgasm can be a harbinger of more intense orgasms to come, each with its own unique set of sensations and moments of excitation and abandonment. To attain this quality of orgasmic experience, lovers can practice achieving a quality of erotic attunement with each other in which minds, hearts, and bodies are totally in sync.

Orgasms with Heart

With all this kissing and touching, warm lingering gazes, relaxing and breathing deeply, two people who love each other will be able to feel sensations of love in their hearts. The unmistakable felt-sense of love is experienced as a kind of swelling or glowing sensation in the chest.

Alexander Lowen, a student of Wilhelm Reich and the founder of bioenergetics, cited evidence to show that in both men and women, a lack of emotional satisfaction during sex is statistically associated with a greater incidence of coronary disease and heart attacks. Lowen referred to climaxes as being full-hearted, half-hearted, or having very little heart, and he suggested that when the heart is open and in touch with love, an individual can have a full-body orgasm that "embraces the heart and . . . approaches the ecstatic." That's what I call a *heartgasm*.

In studies, both sexes identified emotional satisfaction—qualities like a partner's warmth and closeness—as even more critical than orgasm to feel fulfilled in sex. Naturally, it's nice to have both.

Two people in loving erotic attunement are fully present in their bodies and focused on their love. They're "into" each other, and they can feel it. It shows in their eyes when they look at each other. Their hearts are pumping, sometimes with a slow steady pounding, sometimes with a fast skipping beat. As their bodies surrender into the excitement, blood flows freely through their bellies and into the pelvic areas, heightening genital excitement.

Ecstasy: Magical Sex

Every once in a while, all the elements just seem to mesh perfectly, and the sex is magical. Maybe you have been away from each other and have longed to be together. Maybe your partner did something especially tender, and you're in touch with powerful feelings of love and gratitude. Your lovemaking feels beautiful, smooth, and natural. You're both on the same wavelength, moving in rhythm, making breathy, passionate sounds as your hearts fill with love. When you start to climax, the orgasms flow one after another and spread throughout your entire body. You completely surrender, abandoning yourself to this exquisite moment. The boundary between you and your partner seems to melt, and you are soaring through space, one-body boundless, in touch with the eternal. You are experiencing an altered state of consciousness.

It's been called knock-your-socks-off sex, peak sex, sacred sex, and cosmic orgasm. When it just happens, it's very special. The high can last for weeks, with repercussions that may last a lifetime.

Canadian author and yoga scholar Georg Feuerstein sent out questionnaires and studied the first-person accounts of men and women who had had extraordinary, mystical, or transcendent experiences during sex. His respondents overwhelmingly described experiences resulting in psychological or spiritual breakthroughs that healed feelings of guilt, shame, and fear and that expanded their creativity, compassion, and ability to love.

For those seeking a more deliberate method to achieving a transcendent state through sexual ecstasy, there are various paths. Tantric yoga, with both Buddhist and Hindu branches, is thought to have originated more than five thousand years ago, and today it is probably the most widespread spiritual sexual system still practiced.

Traditionally, Tantra is a set of rituals two people practice together in a state of stillness and relaxed concentration that begins with honoring each other and the male and female principle—Shiva and Shakti—within them. In a very distilled

version of a basic practice, tantric initiates sit cross-legged opposite each other and engage in gazing at each other and matching
breaths. When the man is erect, they engage in *yabyum*, a sexual
position in which the woman sits on the man, inserts his penis
into her vagina, and crosses her legs around his waist. The traditional practice is for the man to maintain an erection with minimal
movement while reserving his ejaculation.

Modern-day Tantra, or neo-Tantra, has grown increasingly
popular for those who value the spiritual dimensions of sex. Sex
researcher and therapist Gina Ogden advocates the use of some of
the tantric rituals for couples who want to move beyond physical
sensation and into the realm of higher consciousness.

In these Eastern-inspired practices, sex becomes a form of
worship. The couple stays focused and attentive and engages in
a variety of breathing and gazing practices, including penetration
without thrusting. Once again, we can see the principle of containment at work. As Ogden describes it, both the man and the
woman learn to delay orgasm in order to enter "a state of shared
physical and spiritual bliss."

A woman with a strong PC muscle may also be able to contract and relax her vagina around the man's penis in a motion that
can give them both enormous pleasure. The practice, known as
pompoir, or "playing the flute," can be traced back to a sixteenth-
century Indian text in which it was considered an important part
of a woman's training to be a wife.

A woman with the ability to grip the penis and to make rip-
pling and milking contractions with her vagina is called a *kabazzah*.
The man is to remain completely passive as the woman sits on his
erect penis, moving only the muscles of her vagina in an action
similar to milking a cow.

Exploring the Erotic Spectrum

I hope I have conveyed the vast spectrum of erotic experiences
that can be savored and cultivated. It's like developing a taste for

classical music or jazz or becoming an artist or an athlete: it's all about honing a set of skills that can grow over the years.

There's nothing wrong with married sex in bed at night when both people enjoy it as a way to end the day and fall sleep. But as a steady diet, it loses its zest. If year after year, fast food were all you ate, you'd likely lose your appetite. We deserve fine dining at least once in a while.

The time devoted to sharing love and intimate pleasures gives many rewards. When two people are fully present with each other and explore the heights and the depths of physical and emotional pleasure, it's enormously bonding. Everybody knows that it's good for a relationship, but it's also good for each individual. When you're in your body, relaxing and breathing and allowing yourself to feel pleasure, it's personally freeing. Wonderful sex lightens people up.

Step nine elaborates on these activities and offers intimate experiments to enjoy with your partner.

Step Nine: Masterful Lovemaking

Objective: To practice exchanging a wide assortment of empathic and erotically attuned genital pleasures with a lover

Genitals—female and male alike—are delicate and deserve to be approached with respect, even if you like to play rough. The skin in the vagina and on the penis is thin and fragile. The gonads in both sexes, the ovaries and the testes, hurt when thumped. Sudden grabs to the area automatically make people flinch—not the response anyone wants from a lover.

Lovers can build excitement by moving in on each other slowly and mindfully, teasing and making the other yearn to be touched. Once genital contact is made and feels safe, that area can begin to let go, become engorged, and radiate sexual energy. The following are a range of activities to explore with your lover.

Frottage

Lovers brush or rub genitals, often while fully or partially clothed. It can be done lying down, while dancing, or standing and is one of the best uses of a bare wall as a sexual prop. It's about how you look at each other as you press into each other, how you change rhythms as your excitement grows. All of it is like a finely executed dance that can be very hot.

Hand Skills on a Man

Speaking in the vernacular, a hand job for a man is more than simply jerking off. For one thing, the goal is not necessarily for him to ejaculate—it's to stimulate and to give pleasure.

- Forming a sheath with a lubricated hand and fingers and slowly sliding it up and down the shaft of the penis—giving special attention to the coronal ridge and to the head of the penis—can be especially pleasurable.

- The sounds of a man's breaths, as the lover changes rhythms or gently caresses his scrotum and other parts of his body, give clues as to what is most exciting and erotic to him.

Hand Skills on a Woman

The term *fingering* is typically used when applied to a woman, but a woman can enjoy a genital massage beyond just having fingers stroking her clitoris or inserted into her vagina. Recall that the clitoris is more than just the pea-shaped glans. The shaft of the clitoris runs under the pubic bone and the wishbone-like legs, or *crura*, run alongside the vaginal opening.

- Gently squeezing and tugging at the vulva will stimulate a woman's entire clitoral organ and can be especially exciting for her.

- When well-lubricated fingers of one hand are inserted into a woman's vagina, they can add to the pleasure felt while her clitoris is being stimulated with the other hand.

- A lover can experiment with moving at different angles, pressing in different directions, or holding the fingers all the way in and grinding, always being sensitive to the partner's sighs and moans.

- The G spot or a vaginal orgasm may be stimulated through inserting one or two fingers inside a woman and making a come-hither movement along the front wall of the vagina.

Oral Skills

For some partners, taking a bath or washing the whole pelvic area before engaging in oral sex makes the experience more pleasant. In developing oral skills, the giver can use the lips, the mouth, and the tongue creatively to kiss, lick, and gently suck the genital area.

- Men often enjoy their lovers' hands on the penis and testes while being stimulated by the mouth.

- Some women enjoy having the tongue inserted into the vagina or having one or two fingers inserted while the clitoris is licked and sucked.

- A woman may relish having her first release as a clitoral orgasm through oral sex, which may then enhance her ability to enjoy vaginal orgasms through penetration.

- A man may be able to withhold his ejaculation for the duration, or he may ejaculate and rebuild his excitement by staying erotically and energetically connected.

Penetration

For many couples, this is the high point of their sex play, the inter-mingling of the bodies, the ultimate union. When the energy has been supported through continued breathing, and they've stayed sexy, playful, and tuned in to each other, their bodies are in a state of relaxed and energized arousal.

If a man is in good health and capable of an erection, a valuable skill to develop is the ability to maintain his erection long enough to experience a variety of activities and pleasures. The key here is to recognize the point just prior to ejaculation and to stop and relax.

Containing the excitement by breathing into and expanding tense torso and pelvic muscles allows blood flow and reduces the pressure to discharge the energy. This skill can be practiced and developed during masturbation.

Lovers can vocalize their readiness for intercourse or give each other signs through their breathing or eye contact or how they position themselves vis-à-vis the other to show that they are ready.

Skills to hone for both people during penetration include how to enter or receive your lover, how to move, and how to vary the tempo.

ENTRY

Naturally, both people have to be ready, and the whole area of entry and what's being inserted both have to be fully lubricated. The one who will be entered needs to relax and to be open and welcoming.

- The best way for a man to contain his excitation and maintain his erection is to enter gradually and deliberately and to breathe. This is a delicate moment and a time to be mindful and engaged with your lover.

- Breathe deeply and fully, moving chest and torso, feeling the belly and the pelvic area opening and relaxing. Move slowly and stay attuned to the moment of joining.

- A woman who tends to take a passive role in receiving a man may enjoy experimenting with becoming the more active lover during entry, positioning herself to take him into her slowly by sitting on top and guiding him in.

- Since both the introitus and the coronal ridge are the most sensitive areas of the vagina and the penis, respectively, lovers may play at partially inserting and pulling out slowly several times before full penetration. This action may also have the effect of increasing the lubrication between them.

INTERNAL MOVEMENTS

When lovers stay erotically engaged and relaxed, they may be able to maintain penetration for quite a while—fifteen, twenty, thirty minutes, or longer. What are they doing with each other all that time?

- *Tiny motions.* Lovers can relax into each other's arms and legs and savor the moment of fully entering and fully receiving the other. Focus your attention on where you are joined together; breathe and feel. This is a good time to kiss and caress and make very small internal movements of pelvis-to-pelvis communication.

- *Slow thrusts*. The erect penis can slide low along the bottom of the vaginal canal or point up left or right. It can tap and bump the cervix lightly, or it can stay fully inserted and be stirred around in deep inner circles. All of it can feel different and exciting to both lovers.

- *Deep penetration and grinding*. For many women, this pattern is a sure bet for orgasm. It consists of thrusting in as deeply as is comfortable for both, pressing and holding the penis in, and making small grinding motions. However, the penis can also "kick" a woman's gonads and cause pain. For these reasons, the woman may need to control the movement until the man comprehends where to aim and how deeply she can tolerate him.

- *Pompoir*. A woman with a strong PC muscle may also be able to contract and relax her vagina around the man's penis in a gripping and milking motion that can give both of them pleasure. Practice your Kegels to develop these sexy skills.

TEMPO

One of the great ways in which the right music can inspire a sexual connection is that as with dance, a strong rhythm section benefits sexual movements.

- *Slow and easy—full range of motion*. Slow and deliberate allows you to attain complete penetration. This way of moving together permits lovers the greatest opportunity to eroticize the primal intimacies of holding, stroking, breathing together, eye gazing, and deep kissing.

- *Fast and hard—cardio sex*. As men approach orgasm, they are likely to speed up their thrusting movements to the point of ejaculation. Some women have vaginal orgasms during hard pumping, and when they do, the gushing fluid that often accompanies these kinds of orgasms keeps the vagina very wet and adds to the excitement of the moment.

- *Blended patterns*. When lovers want to extend their lovemaking and provide time for a variety of orgasms, the best way is to alternate slow and easy with fast and hard. That way you can slow down and catch your breath, kiss, talk, touch, and build up another head of steam to usher in yet another level of pleasure.

EVOLVING YOUR ORGASMS

Typically, an orgasm is considered the big finish, the climax that everyone aims for that signals the end of the sex. But an orgasm can be just the beginning of yet another level of passion and fulfillment. What does it take to enhance your orgasms? Here are some of the most essential qualities:

- *You have to be willing to have more.* You may be quite satisfied with the quality of your orgasms and not want to do anything different, and that's fine. You may find that your orgasms spontaneously evolve anyway. But if you do want more, you have to stay engaged and make time for it.

- *You can't force an orgasm.* If you tense your pelvic muscles, you may be able to pop out an orgasm, but it won't be much of a release. Relax and let it happen. The best orgasms build slowly and are completely spontaneous.

- *Breathe deeply.* Sighing and panting fills the chest and back and allows feelings of love. Diaphragmatic breathing opens the belly and the genitals and allows feelings of trust. For the man whose heart beats very fast at the point of entry: stop moving and breathe into your chest until your heart calms down. Look into your lover's eyes and take the time to kiss and relate.

- *Slow down to upgrade your lovemaking.* Practice shifting from being active to passive to active again—from being a sensitive-intuitive top to becoming a receptive-responsive bottom. When you feel your lover building toward orgasm, don't stop or change what you're doing. Maintain a steady movement and rhythm.

- *Enjoy simultaneous orgasms.* For heterosexual couples, the most reliable way for two people to orgasm at the same time is if the woman is capable of multiple orgasms and the man is capable of containing his ejaculation. If she orgasms first and he sustains his erection, she can have several orgasms. When he is ready to ejaculate, they will naturally come together.

- *The best orgasms of all end with feelings of love and connection.* Stay engaged. Hold each other, kiss, breathe together, and feel grateful to have this very special kind of love.

10

A Lust for Life

There are those who say that it's impossible to sustain sexual interest in one person forever and that anyone who says different is giving people false hope. I say it's not only possible, it's essential. But that one person is you.

This book has offered a wide spectrum of possibilities to nourish new vistas in you—alone or with a partner—to enhance, gain, or regain sexual aliveness. Not everything offered here will be your cup of tea, nor should it be. But I'll bet some of the things you have read have noticeably perked you up. Those are at least ideas to play with.

Besides, we go through different phases in life. We get older. What we value at one stage, we've completed by a later stage. Energy naturally shifts, ebbing and flowing in response to what's currently going on, and our sexuality varies in the same way. We do not want to pathologize these natural peaks and valleys of interest.

Love and Libido Together Again

What I have especially wanted to communicate is that love and libido are not completely independent but are intricately connected from the beginning of life until its very end. Whether we call them drives, needs, or behavioral systems, emotional attachment and the sex drive are intertwined and linked together in the brain and the nervous system. The dynamics of that connection can affect everything: your moods, self-confidence, and optimism as well as how you handle stress, your resistance to illness, how you get along with a partner, the quality of your orgasms, and your ability to abandon yourself to pleasure and to celebrate life.

The body has always occupied a central role in these explorations. This approach emphasizes body-mind methods to encourage a quality of relaxed and alert presence: breathing and letting go, coming into the moment, being mindful, calming as you energize. It promotes an awareness that the pleasures of love and libido are life affirming and relationship enriching. This approach fits in well with the new emphasis in psychology on the positive—on what makes life worth living and helps individuals and society to flourish.

Flourishing, Resilience, and Loving Connection

According to the dictionary, to *flourish* is to be strong and healthy, to thrive and prosper. Psychologists Barbara Fredrickson and Marcial Losada have defined flourishing as "living within an optimal range of human functioning, one that connotes goodness, . . . growth, and resilience."

In examining the dynamics of human flourishing, these researchers cited a broad range of evidence that good feelings have multiple benefits. These benefits include generating positive moods, widening the scope of attention, altering people's mindsets, broadening behavioral repertoires, and increasing intuition and creativity. The research clearly demonstrates that a key pre-dictor of flourishing is simply the degree to which a person's posi-tive emotions outnumber the negative ones.

A major benefit of the capacity to sustain positive emotions is that good feelings make us more resilient. *Resilience* is the highly adaptive ability to recover quickly from setbacks or adversity.

The studies showed that positive emotions ameliorate many of the ill effects of negative emotions by lowering the level of cortisol in the blood, reducing inflammation and pain, increasing a subjective sense of happiness, and boosting the immune system. In fact, the tendency to focus on what's good is even predictive of life expectancy.

Naturally, any ongoing stress is not good for you, but stress in a relationship can be particularly damaging. Researchers at the University of Utah found that women in marriages marked by hostility and strife were more likely to be depressed and to suf-fer high blood pressure, high cholesterol, and other factors that significantly raised their risk of atherosclerosis, the narrowing of the arteries that carry blood to the heart.

For men, it wasn't hostility that made the difference, but rather control. Those who had controlling wives or were themselves con-trolling had a significantly higher incidence of atherosclerosis.

In contrast, laughter was found to be good for the heart. In another series of studies, blood flow increased 22 percent during incidents of laughter among volunteers viewing comedy clips and decreased 35 percent while they watched stress-inducing clips.

Clearly, two people who hold and massage each other, look into each other's eyes, are playful, laugh together, and are respectful, appreciative, and generous are dosing each other with the best medicine of all: your own endogenous medicine—endorphins, dopamine, oxytocin, and the right balance of adrenaline and serotonin. Add a few shots of testosterone and estrogen, and you have a veritable elixir of love and a connection that enables you to flourish with each other.

Flourishing in a Secure Relationship

Another factor that consistently correlates with flourishing, resilience, and feelings of subjective happiness is a secure love style. The research of psychologists Phillip Shaver, Mario Mikulincer, and their colleagues has done much to connect the dots between infant development, neuroscience, romantic love, and sexuality.

Their data consistently showed that people who feel secure tend to have a healthy sense of self-worth, are trusting, have positive feelings about their partners, and have faith in their ability to resolve conflict. They are also good at regulating their stress; they deal effectively with disappointment, loss, and trauma and are generally optimistic. Manifesting many of the same attributes as Abraham Maslow's self-actualizers, they are hardy, happy people who enjoy close relationships.

Mikulincer and Shaver have demonstrated how intricately the bonds of love and attachment are intertwined with sex. Their data clearly showed that secure people are more likely than insecure people to enjoy the pleasures of sex and the emotional connection that accompanies it.

For insecure people, despite all the pleasures and benefits of sex, sexual arousal, sexual activity, and orgasm can be accompanied by negative feelings like ambivalence, guilt, or concerns about performance and lovability. Under those circumstances, the inability to regulate intense excitement can generate a sense of urgency for immediate release, which serves to limit the sexual experience.

Worries and anxieties about performance are distracting and distancing. A lack of attunement to a lover or an inability to read the other's cues can result in misreading or being insensitive to his or her desires. As a result, insecure people tend to be less able to enjoy conflict-free sex.

A person's sexual difficulties are a sign of insecurity, and we've looked in depth at what works for becoming more secure or for helping a partner to become secure. Some major components are sustained affectionate connection, the willingness to self-regulate, and the generosity to help a partner regulate his or her bodily stress.

In a sense, security is learned, and if both partners are insecure, it can help to seek the guidance of a good relationship therapist. Albert Einstein once said, "The mind that created the problem can't solve the problem." It helps to have another set of eyes and ears to see what does or doesn't work to promote intimacy. A couples therapist can offer a more realistic set of expectations and guidelines about how to maintain a loving relationship.

A Good Relationship Is Healing

Highly successful people who show impressive resilience in the face of childhood hardship can usually identify someone in their past who was sympathetic, caring, and simply "there" for them. A loving adult relationship can have the same impact. Stony Brook psychologists Arthur Aron and Elaine Aron cited evidence that when people develop greater security not as children but as adults, the most consistent positive influence is also a close relationship with another person. In essence, a relationship is therapeutic when it helps people to revise their distorted mental models of themselves and their unrealistic models of relationships.

Obviously, the relationship that has the greatest potential to be that kind of positive influence for someone insecure is the one with the person he or she loves. A more secure partner can help a less secure partner feel lovable, deserving, and special—especially when the insecure partner is motivated to learn and to grow.

Aron and Aron observed that people who earn their security through their intention to do so "can enjoy a level of depth and insight rarely found in those who have been continuously secure." In this sense, overcoming insecurity may actually bestow an evolutionary advantage. The researchers suggest that it may be that insecure people who are motivated to grow have a greater incentive than consistently secure people to expand the self and to find meaning in their pain.

Flourishing and Sexual Aliveness

A rich sexual experience is all about the abundance of emotions, sensations, and qualities of experience that are possible through physically intimate erotic play and sexual pleasure. There is a wealth of evidence that marital satisfaction and stability is greatest when both partners are sexually gratified. Mikulincer and Shaver cited an interesting study that tested the effect of sexual experience on the perceived quality of a relationship.

Cohabiting partners were asked to keep a diary for forty-two days and to indicate how they felt about the quality of their relationship each day. They were also asked to record each time they had intercourse and to report their thoughts and feelings about it. The results showed that experiencing positive feelings during intercourse one day had a significant positive effect on the partners' interactions the next day and on how they rated the quality of their relationship.

Now, if we broaden our definition of sex to include kissing, stroking, caressing, massaging, and erotic play, we can add a reliable and ongoing source of good feelings in everyday life.

New Models of Marriage and Partnership

In the summer of 2009, social commentator and *Los Angeles Times* contributing editor Gregory Rodriguez wrote a thoughtful column about the decline in the divorce rate during the economic crisis. He suggested that it wasn't necessarily a sign that people were working things out better, but rather that they were staying together because they couldn't afford to part. He predicted that once the economy recovered, we'd be back to our "astronomical" divorce rate. His take on why the national divorce rate was so high was that "in a rapidly changing society, it's harder to figure out what kinds of arrangements we should make with our spouses."

Rodriguez reflects that with more women in the workplace, with the ability to outsource household tasks (such as cleaning and cooking), and with some men at home while their wives work, modern realities can strain the traditional notions of marriage. Although he acknowledges that many couples have found happiness making peace with untraditional marriages, he adds, "We haven't figured out a new marriage model that takes into account the greater range of choices for both women and men."

That may be because marriage is no longer a one-size-fits-all institution. A greater range of choices naturally begets a greater range of models for how to be in a committed relationship. Here we are in the twenty-first century. We're a diverse crowd. We can customize.

Renegotiating Your Contract

Renegotiating your contract in a relationship may be a new concept for people who aren't aware that they ever negotiated a contract in the first place. They probably didn't. Maybe both partners silently assumed that they were on the same page about what was expected of them. In this new era of relationship awareness, people are recognizing that they can discuss the kind of relationship they want.

Some couples have explored open marriage, in which the partners give each other permission to be sexual with others, within certain parameters. The rules may be that you can flirt, but no touching; that it's okay to kiss and fool around a little, but no intercourse; or that you can do whatever you want with people I don't know when you're out of town. These are all possibilities that work for some people. When it stops working for them, they can reassess it.

I was recently interviewed for an article on alternative lifestyles for a women's magazine. The journalist was asking me about a young couple who had met at a swing party, had fallen in love and married, and had continued that lifestyle. Weren't the partners playing with fire if they truly loved each other and wanted the relationship to last? Not necessarily, I said. They both seemed to be into it, they were in their twenties, and their responses to the journalist's questions indicated that it was a life-style and a social community with friends they both valued. It seemed to be working for them.

However, I added, it may or may not continue to work for them. Priorities change as we get older or have children, and at some point that couple might choose to renegotiate the contract. The best thing they could do is to keep checking in with each other on how it's going for them.

The journalist then described another couple with a young child, who had decided to open up the relationship but weren't doing well. The partners argued about it. She thought that he was always on the make, so she would punish him by feigning interest in men who threatened him.

I told the journatlist that this couple seemed to have some real issues. The partners seemed incapable of setting boundaries in a loving way and instead were emotionally blackmailing each other to gain an edge. I wondered whether they even enjoyed having sex with other people or whether the real kicker was just spiting each other.

These two people seemed to need some help, not only in their relationship but also in their personal healing. That kind of pun-ishing behavior is usually indicative of long-term hurt and pos-sibly abuse, and their willingness to put up with such relationship chaos suggests that each may have had a tough childhood. They certainly needed to renegotiate their contract, and if they sought therapy to do that, it could start a process that would be illumi-nating on many fronts.

Eventually, in every relationship, tacit assumptions surface and are challenged, and a process of negotiation may be initiated for the first time. It can be a painful time for people who aren't well practiced in the fine art and grace of give and take, but it can also be an eye-opener and an impetus for growth.

Changing Views of Sex

In this postmodern world of breaking the social molds of the past and crafting new models for singles, couples, and families, more people are willing to explore their sexuality. News magazines have been trying to keep up with the trends.

Periodically they report on the growing incidence of college students and older adults who are experimenting with various forms of sexual activity and sexual nonexclusivity. Same-sex sexual activity by heterosexuals, bisexuality, threesomes, polyamory (maintaining two or more ongoing intimate relationships), and the increasingly acceptable phenomenon of older women with younger men are just a few of the possibilities in the sexually diverse panoply.

Under the circumstances, does it make sense for modern women and men to assume that once they become part of a couple, they have to define the relationship according to the old standards and then stick to them forever? That doesn't seem right to psychotherapist Esther Perel.

Appreciating the wealth of intimate configurations available today—marriage and domestic partnerships, successive marriages, serial monogamy, cohabitation, or never marrying—Perel has assailed a "monolithic monogamy" of absolute sexual exclusivity. Instead she has encouraged an acceptance rather than a denial of the lure of the other, "the shadow of the third."

For some couples, she noted, just the acknowledgment that one partner has his or her own sexuality, fantasy life, and desires that don't include the partner bestows a sense of freedom that may be enough to spice up their sex life. For couples who do experiment with sex outside the relationship, fidelity is defined not by sexual exclusivity but by emotional exclusivity. Perel suggested that the less people choke off each other's freedom, the easier it is for their desire to breathe in a committed relationship.

In my own practice I've noticed a number of creative solutions to resolving sexual dilemmas. For one heterosexual couple in which both partners were in their forties, the man had little interest in sex, and the woman lobbied for change.

She had heard about a lifestyles convention in Las Vegas and suggested that they go to it and see what it was like to be around "a bunch of oversexed people." As it turned out, they really enjoyed it and found themselves having hot sex with each other in their hotel room. From then on, they continued to go to swinging parties but had sex only with each other. She said that they were inspired by the lack of shame and everyone's openness and ease with sex.

In another situation, one very attractive and fit woman in her fifties had been single for many years and missed having sex with a committed partner. Pam had met men through Internet dating services and had been fixed up by friends and coworkers. None of the people she met suited her, and she lamented that most of the men her age were looking for women much younger.

Pam had struck up a friendship with a woman at the gym, and as they discovered mutual interests, they started to spend a good deal of time together. A surprising turn of events occurred one evening after the theater when Pam's friend, Irene, admitted to being a lesbian and to falling in love with Pam.

Pam's initial response was to cut off contact with Irene, but she really missed her. After several weeks of soul-searching, Pam decided to call Irene just to see if the chemistry between them was still there. It was, so Pam and Irene got together again and made love. Pam described it to me as "magical." It took her a while to deal with this late-in-life switch in sexual orientation, and she wondered if this meant that she had always been a lesbian.

I shared with Pam the research that shows that many women demonstrate a flexible sexuality capable of being responsive to both men and women as objects of desire, yet often they don't let themselves become aware of it. There are also women who do notice that they can become turned on to another woman and who enjoy the feeling, but they choose to make nothing of it because they prefer to mate with a man.

That information appeared to reassure Pam that she had not been lying to herself all these years. When she finally came out to her friends and her grown sons, Pam was doubly shocked to discover that everyone was happy for her and supported her love relationship with a woman.

Pam and Irene have now been in a domestic partnership for more than five years, and they are one of the happiest couples I know. Pam has also confided to me that sex with Irene is the most loving and fulfilling sex she has ever experienced.

Cultural Sexual Evolution

Today's young women and men have benefited from the sexual culture wars of the last decades and the ongoing sex scandals and civil rights issues that sustain a national dialogue on sex. Open discussions of oral sex, infidelity by public figures, purportedly heterosexual (and publicly antigay) men seeking sex with other men, the controversies over whether sex can be an addiction, as well as the current battles over gay marriage, gay parenting, and homosexuals in the military, have all been newsworthy topics. This generation is already more flexible in its understanding of sex and is redefining for itself a new set of sexual standards.

On the blog site Collegecandy.com, Kelly from Simmons College gave the following advice to college students exploring sex: "It's completely normal to be a virgin in college, and you shouldn't feel pressured to lose it. . . . There are more than three sexualities, gay, straight, or bi. Sex is on a spectrum from completely heterosexual to completely homosexual (Kinsey would agree). . . . Casual sex can be hard if one person cares more than the other." She also offered that "monogamy is not the gold standard" and suggested that college students should "explore open relationships and multiple relationships. Find out what type of relationship makes you happiest and pursue it."

Love, Sex, and Getting Older

It's not only the hormonally fueled younger generation whose attitudes are changing. Older adults are also getting in on the action.

Contrary to popular myth, we never have to outgrow our enjoyment of loving sex. In fact, there's plenty of evidence that sex in midlife and late life may hold even better prospects for sexual satisfaction than in youth. When people work through insecurities that held them back when they were younger, get past their disappointments, and come to appreciate what they do have, many find that mature sex may be the best of all.

That's what Harry and Marie, who were in their early sixties, were hoping when they came for sex therapy. Harry had recently recovered from a life-threatening illness and had told Marie that he was no longer willing to live without sexual fulfillment.

They both looked scared as they sat on my couch during their first session. Harry told me that his colon cancer had been found early, the treatment was successful, and he was in complete remission. He and Marie had been high school sweethearts, had been married almost forty years, and loved each other very much. They both agreed that sex had been "not great, but good enough" in the early years, but after they started a family it had deteriorated.

Harry felt that Marie gave in to sex to please him but that her heart was not in it. Marie agreed, saying that sex was just not that important to her, but she wanted Harry to be happy. That didn't work for Harry; Marie's lack of enjoyment made sex empty for him, and he believed that his health depended on the joie de vivre after sex that can come only with the full participation of both people.

As we examined the many factors contributing to this couple's stagnant sex life, we found a deep lack of information and imagination about what constitutes enjoyable sexual contact. Marie, who was a virgin when they met, had always been passive, and Harry, who had one sex partner briefly prior to Marie, had assumed leadership in sex from start to finish. They had three children, and once they had begun having babies, Marie became distracted during sex and wanted it to be over as quickly as possible. She had never had an orgasm and had some sadness about that but had given up on it.

We clearly had some catching up to do. We looked at many of the factors that I've raised in this book, all of which were very helpful. We examined how they made love and how Marie's passivity and discomfort with pleasure and Harry's focus on intercourse and ejaculation had contributed to routine and boring sex. We looked at the childhood influences that led them to accept this kind of contact and had allowed them to keep it this way for so long.

Mostly, however, we explored how they might expand their repertoire for being present with each other and playful. They saw that if Harry was less commanding, it would give Marie room to assert herself.

They also decided to experiment with oral sex, and we talked about the basics of how it's done. It worked out amazingly well. Marie had her first orgasm—at sixty-two years of age. Their broad smiles lit up the room when they told me about it.

Loving Sex for All Seasons

Mature sex can be better than young sex when people have learned from their experiences. Sex educator Carol Cassell has observed that more women today, whether married or single, are better at asking for what they want in sex. Many men too can enjoy more fulfilling sex as they get older because the rush to intercourse of their earlier years is tempered by a slower rate of arousal and a desire for emotional connection.

When author Joan Price found herself, at age sixty, having the best sex of her life with a man she loved, she began to research the phenomenon. She discovered a 1998 study by the National Council on Aging on thirteen hundred Americans that found that 70 percent of the sexually active women over sixty indicated that they were as satisfied or more satisfied sexually than when they were in their forties.

Price decided to solicit interviews with other sexually active women over sixty to see what insights they could share. She found that many women were eager to discuss what often amounted to a newly discovered level of sexual pleasure. Price attributed this enhanced sexuality to a variety of factors, including older women knowing their bodies better and accepting themselves, taking the time with their partners to enjoy touching and stimulating each other, and recognizing that "great sex is what's happening between two souls, two minds, two hearts—not just two bodies."

Older women and men of today are healthier and more fit than their parents at the same age. Popular culture is providing more images of middle-aged sex. From Diane Keaton and Jack Nicholson in *Something's Gotta Give* to Meryl Streep and Alec Baldwin in *It's Complicated* to the sexual innuendos between the older characters played by Karen McCluskey and Orson Bean on the television show *Desperate Housewives*, attitudes about age and sex are shifting. No longer disparaged as dirty old men or women, today's sexy seniors are considered healthy and vibrant.

Recent studies are showing that as long as people stay healthy, many men and women continue to be sexually active in their seventies, eighties, and beyond. In one study, almost 25 percent of sexually active adults between the ages of seventy-five and eighty-five reported having sex four times a month.

In a book about love and sex for people over the age of sixty Pulitzer Prize–winning physician and longevity expert Robert Butler and gerontologist Myrna Lewis have suggested that sexual activity provides older people with many benefits. These include the opportunity to express passion, affection, and romance. Enjoying sex, they said, is an affirmation of one's body and of life itself; it provides the impetus to create new excitement and experiences in long-term relationships and to grow in new directions.

The authors suggested that older people may be able to bring love and sex to new levels of development because they have learned from experience and appreciate the "preciousness of life." They are more present-centered because they are less focused on the future, and they usually have more time available that can be used well by focusing on their sexual relationships. Finally, Butler and Lewis suggest that old age can be a time "for bringing the experience of a lifetime and the unique perspectives of the final years of life to the art of loving one another."

Sex educator Peggy Brick, who is in her eighties, has become a major advocate for the sexual health, education, and rights of older adults. She has encouraged people to examine their old scripts about sex and aging, to be realistic and accepting about body changes, and to recognize that sex is much more than just intercourse.

Noting the physical and psychological benefits of sexual activity at all ages, Brick has expressed particular concern about the rights of mutually consenting residents in assisted living facilities to engage in discreet and safe sex. It is especially critical for these couples for the staff to be respectful of their wishes and to provide access to private space if requested.

A minister and pastoral counselor recently shared with me a tender story about one of his parishioners. An energetic ninety-five-year-old woman had come to him to grieve over the passing of a male friend of the same age. The two had become inseparable since they had met in a nursing home five years earlier. The minister comforted her as she cried over the loss of her dear companion. Then when she stood to leave, a wistful smile crossed her face. As the minister helped her up, she leaned toward him and whispered, "I'm really going to miss the sex."

I saved a clipping from an Ann Landers column that's now more than ten years old. In it, "Stunned Sisters in Philadelphia" wrote that one Sunday, when they went to visit their eighty-three-year-old mother at the nursing home, they walked in on her and got the surprise of their lives. They caught her on the sofa in a silk negligee necking with an eighty-four-year-old widower. Even more shocking, their mother announced that she and her friend were getting married. Does it make sense? they asked Ann Landers. Can two people in their eighties possibly be interested in sex? They needed answers.

Landers replied that she thought it was wonderful, and she added, "Whatever they want to do together (or perhaps I should say *can* do together) is their personal business. Be happy for them. If I lived in Philadelphia, I would offer to be the flower girl."

Added Years Mean Added Pleasures

Before the 2010 census, the U.S. Census Bureau projected that there would be 114,000 people living past the age of one hundred. That's more than twice the number of centenarians in 1984. Centenarians are the fastest growing age group in the world. By 2050, there may be at least six million people worldwide over the age of one hundred. If we take care of ourselves, we can look forward to long and healthy lives, and we want to live them well.

That's the realization that Harry had when he told Marie that he felt that loving sexual pleasure was crucial for his health and vitality. Getting sick had been a wake-up call. He realized that he had been accepting much less than he really wanted in a lot of areas in his life and that he had been given a second chance. He loved Marie dearly and would never leave her, but he couldn't continue to have sex with her if things didn't change. He believed that his continuing survival depended on fixing their sex life—and they did it in their sixties.

A midlife crisis can be a correction rather than a crisis—a midcourse correction. Many of us get very caught up in the fast pace of the full lives we've created for ourselves. Often, our lives are fueled by adrenaline and stress, and we rely on automatic pilot to get everything done. When something comes along that makes us question how we have lived our lives thus far, that's a good thing. It's a sign of waking up from a stupor and taking charge, of gaining the courage to explore new options, and of a willingness to make choices and changes toward what's truly nurturing and life affirming. That's evolution in action.

People may also reach a point in life when they can no longer tolerate living an inauthentic existence. Maybe they have put up with bad treatment from their partners or have been denying an aspect of themselves that can no longer remain submerged. The hunger to be true to oneself is a powerful motivator—it's a yearning to be wholehearted and undivided within.

Then there are people who are lying not just to themselves but also to a partner. What happens when one discovers a partner's infidelity or a hidden life of infidelities? Can that be repaired, or has the relationship been so damaged by the scope of the situation that it is impossible to repair?

That depends on many factors specific to each couple. Not the least of these is whether the partners have young children and want to keep the family together. Another major factor is whether they genuinely love each other and want to work it out. If they have the will to see it through, then all it takes is patience, remorse, forgiveness, self-forgiveness, courage, and determination. Clearly, it's not easy.

I have witnessed many couples in crisis as the result of one partner discovering the other partner in an affair. I have gone with each couple through the multiple layers of anger, grief, guilt, and shame, the slow gains and the sudden tailspins that put the relationship back at risk. I have also seen such couples come out of it better and more in love than they had ever been before. As it says over and over in the *I Ching*, the ancient Chinese book of wisdom, "Perseverance furthers."

Flourishing in a Fulfilling Intimacy

Taking a relationship to a new level of satisfaction entails more than just resolving problems. As psychologist Diana Fosha has pointed out, when people have expressed stuck feelings and worked through their distress, the next stage of growth is a naturally activated process of transformation, what she calls "wired-in dispositions for self-healing." These are pleasurable feelings that release great stores of vitality and energy. When partners work on their insecurities and come to a loving and trusting place in their relationship, the emphasis in life changes from fixing what's not working or is missing to enhancing what they have.

New research in the science of happiness in a relationship has identified several positive factors that make a fulfilling intimate relationship. In a review of the many studies, University of Rochester psychologists Harry Reis and Shelly Gable highlighted several positive interactions that were consistently found to be significant. The four that I want to emphasize here are *accommodation, capitalization, shared fun,* and *affection.*

Accommodation

Accommodation is the tendency to respond in a constructive way to a partner's "bad" or annoying behavior. We examined this in the context of learning to avoid picking up emotional contagion. When one partner can regulate stress during a rapidly escalating stress point, he or she is more likely to respond compassionately, speak nicely, or use humor to voice an objection.

Capitalization

The researchers pointed out a tendency of many couples to let the good stuff slide and to talk only about what isn't satisfying. The research demonstrated the importance of a couple's ability to make the most of—to capitalize on—happy occasions: to celebrate birthdays, anniversaries, and holidays together and to share pleasant experiences.

Shared Fun

One of the most consistent effects in the many studies reviewed was the value of having fun together. Being playful, or enjoying energizing and engaging activity together, is particularly associated with relationship satisfaction.

On a physiological level, doing new and exciting things together stimulates the reward centers of the brain, which releases dopamine. The excitement becomes associated with the relationship, which tends to inspire feelings of romantic love. The research showed that this can happen simply by taking a class together or traveling to new places with each other.

Affection

Also important is the excitement and satisfaction that comes with behaviors and gestures that communicate tender feelings of love, warmth, and appreciation. Reis and Gable cited findings that expressions of affection demonstrated by a couple during the first two years of marriage were predictive, thirteen years later, of whether the couple would stay together or divorce.

Moreover, there is evidence that affectionate contact spurs oxytocin, which in turn increases a person's feelings of connection and the tendency to be nurturing. Physical affection that includes eye contact, hugging, touching, and making love particularly increases oxytocin levels. Oxytocin reduces the stress level and, as we have seen, is associated with multiple health benefits and feelings of well-being.

Reis and Gable concluded that flourishing in a relationship requires a focus not just on solving problems but specifically on enhancing the interactions that make relationships most fulfilling, enjoyable, and growth producing. They emphasize, "Relating well is not the same as not relating badly."

Clearly, the ability to enjoy emotionally gratifying sexual pleasure has much to contribute to flourishing in a relationship.

Truly Great Sex

What does it really take to feel sexually fulfilled? I continually hear people describe great sex as "hanging from the chandeliers," but that sounds like a bunch of rich people having a drunken orgy, and not a very sexy one at that.

Sexologist Peggy Kleinplatz and colleagues at the University of Ottawa set out to shed light on the components of what people consider their "greatest sexual experiences." The researchers were hoping to gain a better understanding of what kinds of sex are worth having and to help individuals and couples access more of what they intuit is possible in sex.

The study was based on a series of interviews with sixty-four volunteers who self-identified as currently having great sex or who had had great sex in the past. The wide sample of people included men and women, older married people, gay men and lesbians, sexual minorities like bondage and discipline (BDSM) players, and sex therapists. The data were analyzed by themes, and eight major components of optimal sex were identified. All of these have been described in various sections of this book. I'll emphasize a few of them again.

The most frequently articulated quality of great sex was "being present, focused, and embodied." The participants said they felt totally absorbed in the moment-to-moment sensations of the experience.

Another component frequently cited was "extraordinary communication and heightened empathy." Here people described being able to respond sensitively and nonverbally by reading their partners' responses through their own bodies.

Many also talked about "authenticity" and "transparency," the freedom to be genuinely honest with themselves and feeling no self-consciousness with their partners. Another vital characteristic for the participants was exploring themselves in the context of "fun and play," having a sense of humor and even enjoying laughter during sex. The participants also said that "allowing oneself to be vulnerable and to surrender to a partner" made sex truly exquisite.

What was most surprising to Kleinplatz and colleagues about the findings was that they painted "a radically different picture of optimal sexuality than portrayed in the mass media." Great sex had little to do with erections, vaginal lubrication, intercourse, or orgasm and everything to do with empathic attunement and being present and focused.

The authors suggested that focusing on sexual performance for those with sexual concerns is counterproductive, because really great sex is all about *"being in* the experience," enjoying the connection, and letting it unfold rather than achieving any particular sexual goals.

Everyday Eroticism Is Everyday Love

In other words, great sex depends not on how the encounter ends— in intercourse or with an orgasm—but on how you get there. When there is intercourse and orgasm as well, that can be the beginning of something more: an opening into a whole new level of physical abandon, exquisite pleasure, and spiritual union. The critical factors are all of the elements that serve emotional and erotic attunement: arousal, affection, focused attention, empathy, humor, generosity, gratitude, and a willingness to relax and physically enjoy the other.

Taking a broader perspective, we can see that what we're looking at here is a style of running a relationship that generates "juice" on a daily basis: energy, enthusiasm, loving feelings, and sexual playfulness. Some days, naturally, will be juicier than other days, but that's just the way it goes.

This is also an attitude that honors the primacy of the body and the crucial role of pleasure. It's supported and informed by the cutting edge of research in the sciences of sexology, psychology, physiology, neurology, developmental neurobiology, and flourishing.

Most especially, this is a way of life. Positive interactions support positive feelings and the capacity to enjoy the pleasures of true love and sexual aliveness.

The Key to Success in Everything: Relaxed Excitement

I hope I've expanded your perspective on love and desire as present-centered, body-based experiences that offer a wide terrain for exploration and a whole lifetime ahead of you to do it in. It's a worthy journey, and it begins with a single breath. As the twentieth-century German playwright Bertolt Brecht wrote, "What has happened has happened. The water you once poured into the wine cannot be drained off. But everything changes. You can make a fresh start with your final breath."

Once again, the key to success in everything is nurturing the capacity to be energized and relaxed at the same time. You do that by remembering to take a few conscious breaths periodically throughout the day, especially when you feel yourself growing tense. Conscious breathing puts you in touch with the moment, and during times of stress it balances the nervous system by triggering the parasympathetic nervous system.

Deep breathing is also a way of self-soothing during difficult times or when you're worried. It's better than popping a pill. Taking just a few complete breaths or deep sighs alters your biochemistry, producing an internally manufactured mood-altering drug that's good for you.

Breathing and relaxing during physically intimate times is at the core of being in touch and attuned to your lover, allowing your sexual desire to build slowly and naturally.

Most important, this is an everyday practice. Relaxed excitement is about breathing and stretching periodically throughout your day to regulate your stress. Checking in with yourself and taking an emotional inventory allows you to deal with things sooner rather than later—before they become big deals. If you have a partner, it's important that you help him or her to do the same.

It has been said that how you do anything is how you do everything. Your patterns follow you everywhere. Practicing emotionally gratifying sexual pleasure is a great way to learn the principle of relaxed excitement. Developing the impulse to breathe deeply, rather than tense up, as your body energizes can have a positive effect on your work, stamina, creativity, optimism, and health as much as on your love life.

All it takes is practice, day by day by day by day.

The New Sexual Evolution

In January 1964, *Time* magazine ran an article on what it called "the second sexual revolution." It identified the first sexual revolution as the era after World War I, the 1920s, known as the Jazz Age. The flapper and the New Woman challenged the double standard and gained the right to vote, to work, and to enjoy sex. Still, the authors noted, it was not a time of marked change in sexual behavior.

The second sexual revolution was the one in the 1960s, and it turned out quite different. What the article saw happening was a complete change in sexual morality. The change was reflected in a new sexual explicitness in books, movies, and the theater; sexual experimentation and nonmarital sexual activity were extolled. Sexual experience, not purity, was becoming an asset.

Just as the birth-control pill separated sex from reproduction, the article's authors lamented, the Sexual Revolution appeared to be separating sex from love. Although they saw many positives to the new movement, particularly that "Americans are becoming more sophisticated, and less inhibited in bed," they also cautioned men that now "American women must be wooed more than ever."

Many people feel a need for a "reaffirmation of the spiritual meaning of sex," the article said, and it ended by suggesting that maybe "it is time that "modern Americans, who know a great deal about sex, once again start talking about love."

Nearly fifty years later, I still don't think we all know a "great deal about sex," but we are learning. Thanks to a burgeoning body of science, we are also beginning to learn a great deal more about love and emotional attachment.

Now all we have to do is make it all work for ourselves. I think of this reuniting love with sexual pleasure as the New Sexual Evolution.

Step Ten: Evolution as a Lifestyle

Objective: To make stress regulation and embodied love a daily practice

Those of us who are moving on to the next developmental stage in life as members of an erotic couple can deepen our love and fulfillment through embodied affection and erotic attunement.

The following exercises are mostly reminders of what you have practiced so far that can be incorporated into a loving, sexy style of daily living.

Self-Regulate: Everyday Embodied Basics

Make the embodied basics part of your everyday life. Take charge of your emotional energy. Be sure to take a few mindful minutes several times a day to breathe deeply and relax, to close your eyes and tune in to your body. Take a felt-sense inventory. Stretch and de-stress.

Home Aerobics

There is no doubt that the more fit we are physically and the better our mobility, the greater our desire for sex. Just as you don't want to relegate sex solely to the bedroom at night, you don't want to relegate your fitness solely to a gym at a particular hour of the day. Figure out how you can stretch, exercise, and practice fitness in every room in your home.

- Find a heavy piece of furniture with a leg that will support you in a squat, a doorway that is good for stretching your arms and chest as you pass through, a stair or a doorstep for stretching out your hamstrings, and several spaces that are good for dancing.

- Conduct your own personal aerobics class with your favorite lively music. Clear a path from one room to another that you can jog back and forth through, even if it's only a few feet long.

Embodied Love

Upgrade your capacity to love, to feel compassion, and to be kind.

- If your parents let you down, forgive them for their inadequacies. They're just ordinary people, not the superhero parents you would have preferred. Given their history, they couldn't have done it any differently. But you can. Give up ideal love and accept real love—flawed but still special.

- Don't allow your partner to be disrespectful. Educate him or her nicely on how you like to be treated.

- Don't take your love for granted. Periodically picture the people you love in your mind's eye and remind yourself about what you love about them and how they enrich your life.

- Feel warmth and gratitude in your heart. See if you can feel love in your throat and belly. Where else do you feel it? If at first you don't feel love in your body, run up and down a flight of steps and then picture him or her again. Once you find the feelings of love in your body, check in with those feelings from time to time.

- Take the time to admire and appreciate your partner. Do little things your partner enjoys and feel his or her pleasure in your heart, and in the rest of your body.

- Always ask for what you want. Always ask nicely. Be willing to take no for an answer. (As long as it's not all of the time.)

Mutual Regulation: The Embodied Couple

Take advantage of the enormous power intimates have to calm each other's stress and help each other feel good, hopeful, confident, grateful, and joyous.

- Renew your loving feelings daily, even for just a few seconds. Stay attuned. Look into each other's eyes when you talk. Smile at each other every so often. Give him or her a hug and a kiss. Lie in each other's arms and breathe together. Touch and stroke each other with listening, empathic hands.

- Help your partner de-stress by holding him or her when he or she is tense. Breathe together. Ask to be held when you're tense.

- Be playful. Make each other laugh.

- Be romantic. Find ways to make your partner feel special—let your lover know those moments when he or she is being the sweetest, cutest, funniest, wisest, most generous, best lover or best friend.

- Enjoy the silence together.

Eroticize Your Daily Life

Be sexy for yourself. Connect with your inner lover and be sweet to the person you see in the mirror.

- Make time for self-pleasuring, even if it's for just a few minutes. Don't aim for an orgasm each time—just a good feeling and maybe a pleasant fantasy.

- Surprise your partner with an unexpected kiss and a warm caress. Let your kisses linger. Make out for a little while and stop while you still want more.

- Come on to each other playfully, without having to do anything immediate about it. Every so often, play dress-up to entice each other.

- Talk sexy. Whatever turns you and your lover on is okay.

- Make time for sex play when you are alert and energetic. Try extending your erotic energy for several days instead of just going for a quickie orgasm before falling asleep at night.

- Every so often, go for a quickie orgasm before falling asleep at night.

- Do what turns you on and gives you both pleasure.

Those of us who enjoy such love are the richest people on earth. Enjoy your good fortune!

References

Acevedo, B. P., and Aron, A. (2009). Does a long-term relationship kill romantic love? *Review of General Psychology, 13* (1), 59–65.

Allen, J. P., and Land, D. (1999). Attachment in adolescence. In J. Cassidy and P. R. Shaver (eds.), *Handbook of attachment: Theory, research, and clinical applications* (pp. 319–335). New York: Guilford Press.

Aron, A., and Aron, E. N. (2006). Romantic relationships from the perpectives of the self-expansion model and attachment theory. In M. Mikulincer and G. S. Goodman (eds.), *Dynamics of romantic love* (pp. 359–382). New York: Guilford Press.

Beach, S. R., and Tesser, A. (1988). Love in marriage: A cognitive account. In R. J. Sternberg and M. L. Barnes (eds.), *The psychology of love* (pp. 330–355). New Haven, CT: Yale University Press.

Beebe, B., and Lachmann, F. M. (2002). *Infant research and adult treatment.* New York: Analytic Press.

Berman, L. (2011). *Loving sex: The book of joy and passion.* London: Dorling Kindersley Ltd.

Berscheid, E. (1988). Some comments on love's anatomy: Or whatever happened to old-fashioned lust? In R. J. Sternberg and M. L. Barnes (eds.), *The psychology of love* (pp. 359–374). New Haven, CT: Yale University Press.

Blackburn, S. (2004). *Lust: The seven deadly sins.* New York: Oxford University Press.

Brick, P., Lunquist, J., Sandak, A., and Taverner, B. (2009). *Older, wiser, sexually smarter: 30 sex ed lessons for adults only.* Morristown, NJ: Planned Parenthood.

Britton, P. (2005). *The art of sex coaching: Expanding your practice.* New York: Norton.

Butler, R. N., and Lewis, M. I. (2002). *The new love and sex after 60.* New York: Ballantine Books.

Cassell, C. (2008). *Put passion first: Why sexual chemistry is the key to finding and keeping lasting love.* New York: McGraw-Hill.

Chivers, M. L., and Bailey, J. M. (2005). A sex difference in features that elicit genital response. *Biological Psychology, 70* (2), 115–120.

Dodson, B. (1996). *Sex for one: The joy of self-loving.* New York: Three Rivers Press.

Doidge, N. (2007). *The brain that changes itself.* New York: Penguin Books.

Eagle, M. (2007). Attachment and sexuality. In D. Diamond, S. J. Blatt, and J. D. Lichtenberg (eds.), *Attachment and sexuality* (pp. 27–50). New York: Analytic Press.

Ekman, P. (2003). *Emotions revealed: Recognizing faces and feelings to improve communication and emotional life.* New York: Henry Holt.

Escoffier, J. (ed.). (2003). Introduction. In *Sexual Revolution* (pp. xi–xxxvi). New York: Thunder's Mouth Press.

Feuerstein, G. (1992). *Sacred sexuality.* Los Angeles: Tarcher.

Field, T. (2006). *Massage therapy research.* Oxford, UK: Churchill Livingstone.

Fisher, H. (2004). *Why we love: The nature and chemistry of romantic love.* New York: Henry Holt.

Fosha, D. (2009). Emotion and recognition at work: Energy, vitality, truth, desire and the emergent phenomenology of transformational experience. In D. Fosha, D. J. Siegel, and M. Solomon (eds.), *The healing power of emotion* (pp. 172–203). New York: Norton.

Fredrickson, B. L. and Losada, M. F. (2005). Positive affect and the complex dynamics of human flourishing. *American Psychologist, 6* (7), 678–686.

Freud, S. (1953). *Three essays on the theory of sexuality.* London: Hogarth Press. (Original work published 1905.)

Givens, D. B. (1983). *Love signals: How to attract a mate.* New York: Crown.

Gladwell, M. (2005). *Blink.* New York: Back Bay Books.

Hartman, W., and Fithian, M. (1986). *Any man can.* New York: St. Martin's Press.

Hatfield, E., Rapson, R. L., and Yen-Chi, L. L. (2009). Emotional contagion and empathy. In J. Decety and W. Ickes (eds.), *The social neuroscience of empathy* (pp. 19–31). Boston: MIT Press.

Hazan, C., and Shaver, P. R. (1987). Romantic love conceptualized as an attachment process. *Journal of Personality and Social Psychology, 52,* 511–524.

Hite, S. (1976). *The Hite report: A nationwide study of female sexuality.* New York: Dell.

Holmberg, D., Blair, K. L., and Phillips, M. (2010). Women's sexual satisfaction as a predictor of well-being in same-sex versus mixed-sex relationships. *Journal of Sex Research, 47* (1), 1–11.

Institute of HeartMath. Entrainment, coherence, and autonomic balance. Retrieved from http://www.heartmath.org/research/science-of-the-heart/entrainment-coherence-autonomic-balance.html.

Jillson, J. (1984). *The fine art of flirting.* New York: Simon & Schuster.

Joannides, P. (2009). *Guide to getting it on.* Waldport, OR: Goofy Foot Press.

Kaplan, H. S. (1979). *Disorders of sexual desire.* New York: Brunner/Mazel.

Kleinplatz, P. J., Ménard, A. D., Paquet, M. P., Paradis, N., Campbell, M., Zuccarino, D., and Mehak, L. (2009) The components of optimal sexuality: A portrait of "great sex." *Canadian Journal of Human Sexuality, 18* (1–2), 1–13.

Koch, P. B., Mansfield, P. K., Thureau, D., and Carey, M. (2005). Feeling frumpy: The relationships between body image and sexual response changes in midlife women. *Journal of Sex Research, 42* (3), 215–223.

Komisaruk, B. R., Beyer-Flores, C., and Whipple, B. (2006). *The science of orgasm.* Baltimore: Johns Hopkins University Press.

LeVay, S., and Valente, S. M. (2005). *Human sexuality.* Sunderland, MA: Sinauer.

Lewis, T., Amini, F., and Lannon, R. (2000). *A general theory of love.* New York: Random House.

Lowen, A. (1988). *Love, sex, and your heart.* New York: Macmillan.

Maslow, A. H. (1962). *Toward a psychology of being.* Princeton, NJ: Van Nostrand.

Masters, W. H., and Johnson, V. E. (1976). *The pleasure bond.* New York: Bantam Books.

Michael, R. T., Gagnon, J. H., Laumann, E. O., and Kolata, G. (1994). *Sex in America: A definitive study.* Boston: Little, Brown.

Mikulincer, M. (2006). Attachment, caregiving, and sex within romantic relationships: A behavioral systems perspective. In M. Mikulincer and G. S. Goodman (eds.), *Dynamics of romantic love* (pp. 23–43). New York: Guilford Press.

Mikulincer, M., and Shaver, P. R. (2007). *Attachment in adulthood: Structure, dynamics, and change.* New York: Guilford Press.

Morin, J. (1995). *The erotic mind: Unlocking the inner sources of sexual passion and fulfillment.* New York: HarperCollins.

Nin, A. (1969). *The diary of Anaïs Nin,* vol. 3 (1939–1944). San Diego: Harcourt Brace Jovanovich.

Ogden, G. (2006). *The heart and soul of sex: Making the ISIS connection.* Boston: Trumpeter Books.

Paget, L. (2005). *The great lover playbook.* New York: Gotham Books.

Panksepp, J. (2004). *Affective neuroscience: The foundations of human and animal evolution.* New York: Oxford University Press.

———. (2009). Brain emotional systems and qualities of mental life: From animal models of affect to implications for psychotherapeutics. In D. Fosha, D. J. Siegel, and M. Solomon (eds.), *The healing power of emotion* (pp. 1–26). New York: Norton.

Perel, E. (2006). *Mating in captivity: Reconciling the erotic and the domestic.* New York: HarperCollins.

Perls, F. (1973). *The Gestalt approach and eye witness to therapy.* Palo Alto, CA: Science and Behavior Books.

Perls, F., Hefferline, R. F., and Goodman, P. (1994). *Gestalt therapy: Excitement and growth in the human personality.* Gouldsboro, ME: Gestalt Journal Press.

Perper, T. (1985). *Sex signals: The biology of love.* Philadelphia: ISI Press.

Planned Parenthood, White Paper (November 2002). *Masturbation—from stigma to sexual health.* New York: Planned Parenthood Federation of America.

Planned Parenthood and the Society for the Scientific Study of Sexuality, White Paper (April 2003). *The health benefits of sexual expression.* New York: Planned Parenthood Federation of America.

Porges, S. W. (2011). *The polyvagal theory: Neurophysiological foundations of emotions, attachment, communication, and self-regulation.* New York: Norton.

Price, J. (2006). *Better than I ever expected.* Berkeley, CA: Seal Press.

Ravussin, E. (January 28, 2005). A neat way to control weight? *Science, 307* (5709).

Reich, W. (1961). *The function of the orgasm.* New York: Farrar, Straus & Giroux. (Original work published 1942.)

———. (1970). *The sexual revolution: Toward a self-governing character structure.* New York: Farrar, Straus & Giroux. (Original work published 1945.)

Reis, H. T., and Gable, S. L. (2003). Toward a positive psychology of relationships. In C. L. Keyes and J. Haidt (eds.), *Flourishing: Positive psychology and the life well-lived* (pp. 129–159). Washington, DC: American Psychological Association.

Resnick, S. (1997). *The pleasure zone: Why we resist good feelings and how to let go and be happy.* Berkeley, CA: Conari Press.

———. (2002). Sexual pleasure: The next frontier in the study of sexuality. *SIECUS Report, 30* (4), 6–11.

———. (2004). Somatic-experiential sex therapy: A body-centered Gestalt approach to sexual concerns. *Gestalt Review, 8* (1), 40–64.

Resnick, S., Warmoth, A., and Serlin, I. A. (2001). The humanistic psychology and positive psychology connection: Implications for psychotherapy. *Journal of Humanistic Psychology, 41* (1), 73–101.

Rodriguez, G. (July 13, 2009). Divorce and hard times. *Los Angeles Times,* Opinion Section.

Rosenberg, J. L., Rand, M. L., and Asay, D. (1985). *Body, self, and soul: Sustaining integration.* Atlanta, GA: Humanics.

Rubenfeld, I. (2000). *The listening hand.* New York: Bantam Books.

Saint Exupéry, A. de (1943). *The little prince.* New York: Harcourt Brace & World.

Satcher, D. (2001). *The surgeon general's call to action to promote sexual health and responsible sexual behavior.* Retrieved from http://www.surgeongeneral.gov /library.

Schore, A. N. (1994). *Affect regulation and the origin of the self: The neurobiology of emotional development.* Mahwah, NJ: Erlbaum.

———. (2001). The effects of a secure attachment relationship on right brain development, affect regulation, and infant mental health. *Infant Mental Health Journal, 22,* 7–66.

Schwartz, P. and Lever, J. (1997). *The great sex weekend.* New York: G. P. Putnam's Sons.

Selye, H. (1974). *Stress without distress: How to use stress as a positive force to achieve a rewarding life style.* New York: Signet Books.

Shaver, P. R., Hazan, C., and Bradshaw, D. (1988). Love as attachment: The integration of three behavioral systems. In R. J. Sternberg and M. L. Barnes (eds.), *The psychology of love* (pp. 68–99). New Haven, CT: Yale University Press.

Siegel, D. (2001). Memory: An overview, with emphasis on developmental, interpersonal, and neurobiological aspects. *Journal of the American Academy of Child Adolescent Psychiatry, 40* (9), 997–1011.

———. (2007). *The mindful brain: Reflection and attunement in the cultivation of well-being.* New York: Norton.

Stark, M. (2009). *The wisdom of the matrix: Regulation, balance and harmony.* Retrieved from http://www.lifespanlearn.org/documents/STARKMatrix.pdf.

Tavris, C. (1982). *Anger: The misunderstood emotion.* New York: Simon & Schuster.

Time (January 24, 1964). The second sexual revolution. Reproduced in J. Escoffier (ed.) *Sexual revolution* (2003) (pp. 419). New York: Thunder Mouth Press.

Trevarthen, C. (1993). The self born in intersubjectivity: The psychology of an infant communicating. In U. Neisser (ed.), *The perceived self: Ecological and interpersonal sources of self knowledge* (pp. 121–173). New York: Cambridge University Press.

Tronick, E. Z. (1989). Emotions and emotional communication in infants. *American Psychologist, 44* (2), 112–119.

Zaviacic, M. and Whipple, B. (1993). Update on the female prostate and the phenomenon of female ejaculation. *Journal of Sex Research, 30* (2), 148–151.

Resources

Your inner resources are your best resources. The more you practice taking mindful moments periodically throughout your day, to breathe deeply and regulate your nervous system, the quieter your mind will be and the better your capacity to love and be loved. The more you open your heart, the more old wounds will heal and the more you can relax into and surrender to erotic pleasure. The following resources are offered to support you in honing these basic skills.

Depending on your needs, goals, and desires, these resources can help to deepen your self-discovery, your fulfillment in your intimate relationship, and your knowledge and skill as a professional.

Personal Growth and Couples Enhancement

The following websites also offer programs for professional development.

My website, www.drstellaresnick.com. Visit my website for more information about full-spectrum therapy and how to work with me in individual, couples, group, or sex therapy. I offer sessions both in my office and via Skype. Access my schedule for the year, locate my blog, and check for workshops or training seminars for professionals in your area. The basic embodiment exercises are available for you to download to your computer.

Esalen Institute, www.esalen.org. Esalen was founded in 1962 as an alternative educational center devoted to the exploration of human potential and the expansion of human capacities. It has become known for its blend of Eastern and Western philosophies, its historical role in the continuing development and practice of Gestalt therapy, the varieties of experiential and didactic workshops it offers, its hot springs, and the spectacular coastline between the Santa Lucia Mountains and the Pacific Ocean in Big Sur, California. Go to this site to find workshops on a variety of issues and interests, including relationships, sexuality, spirituality, entrepreneurship, filmmaking, painting, writing, dance, massage, and nature.

American Association of Sexuality Educators, Counselors, and Therapists (AASECT), www.aasect.org. Go to this site to find a certified sex therapist or educator anywhere in the United States and in many countries around the world.

Association for the Advancement of Gestalt Therapy (AAGT), www.aagt.org. Go to this site to locate a Gestalt therapist in your area and to learn more about Gestalt therapy.

Sexuality Information

**Sexuality Information and Education Council of the United States, www
.siecus.org.** SIECUS was founded in 1964 to disseminate accurate information about
sexuality to young people and adults. It has become a recognized leader in the field
of sexuality education, publishing books, journals, and the *SIECUS Report*, which all
cover key issues in sexual health, research, HIV and AIDS prevention, public policy,
and sexual rights. Go to this site for evidence-based information on comprehensive
sex education, abstinence-until-marriage programs for teens, adolescent sexuality,
teen pregnancy, sexual and reproductive health, sexual orientation, and the benefits
of sexual pleasure and fulfillment.

Planned Parenthood, www.plannedparenthood.org. This is the nation's leading
sexual and reproductive health-care provider, primarily focused on the prevention
of unintended pregnancy, education, testing, and treatment for sexually transmitted
illness. Go to this site for more information on services and for a host of reports on
topics such as women's and men's sexual health, body image, sexual orientation and
gender, masturbation, sex play, and pleasure.

Betty Dodson, www.dodsonandross.com. Betty Dodson is an artist, an author, a
unique sex educator, and a sex coach with a focus on women's sexual pleasure,
masturbation, and orgasm. Carlin Ross, her business partner, is an entrepreneur and
former journalist. Dodson and Ross have created a one-of-a-kind raunchy online sex
information site that features videos of the two in conversation. Go to this site for
sexually explicit instructional videos, articles on controversial topics, a genital art
gallery, a fine art gallery of Betty's paintings and drawings, and a sex boutique that
sells books, DVDs, condoms, lubricants, dildos, and vibrators.

Sex Smart Films, www.sexsmartfilms.com. This site, founded by sexologist and film-
maker Mark Schoen, is dedicated to promoting sexual health and literacy by showcas-
ing hundreds of classic and contemporary films and videos that provide accurate sex
information. They offer videos that are age-appropriate for use in classrooms as well
as erotic videos to guide adult couples in sexual pleasure. Go to this site for videos on
a wide range of sexual interests, including sex and disability, religion and sex, sex and
aging, anatomy and physiology, bisexuality, gay and lesbian sex, and sex ed for teens.

Femme Productions, www.candidaroyalle.com. This is a production company
headed by Candida Royalle, a former erotic film star who produces and directs
erotic films and videos that specifically aim to please women and are couple-friendly.
Go to this site to explore the line of erotic films, videos, and sex toys.

Professional Development

The following sites are professional organizations dedicated to furthering the development of their field and benefiting the larger community.

**American Association of Sexuality Educators, Counselors, and Therapists
(AASECT), www.aasect.org.** This is an interdisciplinary organization of professionals
dedicated to sexual health. It includes psychologists, physicians, lawyers, clergy, social

workers, nurses, allied health professionals, and researchers who keep up with knowledge in the field of sexual health. Membership provides educational opportunities and national conferences, clear professional standards, and supervision and certification for sex therapists, counselors, and educators. Go to this site for information on membership and opportunities for continuing education and student involvement.

Society for the Scientific Study of Sexuality (SSSS), www.sexscience.org. This is an interdisciplinary organization of psychologists, sociologists, anthropologists, biologists, educators, and therapists that is dedicated to advancing knowledge about sexuality through research and to the clinical, educational, and social applications of the research. Go to this site for membership information, access to the *Journal of Sex Research*, information on the national conferences and regional conferences in the Western Region, Midcontinent, and Eastern Region, and opportunities for continuing education and student involvement.

Association for the Advancement of Gestalt Therapy (AAGT), www.aagt.com. This is a multinational organization of psychologists, psychiatrists, social workers, teachers, writers, artists, organizational consultants, and others. The common thread of this international community is the continuing development of theory, philosophy, practice, and research in Gestalt therapy. Go to this site to learn more about Gestalt therapy, and to find regional and international opportunities for professional development.

United States Association of Body Psychotherapy (USABP), www.usabp.org. This is a professional organization dedicated to developing and advancing the art, science, and practice of body-based and somatic psychotherapies. Go to this site for membership information, information on conferences, and access to the *USA Body Psychotherapy Journal*.

Lifespan Learning Institute, www.lifespanlearning.org. This group organizes high-quality conferences and training programs for continuing education for mental health professionals that are typically offered through UCLA Extension. Go to this site for information on future conferences as well as access to interesting books and CDs and DVDs of past conferences.

Other Valuable Resources

Jack Kornfield, www.jackkornfield.com. Jack Kornfield is one of the leading meditation teachers in the United States today. His approach emphasizes compassion, loving-kindness, and the path of mindful presence, all offered in simple, accessible ways in his books, CDs, classes, and retreats.

Tuning Effect, www.melvynbucholtz.com. This is an elegant process of guided meditation and body attunement utilized for psychological healing, personal growth, and enhancement of the creative process. The procedure, developed by psychotherapist Melvyn Bucholtz, integrates Eastern spiritual practices, meditation, and hypnosis into an alternative approach to well-being.

***Gestalt Review*, www.gestaltreview.com.** This publication concentrates on the Gestalt approach to clinical, family, group, and organizational topics. Case studies and papers dealing with specific clinical issues are regularly featured. The journal also publishes original papers dealing with politics, philosophy, culture, and gender.

The Gestalt Journal Press, www.gestalt.org. Updated frequently, this site includes up-to-date information on new books, workshops, and other Gestalt events. The *News and Notes* newsletter is distributed to subscribers monthly by e-mail.

Sex Coach U., www.sexcoachu.com. This is a home-based educational and training program founded by sex educators and coaches Patti Britton and Robert Dunlap to apply the philosophy, principles, and practices of professional coaching to the field of sex therapy. Go to this site for more information on self-directed learning courses in clinical sexology that can lead to certification in sex coaching.

Sexuality and Aging, www.sexualityandaging.com. Sponsored by the Widener University Graduate Program in Human Sexuality, this site is dedicated to enhancing the sexual health, knowledge, and well-being of people in midlife and later life by providing quality sexuality education to individuals, couples, and the professionals who serve them.

Index